International Socialism 136

Autumn 2012

Contributors

Alex Anievas is a postdoctoral fellow at St. Anne's College, University of Oxford.

Paul Blackledge is author of *Marxism and Ethics: Freedom, Desire and Revolution*.

Guglielmo Carchedi is the author of *Behind the Crisis: Marx's Dialectics of Value and Knowledge*.

Esme Choonara is a health worker and socialist activist in east London.

Joseph Choonara is the author of *Unravelling Capitalism: A Guide to Marxist Political Economy*.

Laura Cooke is a socialist activist in east London.

Nick Evans is a postgraduate student and activist at the University of Oxford.

Adam Fabry is a postgraduate student and activist at Brunel University.

Panos Garganas is the editor of the Greek newspaper *Workers Solidarity*.

Nicola Ginsburgh is a socialist activist based in Leeds.

Donny Gluckstein is the author of *A People's History of the Second World War*.

Robert Knox is a PhD candidate in Law at the LSE and an editor of the journal *Historical Materialism*.

Amy Leather is national organiser for the Socialist Workers Party.

Yuri Prasad is a socialist activist in east London.

Sarah Robertson is a socialist activist in east London.

John Rose is the author of *Myths of Zionism*.

Sean Sayers is the author of *Marx and Alienation: Essays on Hegelian Themes* and editor of the *Marxism and Philosophy Review of Books* (http://marxandphilosophy.org.uk/reviewofbooks).

Dave Sewell is a journalist on *Socialist Worker*.

Richard Seymour is the proprietor of the Lenin's Tomb blog and the author of *American Insurgents: A Brief History of American Anti-Imperialism*.

Jeffery R Webber sits on the editorial board of *Historical Materialism*. He is the author of *Red October: Left-Indigenous Struggles in Modern Bolivia*.

Sebastian Zehetmair is a socialist historian in Germany.

Narrowing the bounds of the possible: the US election

Alex Callinicos

In November 2008, after Barack Obama had won in the presidential election in the US, Slavoj Žižek wrote one of his very best pieces: "The reason Obama's victory generated such enthusiasm is not only that, against all odds, it really happened: it demonstrated the possibility of such a thing happening." The election of America's first black president, in other words, showed that the boundaries of what is socially possible are wider than had hitherto been thought. This was a demonstration that could have much more broadly liberating consequences, though Žižek wisely warned: "The true battle begins now, after the victory: the battle for what this victory will effectively mean".[1]

His words seem full of irony now. For Obama's presidency seems to have been designed to suppress the dangerous truth his election revealed and to narrow down the limits of the possible. He took office in January 2009 in the wake of the financial crash following the failure of Lehman Brothers the preceding September—the most dangerous moment for American capitalism since the Great Depression of the 1930s. Obama invited, and sometimes still seeks, comparison with Franklin Roosevelt, who entered the White House in March 1933, when the US banking system was in complete disarray and one in four American workers was unemployed.

Obama today doesn't come out well from this comparison. It would

---

1: Žižek, 2008.

be a huge mistake to idealise Roosevelt. He was a cynical New York patrician whose aim was to rescue American capitalism from a life-threatening crisis; during the Second World War he acted ruthlessly to make the US the dominant global power. Nevertheless, Roosevelt was willing in the 1930s to take on powerful bastions of the American establishment, from Wall Street to the Supreme Court, in order to reconstruct US capitalism along lines that involved a much higher degree of political control of the economy, along with elements of a welfare state (measures that were taken considerably further during the presidencies of Lyndon Johnson and Richard Nixon in the 1960s and 1970s).[2] Compare this bitter recent judgement by the critical theorist David Bromwich: "The Obama presidency has gone far to complete the destruction of New Deal politics which began when Bill Clinton brought Wall Street into the White House".[3]

Elsewhere in this journal Alex Anievas, Adam Fabry and Robert Knox demonstrate the continuities between Obama's foreign policy and that of his Republican predecessor George W Bush. Rather than reining in the imperial presidency, Obama has revelled in the expansion of a global machinery of assassination executed by Predator drones and Navy Seals. A new profile by Michael Lewis focuses admiringly on his decision "effectively [to] invade another Arab country"—ie Libya—last year.[4]

Exactly the same can be seen on the domestic front, where the Obama administration's response to the 2008-9 slump essentially continued the policies hastily put in place by treasury secretary Hank Paulson during the dying days of the Bush presidency. The main thrust of the massive Troubled Assets Relief Programme was, as Thomas Frank puts it, to give "the banks an open-ended guarantee against failing without restricting their activities".[5] The Dodd-Frank Act 2010 reorganised and tightened the regulation of financial markets, but successful lobbying by Wall Street and the White House's timidity ensured that nothing saw the light of day comparable to the Glass-Steagall Act 1933, one of the central planks of the New Deal, which forced the separation of investment and retail banking.

Obama instead focused his energies on healthcare reform, where he ended up caving in to the private health industry's opposition to a public insurance scheme and pushed through a plan modelled on measures introduced in Massachusetts by his eventual Republican presidential opponent

2:   Two interesting studies of the New Deal from very different perspectives are Aglietta, 1979, and Rosen, 2005.

3:   Bromwich, 2012.

4:   Lewis, 2012. See also Sanger, 2012.

5:   Frank, 2012.

Mitt Romney. And in subsequent manoeuvres against the Congressional Republicans over cutting the budget deficit, Obama has essentially accepted their agenda that (in Ronald Reagan's words) government is the problem, not the solution, and must be shrunk.

It is too easy to excuse Obama's caution by citing the objective constraints imposed by the increasingly dysfunctional US political system. Taking office, as we have seen, at a moment of profound crisis, Obama at first enjoyed room for manoeuvre that could have allowed him to act more adventurously—like Roosevelt, to reconstruct the dominant model of capitalism in the US. And he was aware of this power. Frank reports: "When he met with a delegation of Wall Street bankers in April of 2009, the new president told them: 'My administration is the only thing between you and the pitchforks'." [6]

Obama's refusal to throw the bankers to the mob was a matter of political choice, not merely a structural necessity. We can't say we weren't warned. In *The Audacity of Hope* he disarmingly acknowledged his gradual assimilation as a senator to the worldview of the corporate rich he increasingly mixed with:

Increasingly I found myself spending time with people of means—law firm partners and investment bankers, hedge fund managers and venture capitalists. As a rule, they were smart, interesting people, knowledgeable about public policy, liberal in their politics, expecting nothing more than a hearing of their opinions in exchange for their cheques. But they reflected, almost uniformly, the perspectives of their class: the top 1 percent that can afford to write a $2,000 cheque to a political candidate. They believed in the free market and an educational meritocracy; they found it hard to imagine that there might be any social ill that could not be cured with a high SAT score. They had no patience with protectionism, found unions troublesome, and were not particularly sympathetic to those whose lives were upended by the movements of global capital. Most were adamantly prochoice and antigun and were vaguely suspicious of deep religious sentiment... Still, as a consequence of my fund-raising, I know that I became more like the wealthy donors I met. [7]

Acting as president in the interests of this 1 percent, Obama responded to the crisis with the most limited possible measures. His most striking initiative

6:    Frank, 2012.
7:    Obama, 2007, pp113-14.

was the bailout of Chrysler and General Motors (GM), which involved forcing the two auto giants into bankruptcy in April and June 2009 respectively and the US government taking a 60 percent stake in GM. Nevertheless, not only did this once again follow an initial bailout by the Bush administration in December 2008, but the rescue involved the administration extracting massive concessions from the United Auto Workers (UAW).

The administration's attitude to the union, a longstanding mainstay of the Democratic Party, was summed up by Obama's chief of staff, Rahm Emmanuel, when he said, "Fuck the UAW," at a White House meeting in March 2009—exactly the same stance that Emmanuel has taken as mayor of Chicago toward the city's teachers (whose strike was settled as we went to press). Steven Rattner, put in charge of the rescue by Obama, has revealed how weak the administration's hand was in its negotiations with UAW president Ron Gettelfinger:

> Suppose Gettelfinger had simply refused any or all of our demands? We could still force GM into bankruptcy, which would void the UAW contract and, in theory, free GM to start over, either with the UAW or by hiring replacement workers... We did not believe that hiring non-union labourers to replace skilled UAW members was practical. The assembly of cars by GM involved hundreds of teams of five to six people executing highly specific tasks at 45 to 50 second intervals. Nor did we believe that Barack Obama would have been willing to discharge the autoworkers the way Ronald Reagan had fired the air traffic controllers in 1981... I kept wondering why Gettelfinger didn't call our bluff. We had no backup plan, no notion of what we would do in that event.[8]

But in the event Gettelfinger swallowed the concessions. Rattner says: "This was something of a "Nixon goes to China" moment"—in other words, the Obama administration could use its pull with the trade union bureaucracy to carry out a restructuring of the auto industry much more effectively than the Republicans.[9] That restructuring, in the event, allowed a significant revival in the competitiveness of GM and Chrysler (which has been taken over by Fiat). Thus Obama deployed his political capital to rescue an economic system whose failure had been so dramatically exposed in 2008-9. As Frank argues, this allowed the Tea Party right—now represented at the very top of US politics by Republican vice-presidential candidate Paul

---

8:   Rattner, 2010, pp68, 230.
9:   Rattner, 2010, p152.

Ryan—to capitalise on the anger created by the crisis, using it to mobilise in support of the neoliberal capitalism that had produced it in the first place. He calls "the conservative comeback of the last few years...something unique in the history of American social movements: a mass conversion to free-market theory as a response to hard times".[10]

Frank exaggerates: the success of the Tea Party has lain less in its ability to win over new people to extreme versions of economic liberalism than in its mobilisation of an existing constituency.[11] Nevertheless, there is no doubt that the Republican right have been making the running, using their success in the 2010 mid-term Congressional elections to attempt to roll back Obama's very modest reforms and to win control of their party. Their inability to produce a strong candidate in the primaries has left them stuck with an establishment stuffed shirt who used to run a private equity firm, and whose only deviation from the Wasp norm (his Mormonism) makes Christian fundamentalists twitchy. But, to accommodate his base, Romney has shifted sharply rightwards in the course of the year, as is reflected by his choice as his running mate of Ryan, who is celebrated for, among other things, writing an article entitled "Down with Big Business" that denounced Washington imposed "crony capitalism".[12] Ryan, a devotee of the ultra-liberal ideologue Ayn Rand, tried to privatise Social Security (the federal pension system) in 2005.

The sheer ferocity of the renascent right is, of course, one of the main reasons for left liberals' willingness to give Obama the benefit of the doubt. Thus Bromwich despairingly writes:

> And yet there is no alternative to Obama. Supporters who realise that he is not what he seemed in 2008 are reduced to saying (as two of them, a historian and a lawyer, said to me separately in the last few days): "He's not a good president, and doesn't deserve to be re-elected, but he must be re-elected." The short name for the reason is Mitt Romney; the longer and truer name is what the Republican Party has become. It is the party of wars, prisons and the ever expanding riches of the very rich. Romney's foreign policy advisers are graduates of the workshop of Dick Cheney and the various American outworks of the Likud or the neoconservative American Enterprise Institute... As for Romney's economic ideas, every backward step towards the finance economy of 1920 which Obama has worked half-heartedly to

---

10: Frank, 2012.

11: See Megan Trudell's careful analysis in Trudell, 2011.

12: Ryan, 2009. For an incisive analysis of Ryan's politics and the Democrats' role in facilitating his rise, see Selfa and Maas, 2012.

impede, Romney will push to achieve with the greatest vigour. Even if he were otherwise disposed, the ideology of his party commits him to policies of a regressive order that will surpass Reagan.[13]

This is simply the current version of the traditional left case for supporting the Democrats: that they represent a "lesser evil" compared to the Republicans. The argument is reinforced by the fact that the 2012 race is proving to be extremely narrow. The main reason for this is that unemployment remains persistently high, putting Obama at a constant disadvantage even against as clumsy an opponent as Romney. To some degree, he has only himself to blame: Martin Wolf, like other Keynesian economists, criticised Obama's initial fiscal stimulus as "disturbingly modest"; he also warned that, by the time this became obvious, "Mr Obama may have lost the argument and his authority".[14]

This is exactly what happened: since the slump bottomed out in the early months of 2009, the US economy has stagnated, while any further attempts at stimulus have been blocked by the Republican-controlled House of Representatives. The consequences can be seen in the grim announcement that US real median household income fell in 2011 to its lowest level since 1995, 4.1 percent lower than when Obama took office in 2009.[15] Gridlock in Washington has left the Federal Reserve Board alone with the ability to stimulate the economy: in mid-September it followed the example of the European Central Bank and announced a new bout of quantitative easing—buying bonds as a way of pumping money into the financial system—in the hope of cutting unemployment.

The tightness of the race means it will be dispiritingly narrowly focused. After the two party conventions in late August and early September, the *Financial Times* predicted: "Polls show the presidential election in November will be exceptionally close, but the race is even tighter than it looks nationally. It hinges on nine swing states, which both candidates will be visiting repeatedly in the next 55 days".[16] The biggest of these are Florida and Ohio, the key battlegrounds in the 2000 and 2004 elections respectively. Vast quantities of money are being poured into the swing

---

13: Bromwich, 2012.

14: Wolf, 2009. See the detailed critique of the stimulus in Krugman, 2012, chapter seven. Elsewhere in this issue, Guglielmo Carchedi argues that Keynesian measures to stimulate effective demand can in certain circumstances increase output and employment, but in doing so merely postpone the resolution of the underlying crisis of profitability.

15: Politi, 2012.

16: Fifield, 2012.

states: in a reversal of the pattern of 2008, the Republicans' fundraising is running ahead of Obama and the Democrats, partly thanks to the January 2010 Supreme Court ruling that struck down limits on corporate political contributions as an infringement of free speech. Obama's campaign is ahead in its use of social media and the like to "micro-target" voters, but the intention to vote of one key demographic—young voters—has fallen sharply compared to 2008 or even 2004.[17]

Do socialists have a dog in this fight? Bromwich's arguments are unpersuasive. Romney certainly has a pack of neocons advising him, and has tried (on the whole ineptly) to outflank Obama from the right on foreign policy. But there is little evidence that he would diverge significantly from the more temperate defence of empire forced on a chastened Bush administration in its final two years—just as Obama has toed the same line, reneging on his promise to close down Guantanamo Bay and returning to Donald Rumsfeld's original preference for air power and Special Forces as the chief instruments of US power-projection. On the domestic front, the renewed strength of the Republican right is a reality that a president of either party would have to handle. Romney has even recently slid centre-wards on "Obamacare", the right's ultimate hate object, saying that if elected he would keep elements of it.

In his classic critique of the lesser-evil argument Hal Draper wrote:

> The point is that it is the question which is a disaster, not the answer. In setups where the choice is between one capitalist politician and another, the defeat comes in accepting the limitation to this choice … you can't fight the victory of the rightmost forces by sacrificing your own independent strength to support elements just the next step away from them.[18]

This argument still seems relevant. What we see is fear of the Republican right (in the 1960s it was Barry Goldwater and Ronald Reagan; now it is Ryan and the Tea Party) used to shackle the left to a Democratic Party that constantly disappoints and betrays their hopes, thereby helping to feed the development of the very right used as a bogeyman to scare the left to hang onto nurse for fear of something worse.

Draper also sought to explain the fact that in practice Democratic and Republican administrations pursued similar policies:

17: McGregor, 2012, Gallup, 2012.
18: Draper, 1967.

In the three and a half decades since 1932, and before, during and after a second world war which intensified the process, the capitalist system itself has been going through a deep-going process of bureaucratic statification ... Under the pressure of bureaucratic-statified capitalism, liberalism and conservatism converge. That does not mean they are identical, or are becoming identical. They merely increasingly tend to act in the same way in essential respects, where fundamental needs of the system are concerned. And just as the conservatives are forced to conserve and expand the statified elements of the system, so the liberals are forced to make use of the repressive measures which the conservatives advocate: because the maintenance of the system demands it. Just as when Truman vetoed [the anti-union] Taft-Hartley [Act 1947] and then invoked it against striking workers. What is more, because the liberal politicians can point a warning finger towards the right and because the lib-labs will respond to it, they are even more successful than the conservatives in carrying out those measures which the conservatives advocate.[19]

Since the 1970s we have seen a further restructuring of capitalism that has involved, not the scrapping of what Draper calls "bureaucratic stat-ification" (as is shown by the enhanced role of the state in response to the present crisis), but a shift in the balance towards globally integrated market capitalism. And so we see the Democrats and Republicans converging once again: each is equally "the party of wars, prisons and the ever expanding riches of the very rich". The Democrats may be able to rely on the support of the bulk of the trade union bureaucracy, but they lack the roots in the workers' movement that still distinguish genuine reformist parties. Bill Clinton's administration in 1993-2001 marked their full embrace of the neoliberalism pioneered by Reagan during the 1980s; Obama, confronted with a much bigger crisis than Clinton had to deal with, has maintained this stance. As Simon Johnson (ex-chief economist of the IMF) and James Kwak put it, "By 2009, the economic policy elite of the *Democratic* Party was fully won over to the idea that finance was good".[20]

But there is an important proviso to be added. It is essential to distinguish between the objective character of the Democratic Party and of the Obama presidency and the reasons why people support them. The worst thing about the lesser evil argument is that it works. Tens of mil-lions of people will vote for Obama in November because they hate

19: Draper, 1967.
20: Johnson and Kwak, 2010, p185. For a critique of Clinton's economic policy, see Pollin, 2003, especially chapters one to three.

and fear the Tea Party movement and they want to defend Medicare and Social Security against the likes of Paul Ryan—and also, of course, because Obama is the first African-American president, confronting a Republican Party whose base continues to pulse with racism. [21] These are good reasons for loathing the Republicans. The mistake lies in believing that Obama represents a bulwark against them.

Those on the left who reject the lesser evil argument have therefore to make their case in a way that allows a dialogue with those who still accept it. For it is only from the latters' ranks that a genuine mass radical left can develop in the US. In many ways this is a favourable moment to pursue the dialogue. The Occupy movement, short-lived though it was as a mass force, represented a powerful ideological challenge from the left to the neoliberal consensus, giving progressive expression to the immense anger at the banks and their bailout. The nine-day Chicago teachers' strike, which held off Emmanuel's assault on public education, is the latest sign of a revival in the US workers' movement after many years of decline. Finally, disappointment with Obama is palpable, perhaps especially among those who will nevertheless vote despairingly for him in November. So, despite the dismal choice that mainstream politics offers, there is reason to hope that the opening of possibilities that Obama's original victory represented can continue in forms that genuinely challenge the system.

21:   Younge, 2012.

References

Aglietta, Michel, 1979, *A Theory of Capitalist Regulation: The US Experience* (NLB).

Bromwich, David, 2012, "Diary", *London Review of Books* (5 July), www.lrb.co.uk/v34/n13/david-bromwich/diary

Draper, Hal, 1967, "Who's Going to be the Lesser Evil in 1968?", *Independent Socialist* (January-February), www.marxists.org/archive/draper/1967/01/lesser.htm

Fifield, Anna, 2012, "US: And Then There Were Nine", *Financial Times* (11 September), www.ft.com/cms/s/0/775e860c-fc03-11e1-af33-00144feabdc0.html

Frank, Thomas, 2012, *Pity the Billionaire: The Hard-Times Swindle and the Unlikely Comeback of the Right* (Vintage Digital).

Gallup, 2012, "Young US Voters' Turnout Intentions Lagging" (13 July), www.gallup.com/poll/155711/Young-Voters-Turnout-Intentions-Lagging.aspx

Johnson, Simon, and James Kwak, 2010, *13 Bankers: The Wall Street Takeover and the New Meltdown* (Pantheon).

Krugman, Paul, 2012, *End this Depression Now!* (W W Norton & Co).

Lewis, Michael, 2012, "Obama's Way", *Vanity Fair* (October), www.vanityfair.com/politics/2012/10/michael-lewis-profile-barack-obama

McGregor, Richard, 2012, "Inside Obama's HQ", *Financial Times* (14 September), www.ft.com/cms/s/2/0df7cc4a-fd35-11e1-a4f2-00144feabdc0.html

Obama, Barack, 2007, *The Audacity of Hope: Thoughts on Reclaiming the American Dream* (Canongate).

Politi, James, 2012, "US Median Income Lowest since 1995", *Financial Times* (12 September), www.ft.com/cms/s/0/ed14fc70-fc51-11e1-aef9-00144feabdc0.html

Pollin, Robert, 2003, *Contours of Descent: US Economic Fractures and the Landscape of Global Austerity* (Verso).

Rattner, Steven, 2010, *Overhaul: An Insider's Account of the Obama Administration's Rescue of the Auto Industry* (Houghton Mifflin Harcourt).

Rosen, Elliot A, 2005, *Roosevelt, the Great Depression, and the Economics of Recovery* (University of Virginia Press).

Ryan, Paul, 2009, "Down with Big Business", *Forbes* (11 December), www.forbes.com/2009/12/11/business-government-politics-reform-opinions-contributors-paul-ryan.html

Sanger, David, 2012, *Confront and Conceal: Obama's Secret Wars and Surprising Use of American Power* (Crown).

Selfa, Lance, and Alan Maas, 2012, "How a Right-Wing Fanatic Got to Centre Stage" (14 August), http://socialistworker.org/2012/08/14/right-wing-fanatic-at-center-stage

Trudell, Megan, 2011, "Mad as Hatters? The Tea Party Movement in the US", *International Socialism 129* (winter), http://www.isj.org.uk/?id=698

Wolf, Martin, 2009, "Why the G8 Must Focus on Sustaining Demand", *Financial Times* (11 March), www.ft.com/cms/s/0/b05253d6-0ddb-11de-8ea3-0000779fd2ac.html

Younge, Gary, 2012, "This is Shaping to be the Most Racially Polarised Election Ever", *Guardian* (9 September), www.guardian.co.uk/commentisfree/2012/sep/09/us-most-racially-polarised-election-white

Žižek, Slavoj, 2008, "Use Your Illusions", *London Review of Books* (14 November), www.lrb.co.uk/2008/11/14/slavoj-zizek/use-your-illusions

The crisis of black leadership

Esme Choonara and Yuri Prasad

Nothing illustrates the weakness of black political leadership today more starkly than a comparison between responses to the Tottenham riots of 1985 and the wave of rioting that began in Tottenham in 2011. On both occasions it was the death of a black person unfortunate enough to have had contact with the police that was the spark for major disturbances.

Before the smoke had cleared in 1985, Bernie Grant, the then Labour leader of Haringey council, spoke out, saying, "The youths around here believe the police were to blame for what happened on Sunday and what they got was a bloody good hiding".[1] The press and politicians went ballistic, labelling him "Barmy Bernie", but to many young people in the inner city he became a hero, someone who despite being of their parents' generation, had the guts to stand up for them. Two years later Grant was elected MP for Tottenham, one of just four black parliamentarians at the time.

The response of the current MP for Tottenham, David Lammy, to the riots that began after the police shot and killed Mark Duggan could not have been more different. Those who pelted the police with rocks were "mindless, mindless people", he cried, before explaining that the rebellion was the result of too much social liberalism: "Many of my constituents came up to me after the riots and blamed the Labour government, saying, 'You guys stopped us being able to smack our children'".[2]

1: BBC, 8 April 2000, http://news.bbc.co.uk/1/hi/uk_politics/706718.stm
2: Interview with LBC Radio, 29 January 2012.

Lammy's speedy intervention helped the political class and the media create a narrative for the disturbances. This wasn't political, they insisted—this was "criminality, pure and simple".[3] Diane Abbott, the veteran black Labour MP for Hackney North, where the riots had quickly spread, joined the chorus. "Looting is theft and the people who came out to loot last night were thieves," she said. "You are trashing your own communities... Who is going to invest; who is going to give jobs to communities where this sort of lawlessness occurs?"[4]

Such was the unanimity that in the weeks following, few black and Asian people in positions of influence—local councillors, writers, commentators, lawyers, religious leaders, community workers, academics, musicians, etc—were willing to speak up for those who had rebelled. Despite the most draconian of crackdowns, and an outpouring of racism in the media directed primarily at young African-Caribbeans, rioters stood almost entirely on their own.

The response to the riots proved that both black and Asian politicians, and the social layer of black and Asian authority figures around them, are utterly disconnected from the most oppressed sections of society. How did this come to be? To understand why it is important to grasp the circumstances that produced previous generations of black leadership, the way in which the state moved to either marginalise or co-opt them in the wake of the riots of 1981, and the political consequences of the move into the Labour Party that much of the left and many black activists made subsequently.

Beginning in 1962, when the government passed the first of many immigration laws that specifically targeted black and Asian workers from the Commonwealth, Britain saw rising opposition to racism. There were movements to repeal racist laws, defence campaigns for the victims of racist policing and the justice system, support for those threatened by fascist violence, protests against the rampant discrimination in the education system, and all manner of local and national groups that sought to channel the anger of black workers and black young people.

The new groups produced newspapers, magazines and journals and a plethora of organisations. Many of the key organisers were influenced by black nationalist politics and drew inspiration from struggles in the US and from the Pan-Africanist movements that followed the end of colonial rule. But there was also a strong strain of Marxism running through

---

3:    David Cameron, press statement, 9 August 2011.
4:    Interview with Sky News, 9 August 2011.

the movements that led to a focus on the working class and socialism as the means to achieve liberation. The term "black", as a political category that could unite all those who faced racism because of the colour of their skin, emerged from the needs of these struggles. It was an attempt to give concrete expression to the ad hoc unity that often emerged when different minority ethnic communities came under attack from racism.

All this took place against a background of rising working class militancy and the growing threat of the new Nazis of the National Front. Resisting racist attacks and racist policing became crucial organising points for black and Asian communities, with a feeling that the state was at best incapable and at worst unwilling to defend them. Most of the campaigns were of a temporary nature but nevertheless could be a powerful instrument. An illustration of the potential of this form of resistance can be seen in the protest that followed the New Cross fire in 1981. The blaze had killed 13 young black people and was widely suspected to have been the result of a fascist attack but the police refused a serious investigation. The demonstration that followed saw up to 20,000 people march from south east London to Hyde Park to demand action from an indifferent Metropolitan Police. It was an extremely militant affair, drawing in many who had never taken action before and combining them with others who had already cut their teeth in the fight against the police and the fascists. The protest was repeatedly attacked by the police and then demonised by the press.

Longstanding Race Today Collective activist John La Rose, who chaired the action committee that organised the march, explained what motivated him: "The organisation to which I belong makes its position absolutely clear. We are part of the perspective of struggle to change British society—it is part of the working class, the black working class and unemployed perspective in Britain, and we are in opposition to the black middle classes whose function is to police that black working class—and act as intermediaries for the state".[5]

La Rose's scathing attack on the black middle class reflected growing anger among radicals at the way the state sought to buy off a minority with jobs in what was becoming known as the "race relations industry"[6] while leaving the majority to suffer. His views were echoed among many grassroots

---

5:    Quoted in John, 2011.
6:    The Commission for Racial Equality was established by the 1976 Race Relations Act and sought to resolve issues of discrimination through a legalistic framework. It spawned an array of local race equality councils which mixed community activists with local councillors. Many black activists who participated were later employed by local council race equality departments and became increasingly detached from black communities.

activists who viewed the state as an enemy, not a potential ally, in the fight against racism. Dub reggae poet Linton Kwesi Johnson even wrote a song about it, which he entitled "Di Black Petty Booshwah".[7]

Like the New Cross Action Committee, every anti-racist campaign developed organisation, however limited, and threw up spokespeople and leaders. Those who successfully articulated the rage of one group were often eagerly sought after by others. The attitude of the state to the emerging leaders was contradictory. On the one hand it viewed them as threats who must be first criminalised and then neutralised. This was particularly true as the question of defending black communities under threat of racist violence came to the fore. But on the other hand the state also found community leaders useful—they were people you could negotiate with. The need for such "intermediaries" became paramount after riots exploded across Britain later in 1981.

Major disturbances in Brixton, Handsworth, Toxteth and Chapeltown were joined by smaller ones in scores of towns and cities, creating the most serious civil disturbances since the end of the Second World War.[8] The combination of deep political alienation with vicious police racism and rocketing youth unemployment was a lethal cocktail, leading to firebombing, looting and widespread attacks on the police, shops and offices, and any visible symbol of authority. The Tories feared the inner city rebellion could feed into growing working class anger at cuts and job losses and moved quickly to appoint a high court judge, Lord Scarman, to investigate the riots' causes and what could be done to prevent their recurrence.

Scarman's report provided the liberal whitewash that the establishment had expected of him. It refused to accept there was such thing as institutional racism and instead chose to highlight the so-called deficiencies of Caribbean and Asian families. Nevertheless, Scarman did acknowledge that the police's use of sus laws (which allowed police to stop and search on grounds of suspicion alone) were the spark that ignited the disorder in Brixton, and concluded that economic disadvantage and racism had created a ready fuel for the uprising. His report called for a carrot and stick approach, where heavy policing would be accompanied by a new approach to law and order, dubbed "community policing". He also advocated a massive programme of investment in the inner cities. These new

---

7:    Linton Kwesi Johnson was a member of the Race Today Collective and his work from this period paints a brilliant picture of black Britain. In particular listen to Sonny's "Lettah", "Di Great Insohreckshan", "New Cross Massahkah" and "Reggae Fi Peach".

8:    See Harman, 1981.

strategies marked an acceleration of the state's attempts to create a buffer between itself and working class black communities.

Kalbir Shukra summarises it this way:

> Scarman accepted that "hard" policing (such as stop and search operations) would still be necessary in the future in areas characterised by severe social problems. The question for Scarman was how policing could be enforced without provoking further outbreaks of disorder... Some of the report's recommendations were implemented through a new dual state strategy of repression and containment. This meant that running concurrently with increasing repression in the form of hard policing measures were new state interventions which were designed to create greater public trust and confidence in official institutions.[9]

The Tories approved over 200 new "ethnic projects" in the year after the riots, while traditional spending on similar "ethnic schemes" more than tripled.[10] In London, Ken Livingstone's Greater London Council (GLC) set up the Ethnic Minorities Committee in 1982. It received more than 300 requests for project funding in its first year and subsequently had its budget tripled.[11] For the Tories in central government, the aim of such funding was to create a range of self-help organisations and businesses in which black entrepreneurs would play a key role. This new black middle class would have a stake in the system and could be encouraged to neutralise threats to its stability.

For Labour left wingers, now in charge of (as well as the GLC) most London boroughs and many metropolitan and city councils, the reasoning was different. They argued that drawing community groups into a closer relationship with the local authority through grant funding and more open decision making was a way of extending democracy and giving black people political power. It was also a way of developing a channel of communication with black activists so that their views could shape policy in local government. The rhetoric was radical even if the reality was somewhat different.

A minority of black activists smelt a rat and ridiculed the incorporation policy as little more than an attempt at divide and rule.[12] But the increasingly

9: Shukra, 1998, p54.
10: Sivanandan, 1990, p94.
11: Gilroy, 1987, p138.
12: A Sivanandan even spoke to the GLC's Ethnic Minority Unit in 1983 only to denounce them, saying he was a "disbeliever in the efficacy of ethnic policies and programmes to alter, by one iota, the monumental and endemic racism of this society"—Sivanandan, 1990, p63.

black nationalist alternative advanced by groups such as the Race Today Collective offered little. Attempts to persuade black workers to organise their own workplace struggles separate from whites came to nothing, while black-only community defence campaigns tended to be short-lived affairs that did not reflect the multi-racial reality of the struggles.[13] Even those who refused to accept the state's embrace began to narrow their horizons, no longer believing their struggles could end racism once and for all, and instead accepting that only small-scale reforms of the system were possible now.

The use of state funding as a means of incorporation was given a further twist as local authorities started to move against the use of "black" as a political category in favour of a series of ethnicities. The logic of combining all those affected by racism was broken down as councils insisted that black was divided into first black and Asian, and then ever small units until Asian became Pakistani, Indian, Bangladeshi, Chinese and Other Asian. Community groups bidding for council funding now had to prove they represented particular ethnicities and then join the fierce competition for ever-declining resources.

The changes were embraced enthusiastically by proponents of identity politics, a fashionable spin-off from the postmodernism that had begun to grip the academic left. Breaking down the unity of the term "black" was essential, they argued, because all forms of collective struggle were simply a mask that covered "differing realities". Over the course of the 1980s identity politics swept through the left that ran the Labour councils and pretty soon it had inspired such a wave of delinking that even specific ethnicities had to be further compartmentalised by their gender and sexuality. By encouraging the notion of multiple competing identities, the postmodernists and their allies derided the notions of solidarity that underlined the use of the term "black" and so aided those in the state who wanted to incorporate black struggle.

There were other strong factors acting in favour of the strategy of co-option. With working class struggle on a sharply downward trajectory from the late 1970s onwards, many on the radical left had drawn the conclusion that independent socialist organisation was doomed and that they would be more influential inside the Labour Party where they could help shift the party to the left. Tony Benn's battle for the party's deputy leadership in 1981 accelerated the process and drew in many who were sharply critical of Labour, particularly over questions of race and immigration.[14]

13: Far from being race riots, the uprisings of 1981 were multi-racial and around half of all those arrested were white. See Harman, 1981.

14: See, for example, Tariq Ali's "Why I'm Joining the Labour Party", and replies—Ali, 1981.

For those activists now working within the state or as part of state-funded community or anti-racist groups the logic of joining the Labour Party Black Section (LPBS) was even stronger. If the state could now be considered a vehicle for anti-racism, and Labour in government could be considered its director, then being in the party and seeking elected office made sense. But over time the struggle to shift Labour to this agenda became an end in itself and those who had set out to change Labour found that they had only succeeded in changing themselves. As Kalbir Shukra puts it:

> LPBS's electorally orientated politics turned political issues and black anger into a question of black faces in office. Whereas "mobilisation" had once signified the gathering of forces in readiness for confrontational activity, LPBS's usage of it turned it into a term which denoted bureaucratic activity… The success in electing hundreds of black councillors and four black MPs in 1987 reinforced the view that black representation, rather than mobilisation, could achieve change for black people.[15]

And once inside the party black activists found themselves prisoners of the Labour leadership which forced them to toe an increasingly right wing line. When Bernie Grant spoke out in 1985 he already cut a somewhat isolated figure in the party nationally. Other black party members who refused to obey the top of their party found themselves subject to harsh disciplinary measures.[16] The emergence of Tony Blair and New Labour in the mid-1990s accelerated the process to the point where Labour's black MPs, previously known for being on the radical left of the party, increasingly found themselves lured to the centre by offers of cabinet and committee posts.

Once there, they defended the New Labour line that talked of balancing "rights" with "responsibilities" but in reality meant absolving the state of the responsibility of what were now considered to be the failings of individuals.[17] Issues that had once galvanised anti-racists into action—such as the way schools continue to fail black children, the lack

15: Shukra, 1998, p73.

16: For some examples of black Labour candidates who were barred by the party machine, see Holloway, 2012.

17: Paul Boateng became Britain's first black cabinet minister in 2002. He had once been known as the firebrand young lawyer of the Scrap Sus Campaign but made no further mention of sus after being elected to the Commons in 1987. Keith Vaz, chair of the Home Affairs Select Committee and Labour's Black, Asian and Minority Ethnic group advanced the cause of anti-Muslim racism by voting in favour of 42-day detention without charge of suspected terrorists.

of black people in good jobs and in public life, and even the criminalisation of young black people—were now seen, not as the consequence of institutional racism, but of nihilistic black youth cultures and "the failure of the black family".[18]

That New Labour cast such a long shadow over anti-racist struggle did not prevent new battles over racism, but it did mean that the public figures that many people looked to for a lead—the black MPs, councillors, community organisers, etc—increasingly sought to neutralise any potential threat to the establishment by limiting the aims of the struggle to small-scale reforms, while urging black people to look to themselves for explanations as to why they suffered.[19]

In this sense, black MPs' unanimous condemnation of the riots, and the silence of so many other black and Asian figures, does not itself mark a watershed—it merely showed us how far they have travelled on the road to being part of the problem, rather than part of the solution.

Bradford: a tale of two crackdowns

If the tale of the responses to the two Tottenham riots illustrates the current weakness of black African-Caribbean politics, the tale of two crackdowns in Bradford starkly reveals the decline of Asian militancy and organisation over the past few decades.

In the summer of 1981, 12 young Asian men were arrested in dawn raids across Bradford after police found a crate of home-made petrol bombs. They were charged with conspiracy to cause an explosion and endanger lives, crimes that carried a potential life sentence. Instead of denying their involvement, the accused argued that they had a right to defend their community from fascist attack—that self-defence is no offence. After a huge national campaign, they were acquitted and made legal history, enshrining the right to community self-defence in law.

Skip forward 20 years almost to the day to Bradford in 2001 where hundreds of Asians were caught up in riots provoked by fascists and the police. The crackdown that followed saw the courts throw more than 200 young people in jail, with sentences totalling more than 604 years, for defending their community with sticks and stones.[20] Rather than turning out to support their youngsters as happened 20 years earlier, many of the

---

18: All of Labour's black and Asian MPs have made statements to this effect, but David Lammy's book on the riots explicitly links hip hop and grime to criminality and delinquency—see Lammy, 2011.

19: For a balance sheet of racism under New Labour, see Mahamdallie, 2002.

20: Prasad, 2010.

older generation encouraged their children to hand themselves in, wrongly believing they would be dealt with more leniently. Although some of the left took up the issue of the punitive sentences, the campaign on the ground was weak and defensive.[21] So what happened in those intervening 20 years to create such a contrast?

The campaign for the Bradford 12 was part of a larger wave of struggles against racism, including confrontations with the National Front, some significant strikes involving Asian workers and in particular the Asian youth movements of the 1970s and 1980s. These youth movements were made up of a new generation who were unwilling to put up with the racism they saw their parents endure and determined to defend themselves from the growing harassment by fascist thugs and the police. Like other black activists of the time, they were informed by international struggles—by Vietnam, South Africa, Zimbabwe and Palestine and by the legacy of the US Black Power movement. They were also influenced by the left—several of those involved in founding the Asian youth movements had been members or were close to organisations such as the International Socialists (forerunner of the Socialist Workers Party).[22]

The first of the youth movements was formed in Southall after the racist murder of Gurdip Singh Chaggar in June 1976. New groups followed in many towns and cities including Bradford, Manchester, Birmingham, Sheffield, Nottingham, Leicester, Luton, Burnley and east London.[23] Although many of the groups called themselves Asian movements, they saw themselves as part of a wider struggle by all black people. Balraj Purewal, one of the founders of the Southall Youth Movement, explains: "In terms of the Afro-Caribbean youth, the link…was very close, and they were part of the Southall Youth Movement".[24]

Groups took on the characteristics of their locality and often worked alongside or in cooperation with other left organisations. They were part of a wider campaign of direct action against the NF, which included, for example, the historic confrontation in Lewisham in August 1977 and subsequent mass mobilisations by the Anti Nazi League. Groups also took up the fight to support families torn apart by racist immigration laws along with

---

21: For example, the campaign set up in 2002 to try to get the Bradford defendants' sentences reduced includes the assurance that "all those convicted of their involvement have shown remorse for their activities"—www.fairuk.org/docs/Fair%20Justice%20Campaign.pdf
22: Ramamurthy, 2006, p43.
23: Ramamurthy, 2006, p44.
24: Balraj Purewal in Ramamurthy, 2007, p15. The website www.tandana.org carries a digitised archive of Asian Youth Movement leaflets, posters and other political ephemera.

other issues such as the increasing tuition fees for overseas students. The Asian youth movements were seen as more radical than the organisations of their parents' generation. While many of the young activists' parents would have harboured dreams of returning home, this was a generation that had grown up in Britain and was "Here to stay—Here to fight!" as one of the most prominent slogans put it.

The campaign for the Bradford 12 was a key moment for the Asian youth movements.[25] Those arrested and charged were members of the United Black Youth League, a split from the Bradford Asian Youth Movement. The campaign to support the Bradford 12 grew with mass meetings, demonstrations and pickets of the court every day during the nine-week trial.[26] It drew in support from all sections of the local community, as campaign solicitor Ruth Bundy recalls:

> I remember going to one very, very early meeting when all the defendants…
> were locked up in Armley prison, and there were Sikhs in their seventies
> and eighties and elderly Muslim parents, a whole range of support saying,
> in a sense, these are our children, support them, defend them, and that's
> something that over the years I have never quite seen again.[27]

The youth movements were one of the high points of a long history of Asian struggles in Britain but went into decline in the 1980s as part of the general downturn. The success in driving the NF back also partly removed a focus that had united those involved. Like the black African-Caribbean groups, the Asian youth movements had organisational and political weaknesses that the state was keen to exploit. Despite cooperation between different groups, they mostly remained local in organisation and were also subject to splits and arguments over the question of state funding.[28] Some members of the movements turned their attentions to setting up community centres in Bradford and Manchester, moving away from political confrontation with the state to competing with rivals for funding while devoting their energies to organising official

---

25: For a sense of the times, it is well worth reading the excellent novel *While There Is Light* by Tariq Mehmood, one of the Bradford 12.

26: Shahnaz Ali, who was arrested with the Bradford 12 but later released without charge, reflects on growing up in Bradford, the impact of the youth movements and the contrast with Bradford 2001 in a very interesting podcast at http://blog.plain-sense.co.uk/2011/07/30-years-on-bradford-twelve.html

27: Ruth Bundy in Ramamurthy, 2007, p24.

28: Ramamurthy, 2006, p56.

community and youth groups. This "scramble for government favours and government grants"[29] helped to fragment the groups.

As with other black activists, there was also a pull towards the Labour Party. As collective struggle declined, the lure of reformism grew. Many Asian activists joined the Labour Party. For example, Marsha Singh, a former member of the Bradford Asian Youth Movement, went on to become the Labour MP for Bradford West.[30]

The period of the 1990s and the 2000s saw both similarities and differences between Asian and African-Caribbean organisations. The striking similarities were the state's continued dual strategy of repression and co-option. The differences were in the way they were employed and the specific impact of the "war on terror" on Britain's Muslims.

Muslims and the "war on terror"

Although there have been Muslims in Britain for centuries, the creation of a specific Muslim identity—by either the state or by Muslims themselves—is a fairly recent phenomenon.[31] The impact of imperialism, in particular the New World Order of the early 1990s, the arguments around the publication of Salman Rushdie's *Satanic Verses* and the more recent "war on terror", along with the growing racism against Muslims worldwide have all played a part in the creation of a distinct category and identity.

The British Muslim identity has also been strengthened in a more positive way. As Parveen Akhtar puts it, "There is doubtless at present growing anti-Muslim sentiment in many quarters of Britain...many youths consequently take up a publicly expressed 'Muslim' identity purposefully, to fly in the face of this growing racism".[32] Nevertheless, Muslims in Britain do not form a single homogeneous group: they are divided by ethnic origin, class, age, politics and many other features.

Over the past two decades Muslims have been subject to an onslaught of accusations of self-segregation and harbouring a disloyal "alien" culture, as British politicians have bolstered a very exclusive version of nationalism. The terms of this onslaught have shifted from attacking "Asian" culture to specifically targeting "Muslims". This campaign has been more than simply rhetorical.

In the summer of 2001 fascist provocation and racist policing sparked

29: Sivanandan, 1990, p94.
30: Ramamurthy, 2006, p56. Interestingly, it was Marsha Singh's resignation due to ill health in March 2012 that prompted the by-election that George Galloway won so decisively.
31: Mahamdallie, 2007.
32: Akhtar, 2005, p169.

rioting not just in Bradford but in Oldham, Burnley and Leeds. Arun Kundnani describes the sentences handed out in Bradford as an attempt to "discipline an entire community".[33] The crackdown was combined with a continued ideological offensive from New Labour that painted the community's lack of integration as the cause of the riots. The Cantle report into the riots said that Muslim communities had deliberately segregated themselves from the rest of society, and this was the cause of racism. Among other recommendations it argued that immigrants should take an oath of allegiance that establishes "a clear primary loyalty to this Nation",[34] a proposal enthusiastically embraced by then home secretary David Blunkett. It also argued that funding of community groups should be "rebalanced" towards those that promote "citizenship" and "community cohesion". So the response to the northern riots was both stick (brutal sentences) and carrot (the promise of funding for groups promoting the government's agenda).

Arun Kundnani also points out the failure of so-called "community leaders" to defend the 2001 rioters: "Following in the government's path, a hundred other voices rushed to condemn the rioters, while little was heard from young mill-town Asians themselves. The community leaders blamed a lack of discipline, a decline in Muslim values and the undue influence of Western values which, to them, was a threat to their own authority. The Asian middle class in the rest of Britain, forgetting that their own secure place in society came about because of those who had taken to the streets in the 1970s and 80s, blamed the 'village mentality' of Asian communities not as lucky as their own".[35] It seems that in the 20 years following the Bradford 12 victory the state had succeeded in dividing, intimidating and co-opting away effective opposition to their brutal treatment of young Muslims.

The "war on terror" has built on the agenda of depicting Britain's Muslims as a self-segregating insular community hostile to "British values".[36] The anti-war movement which culminated in the huge demonstrations of 2003 brought many thousands of Muslims into political activity alongside left and peace activists. As Salma Yaqoob points out, the participation of so many Muslims was not an automatic outcome, but required

---

33: Kundnani, 2002. See also Amy Leather's review article on the Bradford riots elsewhere in this issue.

34: Cantle, 2001, p16. See also the BBC summary of the northern 2001 riots at http://news.bbc.co.uk/1/hi/england/1703432.stm. Note that the BBC insisted on calling these disturbances "race riots", even though they could more accurately be described as anti-racist riots (quite apart from the other social issues that fuelled the disturbances).

35: Kundnani, 2001.

36: For a demolition of the myths of self-segregation see Finney and Simpson, 2009.

argument, organisation and standing up to sections of the left who were hostile to working with Muslims.[37]

Tony Blair's New Labour government responded to the terror attacks of 9/11 and London's 7/7 by pushing the onus onto all Muslims to tackle the "evil ideology" in their midst.[38] The state's strategy was to divide Muslims and their organisations into "moderates" and "extremists". This policy was institutionalised through funding attached to the Preventing Violent Extremism programme, commonly known as Prevent.

From its inception in April 2007 to its recent revamping by the Tories, Prevent embodies the view that all Muslims are part of a "suspect community".[39] With a cross-departmental annual budget that has run into the millions, Prevent has continued to use funding for local authority and voluntary projects to bolster groups that fit in with the government's agenda.

The state uses Prevent to foster compliant Muslims groups and reliable "community leaders" while those in disagreement with the government are isolated and designated as extremists. The strategy has also been used to promote particular theological strands that the government favours. It has embedded security services in the provision of local services and attempted to turn teachers, lecturers and other state employees into government spies. Alongside the bribery of funding and official sponsorship, the state has continued the repression against Muslims, with a huge rise in stop and search of young Asian men and numerous high-profile "terror raids" that often amount to nothing. This is part of an attempt to stoke up fear and isolate Muslims from other working class communities.

This mixture of co-option, blackmail, bribery and repression provides the context to responses by Muslims to provocations by the English Defence League (EDL) in recent years. The state has tried a number of approaches to counter-protests against the EDL—including ignoring them, heavy repression, banning marches, courting, intimidating or pressurising community and mosque leaders to discipline their young people, and attempting to divide Muslims from the rest of the anti-fascist movement.[40]

In some areas their strategy has been effective in limiting anti-EDL protests. In other areas, most notably Tower Hamlets in 2011 and Waltham Forest in 2012, there have been large united demonstrations.[41] The balance

---

37: Yaqoob, 2003.

38: *Guardian*, 14 July 2005.

39: Kundnani, 2009, p8.

40: *Socialist Worker* has an archive collecting reports of the different struggles against the EDL in recent years at www.socialistworker.co.uk/topic.php?id=10

41: Khan, 2011.

of forces varies, but the factors determining the level of Muslim participation include the political leadership of the mosques in the area, the growing pressure from young Muslims who want to confront the EDL and the role of the left and wider anti-fascist movement. How these factors will continue to play out will be seen in practice in future flashpoints.

The Bradford backlash

The racist notion of almost timeless British Muslim communities with official leadership handed down from one generation to another was delivered a massive blow by the election of George Galloway to the Bradford West seat in 2012. Labour wrongly thought it could rest its election campaign upon longstanding self-proclaimed figures of authority in the city. Even Labour MP Sadiq Khan admitted the party had been arrogant to take Muslim votes for granted and had wrongly relied on the patronage of community elders and mosque leaders to mobilise votes.[42]

Galloway's campaign tapped into another form of leadership—that based, even in a small way, on struggle rather than accommodation. The support for Galloway did not come just from Muslims, but the campaign's energetic appeal to class anger over austerity and attacks on education as well as the issues of war and imperialism chimed with a generation of young working class Muslims angry at a lack of opportunity and lacking a mainstream voice.

For many years Labour felt able to count on Muslim votes despite delivering precious little. Its handpicked Muslim local councillors and occasional prospective parliamentary candidates were the beneficiaries of previous waves of black and Asian struggle. There is now more Muslim representation than ever before. The last election saw the first three Muslim women elected to parliament. Yet, as with black African-Caribbean MPs, the gap between them and the people they represent has never been greater.

Conclusion

In addressing today's crisis of black leadership, it is important not to collapse into nostalgia for the past. The 1960s and 1970s were difficult times for black and Asian people with brutal racism and fascists organising on the streets. The struggles of those decades were inspirational, but they were a product of their time. Every generation has thrown up struggles against racism and as part of wider class struggle.[43] The important thing is to learn from the past in order

---

42: *Independent*, 3 June 2012.
43: The best account of these struggles remains Fryer, 1984.

to avoid the pitfalls and political mistakes of previous generations—including the danger of collaboration with the state and the pull of reformism.

As we have seen, state strategies of co-option and repression have attempted, with some success, to fragment struggles, criminalise black and Asian youth, and isolate Muslims and other black people from wider forces. The question for the left is how to overcome this.

The key to solving the problem is the use of united front campaigns that can reach out to wider forces. Even in the political climate of the 1990s such strategies were sometimes possible—most notably the Stephen Lawrence campaign led by his parents, Doreen and Neville. The long battle mobilised thousands of activists—black, white and Asian—into petitioning, protesting, holding meetings and attempting to hold the police accountable. It involved the trade union movement, which provided much of the funding for the campaign, as well as a militant 60,000-strong march on the Nazi BNP's headquarters in Welling, very close to where Stephen was murdered. The Lawrence campaign had the spirit of a united front campaign—though it remained an informal one. It succeeded in shifting both the Labour Party and the police, famously establishing the recognition of institutionalised police racism through the Macpherson inquiry.

Today there is a new generation of justice campaigns, led by families of black people who have died in police custody. An interesting feature of these is their ready interaction with the wider left, for example through the Defend the Right to Protest campaign. Many black justice campaigners have made common cause with victimised student protesters and with the struggles of the family of Ian Tomlinson, a white working class man who died after being struck by a police officer at the 2009 G20 protests in London. These signs of ready cooperation reflect the way in which the weakness of black separatist politics today throws up a chance to generalise and widen the struggles that would once have been seen as more narrowly focused black self-defence campaigns.

At their best, united front campaigns involve the revolutionary left working alongside reformists, black and Asian organisations and many other individuals to overcome the attempts to isolate and divide us. They do this by mobilising wider social forces and revealing the scale of potential allies. They are also arenas in which various strategies informed by different political outlooks can be put to the test in practice. United multi-racial campaigns can also lay the basis for militant class-based struggle instead of identity-based politics.

The Stop the War Coalition that reached its height with the huge marches of 2003 involved thousands of Muslims alongside the revolutionary left, many Labour supporters, trade unionists and others. It showed that it was possible to break down some of the isolation of Muslims under attack by the state, media and wider racist ideology.

The most dramatic recent struggles against racism have involved united fronts against the EDL, where revolutionaries have reached out to those to their right politically—to Labour MPs, trade union leaders, and community and religious organisations—in order to mobilise wider social forces. This is not an accommodation to reformism, but a serious attempt to draw in wider numbers to a radical and effective struggle against fascism.

The movement has broken down some of the isolation of Muslims. As Dilowar Khan put it after the 5,000-strong protest against the EDL in Tower Hamlets, "I get a sense recently that the spirit of united resistance that was there in the 1970s is coming back. People, including many non-Muslims, are saying that they will not leave us to stand alone. You can see that in the way people came together to defend the community, and the East London Mosque in particular, from attack by the English Defence League".[44]

The global economic crisis and shift to austerity have seen a return of both crisis at the top of society and a resurgence of the question of class. This, combined with the weakness of black nationalism and black reformism as credible frameworks for resistance, offers new chances to build alliances and a multi-racial grassroots leadership that emerges from the real struggles of our times.

The fate of the fight against racism is ultimately tied to the dynamics of wider class struggle. That is not to say that rising struggle automatically deals with racism—in many of the strikes of the 1970s, for example, Asian workers had to battle against racism in the trade union movement as well as from their employers and the state. But class confrontation creates a culture of resistance—and opportunities for solidarity and a chance to overcome racist divisions.

The anger against racism and the system that exploded in the riots in 2011 is not just confined to those who took part. The growing bitterness at austerity is spread across the whole working class. Despite the success of a number of black and Asian individuals who have joined the ranks of the middle class or the political or business establishments, the vast majority of black and Asian people remain concentrated among the working class and often among the poorest sections of the population. Among the millions of people who have taken strike action, campaigned for justice, protested, demonstrated or confronted the EDL, there is a potential new generation of

---

44: Khan, 2011, p198.

black leadership who can form part of a vibrant and combative multi-racial left. Only such a combined working class force is capable of not just challenging, but defeating, both racism and the capitalist system that breeds it.

References

Akhtar, Parveen, 2005, "'(Re)turn to religion' and Radical Islam", in Tahir Abbas, *Muslim Britain: Communities Under Pressure* (Zed Books).

Ali, Shahnaz, 2011, "30 Years On—The Bradford Twelve", *Just Plain Sense* podcast, 12 July 2011, http://blog.plain-sense.co.uk/2011/07/30-years-on-bradford-twelve.html

Ali, Tariq, 1981, "Why I'm Joining the Labour Party", *Socialist Review* (December), www.marxists.org/archive/harman/1981/12/ali.htm

Cantle, Ted, 2001, *Community Cohesion: A report of the Independent Review Team* (Home Office), http://image.guardian.co.uk/sys-files/Guardian/documents/2001/12/11/communitycohesionreport.pdf

Finney, Nissa, and Ludi Simpson, 2009, *Sleepwalking to Segregation? Challenging Myths About Race and Migration* (Policy Press).

Fryer, Peter, 1984, *Staying Power: The History of Black People in Britain* (Pluto).

Gilroy, Paul, 1987, *There Ain't No Black in the Union Jack* (Hutchinson).

Harman, Chris, 1981, "The Summer of 1981: a Post-Riot Analysis", *International Socialism* 14 (autumn), www.marxists.org/archive/harman/1981/xx/riots.html#f4

Holloway, Lester, 2012, "Britain's 'Obama moment' 25 years ago demands reflection" (27 May), http://cllrlesterholloway.wordpress.com/2012/05/27/britains-obama-moment-25-years-ago-demands-reflection/

John, Gus, 2011, "30 years after the New Cross fire: challenging racism today", *Socialist Worker* (10 September), www.socialistworker.co.uk/art.php?id=26904

Khan, Dilowar, 2011, "Never On Our Own: The Experience of Uniting a Community Against the EDL", in Hassan Mahamdallie (ed), *Defending Multiculturalism* (Bookmarks).

Kundnani, Arun, 2001, *From Oldham to Bradford: The Violence of the Violated* (Institute of Race Relations), www.irr.org.uk/news/from-oldham-to-bradford-the-violence-of-the-violated/

Kundnani, Arun, 2002, "IRR expresses concern at excessive sentencing of Bradford Rioters" (Institute of Race Relations), www.irr.org.uk/news/irr-expresses-concern-over-excessive-sentencing-of-bradford-rioters/

Kundnani, Arun, 2009, *Spooked! How Not to Prevent Violent Extremism* (Institute of Race Relations), www.irr.org.uk/pdf2/spooked.pdf

Lammy, David, 2011, *Out of the Ashes* (Guardian Books).

Mahamdallie, Hassan, 2002, "Racism: Myths and Realities", *International Socialism* 95 (summer), http://pubs.socialistreviewindex.org.uk/isj95/mahamdallie.htm

Mahamdallie, Hassan, 2007, "Muslim Working Class Struggles", *International Socialism* 113 (winter), www.isj.org.uk/?id=288

Mehmood, Tariq, 2003, *While There Is Light* (Comma Press).

Prasad, Yuri, 2010, "Nazis and police provoked the Bradford riot of 2001", *Socialist Worker* (14 August), www.socialistworker.co.uk/art.php?id=22063

Ramamurthy, Anandi, 2006, "The Politics of Britain's Asian Youth Movements", *Race and Class* (Institute of Race Relations), 48(2).

Ramamurthy, Anandi, 2007, *Kala Tara: A History of the Asian Youth Movements in Britain in the 1970s and 1980s* (Tandana), www.tandana.org/kalatara2000.pdf

Shukra, Kalbir, 1998, *The Changing Pattern of Black Politics in Britain* (Pluto).

Sivanandan, A, 1990, *Communities of Resistance* (Verso).

Yaqoob, Salma, 2003, "Global and Local Echoes of the Anti-war Movement: a British Muslim Perspective", *International Socialism 100* (autumn), http://pubs.socialistreviewindex.org.uk/isj100/yaqoob.htm

Democracy: fact and fetish

Donny Gluckstein

Democracy is one of the most popular yet disputed ideas around. Invoked by the US to justify invasions, it is also the stated aim of the Arab revolutions. Israel claims democratic elections give it the right to murder Palestinians, while they themselves struggle for the democratic right of self-determination. Even on the left democracy is sometimes controversial. Many in the Occupy movement consider majority decision-making and representative structures to be flawed and oppressive. They therefore fall back on consensus reached within relatively small groupings. Still others simply opt out, deeply disillusioned by the contrast between the rhetoric and actual operation of the current political system.

This article will argue that democracy is not only possible but essential if ordinary people are to collectively control their destiny. Today economic crisis exposes the web of interconnections linking humanity across the globe. That urgently poses the issue of how key decisions are reached, and what they should be. To stand aside from this is to leave unchallenged the 1 percent who dominate the 99 percent. Yet the difficulties remain. Parliamentary democracy is rightly contrasted with the fraudulent procedures of dictatorships such as Nazi Germany or Stalinist Russia. But does it follow that where "fair" elections occur poverty and inequality exist because most people want it?

One common explanation for the failure of democracy under capitalism is subversion due to infrequent elections, lack of mechanisms for accountability, the appointment of civil servants, judges, army generals and so on. Ralph Miliband sees one source of the problem arising from:

the *personnel* of the state system, that is to say the fact that the people who are located in the commanding heights of the state, in the executive, administrative, judicial, repressive and legislative branches, have tended to belong to the same class or classes which have dominated the other strategic heights of the society, notably the economic and the cultural ones.[1]

This has merit, but replacing the personnel or altering recruitment procedures would not solve the fundamental problem. Indeed, as Lenin argued, "The *more highly* democracy is developed, the *more* the bourgeois parliaments are subjected by the stock exchange and bankers".[2]

Bourgeois democracy does not fail the majority because of some flaw in the constitution. If capitalists control the means of production, then whatever electoral façade is in place, the majority's interests are nullified. Through such control capitalists dominate information channels, and the means of persuasion, education and coercion. Fear of unemployment, blackmail by the money markets, divide and rule (racism, sexism and so on) and a host of other devices are used to influence majority choices, limiting the scope of dissent and leaving the real levers of power in other hands, especially the coercive powers of the state.

Rosa Luxemburg explained the situation well over a century ago:

What parliamentarism expresses here is still capitalist society, that is to say, a society in which capitalist interests are dominant—and it is these that parliamentarism expresses. The institutions which are democratic in their form become, therefore, tools of the interests of the ruling class in their content... parliamentarism [is] a specific means employed by the bourgeois class state.[3]

Democracy cannot get round, jump over or ignore the social reality in which it is embedded.

Therefore the conundrum of democracy can only be resolved if it is seen as a specific form of social organisation rather than an unchanging, abstract principle. The degree to which its formal arrangements equate to genuine democratic content depends on three elements: how representation and decision-making are structured, power and the social context. This article identifies three fundamentally different types in history—ancient, bourgeois and proletarian, each expressing a different class interest.

1:   Miliband, 2004, p68.
2:   Lenin, 1976, p22.
3:   Howard, 1971, p84.

"Perfect democracy" in context

Democracy was invented in ancient Greece and combines the word for "people" (*demos*) with "rule" or "power" (*kratei*). Between 508 and 322 BC the entire male citizenry of Athens directly controlled state business. The result was, as one historian puts it, a "phenomenon of democracy that was 'true'—in the sense of being a relatively stable and long-lasting system of government 'by the people' that operated without an overt or cryptic ruling elite".[4] This refutes the idea that only a small minority of superior people with intelligence and experience (or more likely cash and "breeding") can ever rule, and the majority should leave governing to their "betters".

Athens's breakthrough was the product of deep-rooted development. Greece's mountainous and island geography, plus lack of major rivers such as the Nile, hindered the emergence of large-scale centralised states. Its numerous hereditary kings were weak and by the 590s BC oligarchies and tyrants (whose ascendancy did not depend on lineage) were displacing them. Athens had only the small Attica region as hinterland and it was here that a revolution, in 508-7 BC, inaugurated collective control.[5]

All male citizens of Attica were entitled to attend an assembly that met 40 days per year, had a quorum of 6,000, and took every key decision. Paid to appear, one quarter regularly managed to do so. A council of 500, selected by lot annually, drafted the agenda. The chair for the day was also selected by lot. Any citizen could speak or move motions, and a simple majority in a show of hands decided. Courts had no judges, but a 200 to 300 strong jury, selected by lot and paid.[6] It did not stop there:

> There were not only two elected commanders of the cavalry and the elected commanders of the tribal squadrons. There was an elective board of ten who enrolled the troopers...all the higher military officers [such as the ten generals] were elected...an elective sub-committee of ten [ordered the triremes (warships)]. The naval architects were elected by the people. The superintendents of the dockyards, who saw to the maintenance of the ships and their tackle, were probably one of the usual boards of ten chosen by lot... The festivals were directed by magistrates or boards chosen by lot, partly by elective boards... More surprisingly finance, both imperial and domestic, was...run entirely by boards chosen by lot, supervised by the council, until, in the latter half of the 4th century, an elective treasurer

4:   Ober, 1996, p5.
5:   Davies, 2004, pp260-286.
6:   Ober, 1996, p23.

of the military fund and elected managers of the theoric fund [to finance festivals] were created.[7]

Citizens used these popular checks to prevent the rich exploiting them or dominating the state. They shunned deference and generated a mass self-confidence which, contrary to the belief that collective power produces uniformity, promoted the flowering of the individual. The result was a cultural explosion in philosophy, political theory, drama, sculpture, architecture, the writing of history, and many other areas. This differentiated Athens from the rest of Greece and underpins much of our culture today.

Though this elaborate system was a spectacular success for its participants, it did not escape the class circumstances. Firstly, the "people" was precisely defined. Citizens were a minority of the overall population and kept it that way. Only the 20,000-30,000 boys who could claim both fathers and mothers of citizen descent themselves could aspire to that honour when they became adults.[8] All others—women, foreigners and slaves—were permanently excluded.

Most citizens were small property owners who could not afford expensive commodities like slaves and lived "by the work of their hands, as peasant farmers, craftsmen, shopkeepers".[9] Oligarchs and aristocrats found the very strength of democracy led to "the relative unavailability of Athenian free producers for exploitation [and] was itself a critical factor leading to the growth of slavery. In a sense, the free time of the poor was won at the expense of slave labour for the rich".[10] Therefore:

> we find a more intense development of slavery at Athens than at most other places in the Greek world: if the humbler citizens could not be fully exploited...then it was necessary to rely to an exceptional degree on exploiting the labour of slaves. This explains "the advance, hand in hand, of freedom and slavery".[11]

So poor citizens did not vote out slavery; they believed in private property, even if that included human beings. The scale of slavery is shown by Attica's demography:[12]

7:    Jones, 1969, pp99-101.
8:    Davies, 2004, p18.
9:    Jones, 1969, p17.
10:   Wood, 1988, p61.
11:   Ste Croix, 1983, p141.
12:   Wood, 1988, p43.

	431 BC	323 BC
Total population of Attica	310,000	260,000
Citizens (including their families)	172,000	112,000
Foreigners (including their families)	28,500	42,000
Slaves (they were forbidden families)	110,000	106,000

A seaborne imperialism was another feature inextricably linked to Athenian democracy. Its power depended on the trireme, a galley with three banks of oarsmen drawn from the poorer citizenry,[13] who outnumbered the wealthy men constituting the heavy infantry. A 5th century author known as the Old Oligarch explained the poor had an:

> advantage over the men of birth and wealth, seeing that it is the people who row the vessels, and put round the city her girdle of power. For the steersman, the boatswain, the commanders of 50, the lookout-man at the prow, the shipwright—these are the people who engird the city with power rather than her heavy infantry and men of birth and quality.[14]

Peasants are usually geographically dispersed and, as petty producers, in competition with each other. Even when a majority they have difficulty in uniting to impose their will. However, combined together in the navy Athenian peasants possessed a cohesion and coercive strength that secured the long-term democratic gains of the revolution.

The empire's trade and tribute paid for the "marble magnificence" of the Parthenon in 447 BC, and underwrote state pay for jury service and the Assembly.[15] Russell Meiggs suggests that 60 percent of Athens's

---

13: Meiggs, 1972, p439.
14: Quoted in Claster, 1967, p44.
15: Quoted in Meiggs, 1972, p264.

"GNP" came from tribute.[16] Citizens gained land in conquered territories using brutal methods to displace and enslave the locals.[17] Significantly, while there were no political parties as such in the Athenian Assembly, the rich tended to vote against war (as they were subject to a war tax), while the poor did the opposite.[18]

It would be unhistorical to demand of the ancient Athenians an abhorrence of slavery or imperialism. However, it might be expected that poorer citizens would counter their economic inequality vis-à-vis the wealthy. In fact, democracy gave the poorer citizenry a stake in a system based on inequality and exploitation. As Josiah Ober puts it, "Citizens remained unequal in private life. Despite the fears of elite critics of democracy, the Athenian demos never consistently employed its collective power to equalise access to desirable private goods".[19] A H M Jones reinforces this point: "No suggestion was ever put forward for the redistribution of the land or for the cancellation of debts... Nor did 'the liberation of the slaves with revolutionary intent'...ever occur at Athens".[20] Poor peasant farmers did not wish to challenge property itself; they ensured the rich deployed their greater resources to exploit slaves instead.

Bourgeois democracy in the mother of parliaments

For capitalism, as in ancient Greece, democracy is not an abstract concept floating above class relations. Modern parliamentary democracy emerged when the bourgeoisie struggled to achieve dominance over feudalism. As a numerically small group this class had to appeal for support to wider forces and so it spoke in universal terms. In 1776, when Britain's American colonies sought freedom from Britain, the Declaration of Independence stated, "Governments are instituted among Men, deriving their just powers from the consent of the governed."

In 1789 the French bourgeoisie reached out to the vast majority of the French population, the Third Estate, with these words: "What is the Third Estate? Everything. What has it been hitherto in the political order? Nothing." Two hundred years later India, "the world's biggest democracy", declared independence using virtually identical terms: "the Sovereign people of India having solemnly resolved to constitute India into a Sovereign Democratic Republic".

16: Meiggs, 1972, p258.
17: Ma, Papazarkadas and Parker, 2009, p215.
18: Jones, 1969, p131.
19: Ober, 1996, p90.
20: Jones, 1969, pp91-92.

If in 1776 or 1789 there was a gap between democratic rhetoric and institutional arrangements on the ground, did the granting of the vote to all men and women later on mean real democracy had been achieved? This ignores the continuing influence exercised by capitalist control of the means of production. Thus it was Count Otto von Bismarck, an arch-reactionary, who introduced universal male suffrage to Germany in 1871. The US has elections of district attorneys, state referenda and so on, but is the most successful capitalist state and is among the most unequal societies in the world.

Nevertheless the advent of universal suffrage did have an impact. While an evolving bourgeois democracy neither touched the basis of capitalist rule nor gave popular control over the state, its universal language and appeal unleashed a process whereby the ordinary people fought for democracy *as they understood it*. John Molyneux shows that, "broadly speaking, the right to vote was won by working people as a by-product of the revolutionary wave that swept Europe at the end of the First World War".[21] More recently the Arab revolutions have battled for democratic elections in the teeth of vicious opposition.

Why, if universal suffrage does not threaten its control of the state and society, has capitalism sometimes been so resistant to it? And why has it been so popular if ordinary people gain so little? The rising bourgeoisie had to use language that was universal and therefore inevitably ambiguous. A classic example was seen in the French Revolution with its motto "Liberty, Equality, Fraternity".

In gaining parliamentary democracy capitalists won *freedom to exploit* at will, but others could interpret it as *freedom from exploitation*. The slogan of *equality* could mean capitalists were no longer inferior to feudal landowners; but it seemed to hold out the promise of a more equal distribution of wealth for all. Democracy could be seen merely as periodic elections, or signify the right to interfere with capitalist accumulation. Unlike in slave or serf societies, capitalists can gain from a generalised belief that workers are free because sophisticated modern technology relies on motivating workers rather than on labour extracted by brute compulsion, but a sense of having freedom and some rights also provides a space for trade unions.

So even at the time of the bourgeois revolutions the ambiguities of the democratic idea created openings for the expression of a different class interest, for the majority of the population. The diverse elements in the story of bourgeois democracy are expressed well in the world's oldest example—the

---

21: Molyneux, 2012.

"mother of parliaments" at Westminster. Its history shows a class context throughout. In 1264 a baronial revolt gave England the parliamentary system in order to "tie the hands of arbitrary power by imposing on the sovereign a council [composed of] the greatest ecclesiastical and lay figures".[22] Parliament consisted of the House of Lords plus "the elected representatives of the lesser nobility of the shires"—the Commons.[23] Representatives of cities and boroughs joined a year later.[24] Thus far Westminster represented an advisory committee of the feudal ruling class with the nascent bourgeoisie tacked on. Central power remained with the state headed by a king.

The English Revolution took parliament much further. Capitalist relations had matured within the cocoon of feudalism, and by 1640 the bourgeoisie wanted more influence over state decisions. That year military failure in Scotland forced Charles I to summon a parliament. But the Commons, drawn from an electorate comprising one in five of the male population,[25] resented royal interference, the privileged access of the aristocracy to the spoils of exploitation, taxation and religious policies, and a host of other impositions. The dispute at the summit of society created an opening for a mass democratic movement whose centre of gravity lay with the "middling sort of people"—those between the landlord class above and wage earners below.[26]

In December 1641 the monarch tried to arrest leading parliamentarians. Brian Manning writes, "It was a decisive moment in history and the decision lay, not with the king, not with the parliament, not with the nobility and gentry, not with armed soldiers...but with the mass of ordinary people in London...there was now what amounted to a general strike".[27] The king's intention to crush parliament was thwarted by the City of London, but the outcome was double-edged: "The City was now the parliament's—or rather, the parliament was now the City's".[28]

The relationship between the bourgeoisie and those it had to lean on to successfully combat royal opposition was a tense one. When hundreds of poor people presented a petition to parliament in January 1641 that body dared not reject the document openly, declaring that although "there were some things in the petition extraordinary [but] the House of

---

22: Bémont, 1930, p231.
23: Bémont, 1930, p216.
24: Bémont, 1930, p227.
25: 212,200 out of 1,170,400—Morton, 1979, p212.
26: Manning, 1976, pp152-153.
27: Manning, 1976, p96.
28: Manning, 1976, p98.

Commons thinks it not good to waken a sleepy lion; for it would pull on the mischief sooner".[29]

So the English Revolution became more than a dispute between the king and the institution of parliament. Indeed, the latter was merely one organisational focus of struggle. There were others. When civil war erupted the bourgeoisie needed its own military force. Here too success depended on people recruited from outside its ranks. The New Model Army's commander was Oliver Cromwell who, though a wealthy land-owner himself, chose "not such as were soldiers or men of estates, but such as were common men, poor and of mean parentage".[30] In 1645 this army won decisive battles, securing a fundamental transformation in state structure, never to be reversed in its essentials.

The role of parliament in these events was complex. As soon as the immediate threat from Charles I receded, the majority of MPs (the "Presbyterians"), fearful of the revolutionary elements now at large, sought a peaceful compromise with him so as to reconsolidate state power without which:

> the necessitous people of the whole kingdom will presently rise in mighty numbers and whosoever they pretend for at first, within a while they will set up for themselves, to the utter ruin of all the nobility and gentry of the kingdom.[31]

Cromwell rejected such backsliding in the parliamentary ranks as premature. He imposed a "self-denying ordinance" on the MPs excluding them from the decisive matter of military affairs: "During this time of this war no member of either House shall have or execute any [military] office or command".[32] His forces now represented the bourgeois interest more effectively than did parliament, showing there was no necessary correspondence between a representative form (such as parliament) and this class's rule. Indeed the New Model Army purged Westminster no less than six times in a decade to ensure the victory over the king would not be squandered.

Not everyone shared such disregard for democratic forms. Many of the "middling sort" believed in the potential of parliamentary representation.

29: Quoted in Manning, 1976, p109.
30: Quoted in Hill, 1972, p63.
31: John Hotham quoted in Manning, 1976, p216. The Hothams were originally the focal point of resistance to the king in Yorkshire, but when peace did not come they changed to the royalist side.
32: Quoted in Hill, 1972, p71.

They called themselves Levellers and demanded an extension of the franchise. At the Putney Debates of 1647 Colonel Thomas Rainsborough summed up Leveller beliefs in this way:

> that every man that is to live under a government ought first by his own consent to put himself under this government; and I do think that the poorest man in England is not at all bound in a strict sense to that government that he had not had a voice to put himself under...[33]

Paul Foot comments, "In two glorious sentences, Rainsborough summed up the argument for universal suffrage".[34] The idea of a democracy that really worked in the interest of the majority had been expressed.[35]

By 1649 the Levellers were crushed by Cromwell. For him the purpose of the revolution was to enhance the position of rising capitalism, not to empower ordinary people. He arrested the leaders and told the Council of State, "You have no other way to deal with these men but to break them or they will break you...and make void all that work that you have done... [These are] a despicable, contemptible generation of men".[36] With radicalism curbed and the institution of monarchy safely tamed, the capitalist class could re-establish order and authority using that traditional figurehead. The royal title was therefore offered to Cromwell (who preferred to be called Lord Protector), and after his death to Charles II in 1660. That same year the House of Lords, abolished in 1649, was re-established.

If the social transformation brought about by the English Revolution could not be effaced, the memory was. Modern bourgeois historians play up the role of parliament and affirm that "what happened between 1640 and

---

33: Quoted in Foot, 2005, p28.
34: Foot, 2005, p28.
35: There is debate about whether the Levellers advocated full universal male suffrage, or a vote more restricted to the "middling sort". Foot (in *The Vote*) and A L Morton (in Morton, 1979) affirm the former. Manning disagrees: "The Levellers did not attempt to question the assumptions of the patriarchal society in which they lived: voting was to be by household, in which the male head cast the vote for his servants and apprentices as well as for his wife and children"—Manning, 1976, p311. In one sense this is a non-issue. The "middling sort" genuinely believed their interests were universal, something which seemed plausible in the days before the lower classes and women were able to articulate their wishes clearly. There were, however, hints of other possibilities created by the bourgeois revolution and its openings. The Diggers, for example, went even further than the Levellers and advocated communal ownership of the land. During the French Revolution similar radical programmes were advanced by groups such as the *enragés*, and Babeuf's Conspiracy of the Equals).
36: Quoted in Hill, 1972, p105.

1660 is very much in the mainstream of English history; indeed it is crucial to the development of the constitution".[37] The continuity of parliament from Magna Carta to today is a fiction, but one that casts a long shadow. When universal suffrage eventually arrived in Britain, it brought MPs into a House of Commons festooned with the trappings of ancient ritual.

The post-revolution story of universal suffrage was not consistently one of mass struggle triumphing over privilege. Landmark expansions of the vote occurred in 1832, 1867, 1884 and 1918. The 1832 "Great" Reform Act granted the franchise to the new middle class of the industrial revolution. It came after an enormous wave of marches and riots which induced Macaulay, a far-sighted member of the ruling class and MP, to exclaim, "I support this plan because I am sure that it is our best security against a revolution".[38] So even 1832 was *both* a concession *and* the "best security against a revolution".

Chartism followed in the 1840s. This enormous movement attracted millions of supporters and promoted universal male suffrage as a means to radical redistribution of wealth: "What concerns us is that we ourselves be represented in the legislative body and that we employ our own power to emancipate ourselves from the middle [ie bourgeois] class... Become your own governors in the workshop as well as out of it".[39] Alas, Chartist proposals were rejected by parliament time after time. Mass semi-revolutionary pressure did not produce an extension of the franchise.

That came in 1867. There was a riot in favour of the Reform Act, but the movement was far less radical than in Chartist times. Its leaders wanted the franchise so as to "put an end to animosities...amongst the different classes...and weld all classes together by unity of interest into one harmonious whole".[40] The Third Reform Act of 1884 was passed without even the campaigns of 1867, let alone the 1840s, yet it enfranchised the largest number yet—two out of three men (from one in three).

The advent of votes for women in 1918 fits neither the pattern of mass agitation nor unforced concession. As Foot suggests, Suffragette campaigning in the period up to 1914 made a contribution: "The victory of 1918 would not have been achieved without the long years of struggle that preceded it. The militant activities of the suffragettes loosened the ideological hold of men over women".[41]

37: Aylmer, 1963, p162.
38: Quoted in Foot, 2005, p72.
39: Bronterre O'Brien, quoted in Foot, 2005, p96.
40: Quoted in Foot, 2005, p137.
41: Foot, 2005, p236.

However, the Suffragettes stopped their campaign at the outbreak of the First World War to concentrate on patriotic flag-waving (such as the "white feather" campaign against young men who delayed enlisting). Emmeline Pankhurst even went to Russia to dissuade the population there from the Bolshevik demand for peace. The Reform Act received its second reading in May 1917. This was a time when the outcome of the First World War was far from certain. Lloyd George's government realised survival depended on maintaining civilian morale on the home front, thus avoiding the revolution that eventually made Germany sue for peace. Female suffrage was one of a host of promises, such as "Homes fit for heroes", designed to sustain the war and ward off revolution.

In other words, suffrage was sometimes the result of class struggle, sometimes not. Rather than being a sign of workers gaining traction within the state, it was an expense paid for continued domination. Westminster therefore acquired a carefully constructed, if fictitious, image. The Levellers are forgotten, along with the Chartists. Instead our parliamentary system, with a constitutional monarch, House of Lords, feudal rites, pomp and circumstance, exudes social superiority, but gives out the message that it is possible in a class society to successfully combine democracy and deference.

Partly this is due to the compromises described above. Even more important, at the very moment the voting habit reached British workers, this country was the world's greatest imperial power. As Trotsky explains:

> Britain was the first country to take the road of capitalist development and won, thanks to that fact, the hegemony of the world market in the 19th century. The British bourgeoisie became, again thanks to this fact, the richest, strongest, and most enlightened of the bourgeoisies.

Consequently, the British labour movement carried "a heavy conservative tail stretching back into the Middle Ages".[42] All this has given a peculiarly restrained character to voting behaviour.

Its political development therefore took a different route to elsewhere. While fully-fledged socialist parties had been operating across the continent since the mid-19th century, the British Labour Party was only finally established in 1900. At its birth it was so politically timid that it could only be admitted into the Socialist (Second) International by creating a special category of (non-socialist) membership. It was not that the

---

42: Trotsky, 1974, volume I, pp21-22.

British working class was less powerful, but since the defeat of Chartism mass working class radicalism tended to concentrate on trade unionism, out of which the Labour Party itself emerged. This was a reversal of the order seen on the continent where socialist parties set up the unions.

I have written elsewhere that: "The electoral balance between Tories and Labour is rooted, in the final analysis, in the class struggle".[43] The "final analysis" needs emphasising. The correlation of working class struggle and parliamentary elections exists, but is very weak. Sometimes parliamentary progress is in inverse relationship to class struggle. Labour's precursor, the Independent Labour Party, was formed in 1893 as a conscious move towards substituting parliamentary tactics for strike action. Labour benefited electorally from the defeat of the 1926 General Strike. The incredible industrial struggles that brought down Edward Heath's Tory government in 1974 saw its total share of the vote fall 6 percent compared to the previous election. The point is that there is no fixed pattern, because there is no organic connection between the real life of the working class and elections.

This is a problem for socialists who rightly pay heed to the argument of Lenin's *"Left-Wing" Communism: An Infantile Disorder,* that socialists consider standing in parliamentary elections. He proposed this as a means of exposing the permanent gap between what is granted under bourgeois democracy and what the working class wants from it. However, that is not an easy thing to do in Britain, given the historical background described above.

Take the example of the British Communist Party (CPGB). It started as a revolutionary organisation, and despite succumbing to Stalinism remained an effective focus for militants. The CPGB was clearly the radical alternative to Labour and had what pundits call "high brand recognition". The period up to 1935 saw enormous struggles like Red Friday (1925) and the General Strike. Then came the collapse of the second Labour government, defection of the Labour prime minister Ramsay MacDonald to the Tories, and the rout of Labour in 1931. Yet the CPGB vote never rose beyond 0.3 percent of votes cast. The 1945 peak, at 0.4 percent, was less due to its own efforts than the triumph of the Red Army over Hitler in the Second World War. In January 1951 the CPGB published *The British Road to Socialism* setting a course "for decisive action to win a parliamentary majority". Despite this fixation it never broke through the 0.2 percent barrier. The table below presents a depressing picture of a half century of electoral effort by a key party of the British far left.

43: Cliff and Gluckstein, 1988, p382.

Election	Votes	% of all votes	MPs elected
1922	33,637	0.2	1
1923	39,448	0.2	0
1924	55,346	0.3	1
1929	50,634	0.2	0
1931	74,824	0.3	0
1935	27,117	0.1	0
1945	102,780	0.4	2
1950	91,765	0.3	0
1951	21,640	0.1	0
1955	33,144	0.1	0
1959	30,896	0.1	0
1964	46,442	0.2	0
1966	62,092	0.2	0
1970	37,970	0.1	0
1974a	32,743	0.1	0
1974b	17,426	0.1	0
1979	16,858	0.1	0

Compare this to continental Communist parties. In the pre-1914 Tsarist Duma the Bolsheviks won 50 to 80 percent of the working class vote (which polled separately to other social groups). Before destruction by

Nazism the German CP scored 17 percent of the total vote. In 1945, given the outstanding role played by continental CPs in the resistance movements and the Red Army victory over Hitler, the French CP gained 26 percent, the Belgian and Danish 13 percent and the Norwegian 12 percent. In the 1970s the Italian CP reached 34 percent, the Portuguese 14 percent and the Spanish 11 percent.

To judge the CPGB by voting performance would be a serious mistake, however. It played a decisive role in Britain's most important class struggles. In the run-up to Red Friday the CPGB-influenced Minority Movement organisation was instrumental in the election of left union leaders. During the General Strike the CPGB was at the heart of forming Councils of Action. In the 1930s its militants were central to the revival of industrial struggle through the London bus strike of 1937 and the unionisation of car plants. In the 1960s and 1970s the party led national shop stewards' organisations that shook Harold Wilson's Labour governments and toppled Heath.

Stalinism aside, the mismatch between the CPGB's industrial and electoral influence was not due to lack of talent or membership motivation. Nor could it simply be ascribed to the first past the post system with its gladiatorial contest between the big parties. Shop stewards' elections are also based on first past the post. Communists were elected here because their co-workers could see at first hand that they championed working class interests and had practical views about the way forward.

This is not an argument for ignoring elections. Lenin's critique of ultra-leftism for abstaining on principle was absolutely correct. Though parliamentarism is a dead-end it does not mean that:

> "millions" and "legions" of proletarians are not still in favour of parliamentarism in general... We must not regard what is obsolete *for us* as being obsolete *for the class*, as being obsolete for the masses... You must not sink to the level of the masses, to the level of the backward strata of the class. That is incontestable. You must tell them the bitter truth. You must call their bourgeois democratic and parliamentary prejudices—prejudices. But at the same time you must *soberly* follow the *actual* state of class consciousness.[44]

The socialist approach must be related to the "actual state of class consciousness" and this is influenced by the specific historical background, for good and ill.

44: Lenin, 1993, pp67-68.

If the strength of belief in parliamentary elections means they cannot be ignored by socialists, by the same token, unfortunately, many judge the seriousness of a political platform in the light of the election results obtained. An army that indulges in battles that it is bound to lose badly is not necessarily going to inspire bystanders to join it. So a concrete "sober" judgement has to be made on each occasion, weighing up the real forces behind a socialist electoral campaign and the likely results.

Proletarian democracy

Many ancient Greek cities with a similar social structure to Athens had no democracy, just as today some capitalist states do without parliaments. Class rule by a minority neither requires nor excludes "free and fair" elections, because fundamental power derives from control of the means of production regardless of what representative structures are in place. Fritz Thyssen, who bankrolled Hitler, wrote:

> An industrialist is always inclined to consider politics a kind of second string to his bow... In a well ordered country, where the administration is sound, where taxes are reasonable, and the police well organised, he can afford to abstain from politics and devote himself entirely to business.[45]

Exploiters of slaves, serfs or workers remain exploiters, whether they take an equal share in running government or allow a committee, king or dictator to take the initiative on their behalf.[46]

In this regard capitalism has the greatest room for manoeuvre, because accumulation is disguised. Workers are separated from the means of production and seemingly "volunteer" to labour, without the state having to act coercively, as is the case with slaves or serfs. Capitalism does not require state intervention except, of course, when workers fight back, or a crisis demands exceptional measures. Loose control via bourgeois democracy is possible, but fascism, military dictatorship, imperialist domination and so on are equally suitable.

It is different for the working class where liberation depends on the majority class exercising power collectively. Marx and Engels's *Communist Manifesto* explains why:

45: Thyssen, 1941, p62.
46: This explains the phenomenon of Bonapartism, such as discussed by Marx in his *Eighteenth Brumaire of Louis Bonaparte*. Marx describes how, in certain situations of crisis, the bourgeoisie volunteers to relinquish direct rule of its own.

All previous historical movements were movements of minorities, or in the interests of minorities. The proletarian movement is the self-conscious, independent movement of the immense majority, in the interest of the immense majority. [47]

The "immense majority" require an appropriate collective organisational form to exert authority over both the state and the means of production. Here genuine democracy (in the original Greek sense of the word) is an absolute necessity. The exercise of class power at one remove, which is possible for the capitalists due to their control of the means of production, is not an option. How is the striving for this very different type of democracy expressed?

The labour movement has generated various models of organisation, ranging from trade unions to reformist and revolutionary parties, through which workers have attempted to collectively shape their fate. (There are organisational forms such as single-issue campaigns, but these are too dispersed, too varied or too short-lived to develop a consistent pattern of internal structure for analysis here.)

Democracy and the trade unions

Trade unions primarily relate to working life. They are independent of the bosses, unlike parliament, which is essentially an appendage of the capitalist state. Their existence reflects a certain balance. If capitalists were fully dominant then trade unions would not exist. Conversely, if workers clearly understood their common interest and united as a class, then sectional unions fighting for partial gains would not continue. Finally, if workers ran society, then there would be no bosses to negotiate with over pay and conditions. But because there is a balance, a layer of officials arises. It fears the absolute dominance of the bosses (which would eliminate unions entirely) but also the independent action of workers (as that would render its mediating role irrelevant). It functions as an obstacle to full expression of workers' democracy.

Again British history is informative. The mid-19th century was the era of "Old Unionism" involving skilled workers in particular, narrow trades. This "labour aristocracy", some 15 percent of the working class, opposed the employment of unskilled men and women to maximise the price of its own labour. Old Unionism developed the "Junta"—a strong grouping of elected union bureaucrats dedicated to compromise with

---

47: Marx and Engels, 1976, p495.

employers and the avoidance of strikes. As a means of expressing the wish of the majority class to rule Old Unionism was ineffective.

In the 1880s mass strikes created "New Unions" based on class-wide recruitment. They were ambitious in democratic terms. As Will Thorne of the National Union of Gasworkers and General Labourers wrote, by making "international working-class solidarity a reality [for] the under-paid and oppressed workers...we offered...something tangible, a definite, clearly-lighted road out of their misery".[48] However, an employers' offensive ended the New Unionist upsurge. The weakness of the unskilled in the face of determined bosses now made them reliant on negotiations by union officials. By the turn of the 20th century, therefore, a caste of full-time bureaucrats dominated both New and Old Unionism and internal democracy was largely stymied.

In Britain the first conscious drive to break out of this and achieve workers' democracy both within unions and in society generally came from the syndicalists, a group of militants who believed parliament could not be the agent of change. They saw democratic progress coming through workers' own organisations—the unions. Although history has shown this hope to have been flawed, they achieved important insights into the way unions functioned, which are still relevant today.

Active during the Labour Unrest of 1910-14, syndicalists in South Wales published *The Miners' Next Step* which proclaimed "Industrial Democracy the objective" through reformed trade unions. This would not be achieved by applying the rules of bourgeois democratic formalism, because "no constitution, however admirable in its structure, can be of any avail, unless the whole is quickened and animated by that, which will give it the breath of life—a militant aggressive policy".[49]

For syndicalists the way to workers' democracy lay through class struggle:

> The policy of conciliation gives the real power of the men into the hands of a few leaders. Somebody says: "What about conferences and ballots"? Conferences are *only called*, and ballots *only taken* when there is a difference of opinion between leaders... They, the leaders, become "gentlemen", they become MPs, and have considerable social prestige because of this power... Now, every inroad the rank and file make on this privilege lessens the power

48: Kapp, 1976, p323.
49: *The Miners' Next Step*, 1973, p30.

and prestige of the leader. Can we wonder then that leaders are averse to change?... *The leader then has an interest—a vested interest in stopping progress.*[50]

"Militant aggressive" policies included "different methods and ways of striking",[51] and mass meetings (rather than passive ballots), because "the tendency of large meetings is always towards purity of tone and breadth of outlook. The reactionary cuts a poor figure under such circumstances".[52] As well as blowing away the cobwebs of parliamentarism, the pamphlet proposed democratic centralism by advocating "Decentralisation for Negotiating" and "Centralisation for Fighting".[53]

During the First World War the proletarian democratic current was renewed through a movement of engineering shop stewards. Its lessons were crystallised in *The Workers' Committee* by J T Murphy. He provided an acute analysis of union bureaucracy:

> Everyone is aware that usually a man gets into office on the strength of revolutionary speeches, which strangely contrast with those of a later date after a period in office... Now compare the outlook of the man in the workshop and the man as a full-time official. As a man in the workshop he feels every change; the workshop atmosphere is his atmosphere; the conditions under which he labours are primary; his trade union constitution is secondary, and sometimes even more remote. But let the same man get into office. He is removed out of the workshop; he meets a fresh class of people, and breathes a different atmosphere. Those things which were once primary are now secondary. He becomes buried in the constitution, and of necessity looks from a new point of view... Thus we obtain a contrast between those who reflect working class conditions and those who are remote from them.[54]

Murphy aimed "to invigorate the labour movement with the real democratic spirit" by creating a rank and file movement independent of the bureaucracy.[55]

As with *The Miners' Next Step*, Murphy had understood that the workers' desire to shape their working lives was not hampered by badly

50: *The Miners' Next Step*, 1973, p15.
51: *The Miners' Next Step*, 1973, p30.
52: *The Miners' Next Step*, 1973, p31.
53: *The Miners' Next Step*, 1973, p30.
54: Murphy, 1972, pp13-14.
55: Murphy, 1972, p18.

worded constitutions so much as the energy put into struggle.[56] Though formal procedures are far from irrelevant, they themselves reflect the balance between rank and file activity and the bureaucracy. The best provide a channel for pressure to come from below, though the pace of constitutional change usually lags behind developments outside.

Another barometer of union democracy is reflected by the bureaucracy itself. The division between "right" and "left" leaders is not so much "party political" as dependent on whether negotiation or struggle is seen as the union's key function. Left wing and right wing leaders influence the way the organisation operates, but even this cannot be abstracted from concrete conditions. There is no constitutional formula that can prevent sellouts by left wing leaders if the working class itself feels weak or passive and unable to fight. Conversely a militant, active rank and file membership can pressure right wing officials into action, or lead independent union action, if the officials are obstructing the democratic demands of the base. The famous formula of the Clyde Workers' Committee sums it up perfectly: "We will support the officials just so long as they rightly represent the workers, but we will act independently immediately they misrepresent them".[57]

The battle over how strike action is decided illustrates the difference between bourgeois and proletarian democracy. Secret postal ballots allow the pressure of capitalist media and bourgeois individualism more scope than mass meetings, where collective will is to the fore. In the 1980s Thatcher claimed, "The government are anxious to promote trade union democracy" by imposing secret ballots.[58] One Tory MP contrasted the sort of mass meeting envisaged by *The Miners' Next Step* to secret ballots: "Today, a man must be all but a hero to lead a vote, by show of hands…at the average mass meeting of his union." The secret ballot, he said, is a "basic democratic right".[59] These alternative conceptions of democracy were put to a practical test in the miners' strike of 1984-5. As Mike Simons puts it:

> The call for a ballot was not a demand for genuinely democratic debate and decision-making. It was a weapon in a class war… In 1984 the miners' opponents wanted the ballot because they believed it would break the union. In fact the 1984 strike spread to involve the great majority of the workforce through a thoroughly democratic method—miners from one pit

---

56: Murphy, 1972, pp14-15.
57: Quoted in Cliff and Gluckstein, 1986, p34.
58: Margaret Thatcher, *Hansard*, House of Commons debate, 11 February 1982.
59: John Browne (Tory MP for Winchester) in *Hansard*, House of Commons debate, 22 April 1980.

or area going to another to explain face to face why solidarity and unity were essential.[60]

Whatever advances the collective challenge to the rule of the capitalist class is a step to real democracy; whatever encourages passivity hampers that struggle.

Since the defeat of the miners a raft of anti-union legislation has entrenched the secret ballot, and often the choice for union activists is between no consultation of the membership on a pressing issue, or such a ballot. In these circumstances bourgeois democracy is better than dictatorship, and a secret ballot is preferable to no vote. But it is a poor substitute.

Reformist parties

In the battle for proletarian democracy trade unions are important, but they have a key restriction. Sectional bodies focused on wages and conditions are limited in their capacity to transform society, and so secure collective power. It requires an organisation whose members are drawn from the majority, irrespective of employment status, and centred on wider political questions. That means a political party, and historically there have been three main types—reformist, Stalinist and revolutionary.

Whereas unions reflect the balance of class struggle, reformist parties mirror the ideological balance. If workers fully accepted bourgeois ideas, reformist parties would not exist. If they rejected them and made a revolution, the same would be true. Furthermore, to maximise votes reformist parties appeal to a large proportion of the working class, to those who hold ideas ranging from reactionary to left wing. In that sense the reformist party claims to represent the class as it exists under capitalism.[61] This situation underpins the internal regime of reformist parties.

Whatever their intentions, reformist parties become fundamentally undemocratic because they accept parliamentarism. The focus is getting MPs elected, and it is they who dominate, whatever the party's constitution. In turn, by accepting the "rules of the game" they end up running capitalism when in government. The transmission belt runs from the top down, not the other way round, and far from the reformist party serving the working class, the ordinary members end up suffering at its hands. Reformist parties do not capture the capitalist state; it is they that are captured.

The British Labour Party demonstrates this process well. Before

60: Simons, 2004, pp9-10.
61: See Cliff, Harman, Hallas and Trotsky, 1996.

1918 Labour consisted of affiliated trade unions and socialist societies (like the Independent Labour Party). Its MPs were not accountable to party members, and indeed that category did not yet exist. It was mass wartime radicalism at home and fear of the 1917 Russian Revolution that led Labour to establish individual membership and adopt the socialist Clause Four (which, if enacted, would have meant some real democratic control over the means of production). The 1918 constitution set up local branches, a system of annual conferences, the National Executive Committee and the paraphernalia of internal democracy. So it was the external pressure of mass radicalism and revolution that brought about limited democratic advance.

For a long time the leadership consistently ignored conference decisions and members' wishes, but at least the democratic pretence continued. However, union defeats in the 1980s, with a consequent loss of working class confidence, allowed Blair formally to abolish party democracy, at the same time as scrapping Clause Four.

Revolutionary democracy and revolutionary parties

Since trade unions and reformist parties operate within the framework of the system and inevitably sell out, some people, such as the Spanish *indignados*, reject all political parties and trade unions on principle as undemocratic.[62] This label should not be applied to revolutionary parties because they aim to overthrow the capitalist system, so that the collective will of the masses really can rule.

The means to achieving this ultimate goal becomes visible when organs of mass popular democracy emerge during revolutions. There have been many instances, ranging from the Paris Commune to the Russian soviet and beyond.[63] These were not invented by some political thinker, but emerged spontaneously, as a natural form of collective power, from mass struggle.

Whereas parliamentary systems use arbitrary geographical constituencies as the basis for voting, leaving the core power of the capitalists untouched, through the soviet or its equivalents workers exercise collective control of the means of production and the state by electing delegates from workplaces to form organs of state power. Since these workplaces operate continuously delegates can be subject to instant recall. All that is required is a shop meeting to change them. MPs are only accountable once in four or

---

62: See Molyneux, 2011, for a discussion of the anarchist critique of party organisation, and its weaknesses.

63: See Ness and Azzelini, 2011.

five years. Soviet delegates go from workplaces with the salary of those who elect them, so they experience the consequences of their decisions. MPs are insulated and their pay is unrelated to their constituents'.

Even here it is important not to mystify organisational form. Trotsky chaired the first soviet (in 1905 St Petersburg), yet he found "contemptible and sinister" anyone who:

> abstracts only the bare form and converts it into a fetish. This is what has happened to the soviets... As if the soviets cannot be a weapon for deceiving the workers and peasants! What else were the Menshevik–Socialist Revolutionary Soviets of 1917? Nothing but a weapon for the support of the power of the bourgeoisie and the preparation of its dictatorship. What were the social democratic soviets in Germany and Austria in 1918-1919? Organs for saving the bourgeoisie and for deceiving the workers.[64]

So the immediate representative democracy of the soviet creates only the potential for proletarian rule. To go further it has to wish to do so, and that depends on the majority being won to revolution. In Russia this came from the persuasive efforts of the Bolsheviks, from a revolutionary party. When the Tsar was overthrown in February 1917 the Bolsheviks called for "All Power to the Soviet of Workers', Soldiers' and Peasants' Deputies". Although only a minority of the soviet supported this at first, by the autumn the majority did so, and on 25 October, with an almost bloodless insurrection in the capital, now renamed Petrograd, the slogan became a reality.

The combination of a revolutionary party and the soviet led to the greatest leap forward in democracy ever achieved. By overthrowing the minority power of aristocrats and capitalists mass rule became effective, and made possible the Bolshevik policy "Peace, land and bread". While the parliaments of Germany, Britain and France continued with the First World War, a detested, futile war, the Soviet government responded to the urgent demands of the soldiers, and ended hostilities the day after coming to power. Peasants comprised the vast majority of the Russian population, and their longing for land was answered that same day, when seizure of the aristocracy's estates was legalised. In the towns workers were taking control of their factories. By early 1918, 500 had been nationalised and Lenin soon noted that they had taken over more enterprises "than we have had time to count".[65]

64: Trotsky, 1974, volume 3, p185.
65: Lenin, 1964, volume 26, p334.

The breakthrough fed major advances in the rights of women, ethnic minorities, gays and so on. It was possible because, through the interaction of a revolutionary party, the soviet form, and control over the means of production, popular representation, power and the social context were now mutually complementary.

Tragically that did not last. The soviets became an empty shell. Through a purged Bolshevik Party the Stalinist dictatorship ran the state and ruthlessly exploited the masses. What had gone wrong? A common view is this was the inevitable product of Lenin's Bolshevik Party and its methods. The historian Robert Service, for example, asserts that Lenin "had an especially bossy personality",[66] so:

> Bolshevism itself had a predisposition in favour of political, economic and social ultra-authoritarianism; and, even if not Stalin but Trotsky or Bukharin or even Kamenev had assumed the supreme party leadership after Lenin's death, an ultra-authoritarian system of rule would have prevailed. Trotsky, Bukharin and Kamenev—like Lenin—advocated a milder variant of Bolshevism than Stalin's. But it was still Bolshevism.[67]

So the utter destruction of democracy is explained in terms of bossiness and the "predisposition" of Bolshevism, even though Service grudgingly accepts that "the Bolsheviks were a party whose members in 1917, among themselves, acted relatively democratically".[68]

However, if Service is correct, then the inner workings of the party led to dictatorship over society. That runs counter to the argument of this article: that the political system (including the inner functioning of parties) must be understood in relation to the social context, or as Marx put it, the superstructure must be interpreted in relation to the base.[69] How did this operate in Russia?

Due to its collective character in production, both the Bolshevik Party and soviet democracy relied on a militant, but relatively small working class. The peasants, who comprised 80 percent of the population and were spread over the vast countryside, lacked a similar cohesion or collective interest and participated to a lesser extent in the councils of "workers', soldiers' and peasants' deputies".

66: Service, 1997, p94.
67: Service, 1997, p97.
68: Service, 1997, p97.
69: For a thorough discussion of the interrelationship see Harman, 1986.

After the October Revolution there was a brutal civil war. Reds were pitted against Whites and foreign capitalist intervention. 180,000 workers died. Disruption to production meant the working class declined from 2.6 million to 1.2 million. The population of Petrograd, which had pioneered the revolution, fell from 2,400,000 to 720,000. A contemporary commentator wrote, "There is no example in the history of mankind of such a decrease in productive power suffered, not by a small community, but by a great hundred-million strong society".[70] The result was a quarter of the population, 35 million people, experienced acute hunger, and there were even cases of cannibalism.[71] The Whites were beaten in the civil war, but the massive military effort had required a large bureaucracy. At the end of the war the number of state officials stood at 5,880,000—five times the number of industrial workers. [72]

In this situation collective rule would have evaporated whether Lenin was bossy or not. This is not to deny the importance of individuals, for as Marx said, "men make their own history, but they do not make it as they please...but under circumstances existing already, given and transmitted from the past".[73] Lenin, Trotsky and other leaders tried to stem the tide, but had little effect in the face of such odds, because the social context was utterly hostile to their efforts. The working class was completely outweighed by peasants and the state bureaucracy. In the 1920s the latter groups fought for supremacy under the leadership of Bukharin and Stalin respectively. Destruction of Bolshevik Party democracy ran in parallel with the decline of the working class. The internal regime eventually took a fixed Stalinist form that reflected the state capitalist system Stalin ran—a completely dictatorial regime both within the party and in the country generally.

Russia's amazing democratic achievements and their utter destruction offer startling proof of our argument. In 1917 Soviet Russia exhibited all the immediacy of rule seen in Athenian direct democracy but went even further by encompassing, if only momentarily, the majority of a vast society. The Leninist party was an essential component of the great democratic advance of 1917; so the question of how a revolutionary party functions is of huge significance for democracy.

Just as there is a connection between the internal structures of reformist parties and their external environment, so it is with revolutionary parties.

70: Kritsman, 1971, p257.
71: Cliff, 1978, p90.
72: Cliff, 1978, p178.
73: www.marxists.org/archive/marx/works/1852/18th-brumaire/ch01.htm

While both operate under the constraints of capitalism, their relation to these constraints is quite different. In this context the question of leadership is key.

Reformist parties (like trade unions) recruit from the majority of the working class who, to varying degrees, accept the ideas of capitalism. One of these ideas is that the top brass are there to win concessions *on behalf* of the rank and file. This renders the members passive, leaving the leaders as the active factor. The latter are left free to mediate between capitalists and the rank and file, or are incorporated into capitalism through prestige and high salaries. This divorces them from the membership, encouraging personal or ideological corruption.

The Leninist party model is entirely different, and not based on bourgeois democracy but the relationship between ideas, revolutionary goals and its environment. Though aiming to convince the majority class to take control, a revolutionary party is very much a minority, attracting only the most politically advanced to its ranks. They, in turn, seek to act as a vanguard, to win over the reformist majority of the working class. For the minority to do this it must put forward radical arguments, and propose alternative forms of action—in other words to lead. Thus the revolutionary party must aspire to make every member a leader. In that sense the normal definition of leaders/followers breaks down, and it is more accurate to talk about a technical division of labour between a "party centre" and a party rank and file.

The centre may consist of those who have proved their abilities, can bring particular theoretical or practical experience to bear, have the time and opportunity to play a central role in the organisation, and so on. But, in essence, it is not distinct from the rank and file in the way that an MP or union general secretary is. Bourgeois democracy makes a fetish of elections and representation in order to disguise who really rules. The revolutionary party has no use for such a fetish. It does not exist for itself, for the momentary satisfaction individuals might gain from self-expression in a ballot, but for a specific purpose—the transformation of society. Its internal processes are there to assist that process and nothing more.

Revolutionary party members cannot passively wait for the centre to act on their behalf, nor is it in the interest of the centre for the members to be reduced to passivity. The relationship between both must be dynamic and interactive if a party of leaders is to exist. It does not follow that a revolutionary party is automatically immune from bureaucratic degeneration. Protection from that lies not so much in a constitution as in political action. The relationship between internal structure and external context applies here, as elsewhere.

In seeking to engage with those who are at present to its right, a revolutionary party exposes itself to a working class that is majority reformist. So the danger of accommodating to reformism does not disappear just because someone joins. For example, members may hold prominent positions in trade unions; that puts them under pressure from the bureaucracy. Other members might begin with a revolutionary attitude but succumb to bourgeois ideology over time. Revolutionaries must work alongside members of reformist organisations in joint campaigns and may be more influenced by them rather than vice versa.

In this situation the party cannot remain true to its ideal of winning real democracy unless it can prevent this drag to the right. So a primary democratic function of the internal structure is to uphold the revolutionary ideal against pressures on members to accommodate. For this to work all of the party must be accountable for their actions and their politics—both at the centre and in the rank and file. Accountability is absent in reformist parties, because members can hold backward bourgeois ideas, leaders can sell out—and nothing happens. Russia's Mensheviks were originally in the same party as the Bolsheviks (the Russian Social Democratic and Labour Party), but a split occurred precisely over the issue of accountability, which they regarded as unnecessary. When the Bolsheviks achieved their great democratic leap forward, the Mensheviks were in the camp of the Whites, battling through civil war to defeat these gains.

Countering the drag to the right produces an opposite danger—that the party becomes a sect. Till the moment of the revolution itself revolutionaries are constantly swimming against the stream, and so there is a temptation to renounce meaningful interaction with the working class and retreat into a more comfortable isolation. This leaves them preaching at the class from the sidelines rather than trying to lead. This has been the fate of many socialist parties in the past. The internal regime of a sect is sclerotic and tends to lack democratic debate, because all that is required (for both leadership and rank and file) is constant repetition of unchanging general beliefs and strategy. Revolution, which alone can bring real democracy, cannot be achieved if it becomes a sterile belief and is not constantly tested, developed and informed by the struggle for leadership in the working class. So just as the revolutionary party protects itself from the pressure to adapt to its capitalist environment, it must expose itself through intervention.

This requires an internal structure that reflects members' experience in striving to lead within the working class and decides how to act. It is called "democratic centralism". It does not prefigure a workers' state or mass democracy, such as the soviet. Trotsky, whose commitment to proletarian democracy cost him his life at the hands of a Stalinist assassin, was insistent that democratic centralism was not a formal set of constitutional points. There was no:

> formula on democratic centralism that "once and for all" would eliminate misunderstandings and false interpretations. A party is an active organism. It develops in the struggle with outside obstacles and inner contradictions... The regime of a party does not fall ready made from the sky but is formed gradually in struggle. *A political line predominates over the regime.* First of all, it is necessary to define strategic problems and tactical methods correctly in order to solve them. The organisational forms should correspond to the strategy and the tactic.[74]

Here is a classic expression of this article's argument. The key to healthy internal relationships *within* a revolutionary party is the correct political orientation *outside* the party. Such intervention consists of two elements—the formulation of the strategy and its application. The balance was described by Lenin in these terms:

> We must centralise the leadership of the movement. We must also... *decentralise responsibility to the party* on the part of its individual members, of every participant in its work, and of every circle belonging to or associated with the party. This decentralisation is an essential prerequisite of revolutionary centralisation and an *essential corrective* to it.[75]

Democratic centralism is not only a necessity from an internal party point of view. It is an essential counter both at this level, and at the level of the working class as a whole, to the undemocratic centralism of the ruling class.

Whatever democratic figleaf is in place, the capitalist minority of exploiters depend on intense centralism to prevail against the majority. The capitalist state is highly centralised, and most noticeably so in its weapons of coercion—the army and police. Here power is concentrated through a rigid, unelected and unaccountable hierarchy, from privates at the base to generals at the top. But this is mirrored equally in the staggering concentrations represented by giant corporations. For example, in 2007 Walmart, Exxon and Shell were each worth as much as the Greek economy, larger than Denmark, Argentina and South Africa, and so on.

74: My emphasis. From a US Internal Bulletin in December 1937, prior to the formation the SWP (US)—www.marxists.org/archive/trotsky/1937/xx/democent.htm
75: Cliff, 1975, p249.

The working class needs to centralise its efforts if it is to stand up against such accumulations of force. As a class this cannot be achieved on an individual basis. It requires the involvement of as many people as possible and so must also be democratic. In both an abstract and a practical sense, democracy and centralism are contradictory and complementary.

It is easy to talk about democratic centralism in a revolutionary party, but harder to practise it. If that party spends all its time in democratic discussions to find the best approach, it ceases to deserve the name and becomes an irrelevant talking shop and sect. If a party spends all its time implementing decisions that have been taken, but never revises them to fit changing circumstances, it will be out of touch with the needs of the moment—again a sect. The correct balance must be struck, although this changes constantly.

Writing on the subject in 1937 Trotsky said:

> Democracy and centralism do not at all find themselves in an invariable ratio to one another. Everything depends on the concrete circumstances, on the political situation in the country, on the strength of the party and its experience, on the general level of its members, on the authority the leadership has succeeded in winning. Before a conference, when the problem is one of formulating a political line for the next period, democracy triumphs over centralism.

> When the problem is political action, centralism subordinates democracy to itself. Democracy again asserts its rights when the party feels the need to examine critically its own actions. The equilibrium between democracy and centralism establishes itself in the actual struggle; at moments it is violated and then again re-established.[76]

Democratic centralism in the revolutionary party is the opposite of what occurs under the most free and fair parliamentary system. Here the centralism of the rich and powerful and their state, armies, courts and legislatures work to protect the ruling class, all under the pretence of democracy.

Conclusion

It is common to talk about democracy without regard to the specific social context in which it is operating. Hopefully this article has shown that is a profound mistake, and that meaningful discussion must always differentiate between the different types. Because capitalists own the means of production

---

76: www.marxists.org/archive/trotsky/1937/xx/democent.htm

it is inevitable that their version of democracy separates form from content; representation from rule; *demos* from *kratei*; leaders from led. Proletarian democracy unites all of these elements in a dialectical synthesis which alone can bring collective control to the majority and liberate humanity.[77]

The current capitalist crisis poses an unprecedented challenge to those who believe in democracy. In many places the pressure of the money markets and corporations is such that the falsity and superficiality of bourgeois democracy are exposed. At the same time there is a wave of resistance. It takes many forms; but in every case, whether it is a general strike, a popular revolution or a mass movement such as Occupy, the sinews of the popular will to collectively rule can be seen at work. The history of democracy from ancient Greece to present-day Greece shows the potential for genuine rule by the masses once and for all.

77: This runs counter to the classic expression of "separation of powers" developed by Montesquieu before the French Revolution. In his *Civil War in France* Marx praised the merger of executive and legislature in the Paris Commune as a feature of proletarian democracy.

References

Aylmer, G E, 1963, *The Struggle for the Constitution* (Blandford).

Bémont, Charles, 1930, *Simon de Montfort* (Oxford University Press).

Claster, Jill N, 1967, *Athenian Democracy. Triumph or Travesty?* (Holt Rinehart Winston).

Cliff, Tony, 1975, *Lenin*, volume 1 (Pluto).

Cliff, Tony, 1978, *Lenin*, volume 3 (Pluto).

Cliff, Tony, and Donny Gluckstein, 1986, *Marxism and Trade Union Struggle* (Bookmarks).

Cliff, Tony, and Donny Gluckstein, 1988, *The Labour Party: A Marxist Analysis* (Bookmarks).

Cliff, Tony, Chris Harman, Duncan Hallas and Leon Trotsky, 1996, *Party and Class* (Bookmarks).

Davies, John K, 2004, "Athenian Citizenship: The Descent Group and the Alternatives", in Peter J Rhodes (ed), *Athenian Democracy* (Oxford University Press).

Foot, Paul, 2005, *The Vote* (Penguin).

Harman, Chris, 1986, "Base and Superstructure", *International Socialism* 32 (summer), www.marxists.org/archive/harman/1986/xx/base-super.html

Hill, Christopher, 1972, *God's Englishman* (Penguin).

Howard, Dick (ed), 1971, *Selected Political Writings of Rosa Luxemburg* (Monthly Review).

Jones, A H M, 1969, *Athenian Democracy* (Blackwell).

Kapp, Yvonne, 1976, *Eleanor Marx*, volume 2 (Virago).

Kritsman, Leo, 1971, *Die Heroische Periode der Grossen Russischen Revolution* (Neue Kritik).

Lenin, V I, 1964, *Collected Works* (Progress).

Lenin, V I, 1976, *The Proletarian Revolution and the Renegade Kautsky* (Progress), www.marxists.org/archive/lenin/works/1918/prrk/index.htm

Lenin, V I, 1993, *"Left-Wing" Communism: An Infantile Disorder* (Bookmarks), www.marxists.org/archive/lenin/works/1920/lwc/index.htm

Ma, John, Nikolaos Papazarkadas and Robert Parker, 2009, *Interpreting the Athenian Empire* (Duckworth).

Manning, Brian, 1976, *The English People and the English Revolution* (Heinemann).

Marx, Karl, and Frederick Engels, 1976, *Collected Works*, volume 6 (Lawrence and Wishart).

Meiggs, Russell, 1972, *The Athenian Empire* (Oxford University Press).

Miliband, Ralph, 2004 (1977), *Marxism and Politics* (Merlin).

Molyneux, John, 2011, *Anarchism: A Marxist Criticism* (Bookmarks).

Molyneux, John, 2012, "Capitalism vs Democracy", *Socialist Review* (January).

Morton, A L, 1979, *The World of the Ranters* (Lawrence and Wishart).

Murphy, J T, 1972 (1917), *The Workers' Committee* (Pluto).

Ness, Immanuel, and Dario Azzelini, 2011, *Ours to Master and to Own* (Haymarket).

Ober, Josiah, 1996, *The Athenian Revolution* (Princeton University Press).

Ste Croix, Geoffrey de, 1983, *The Class Struggle in the Ancient Greek World* (Duckworth).

Service, Robert, 1997, "Did Lenin lead to Stalin?" in John Rees and others, *In Defence of October* (Bookmarks).

Simons, Mike, 2004, *Striking Back* (Bookmarks).

The Miners' Next Step, 1973 (Pluto).

Thyssen, Fritz, 1941, *I Paid Hitler* (Hodder and Stoughton).

Trotsky, Leon, 1974, *Collected Writings and Speeches on Britain*, 3 volumes (New Park).

Wood, Ellen M, 1988, *Peasant-Citizen and Slave* (Verso).

Fighting Back: The American working class in the 1930s

John Newsinger
Out now £12

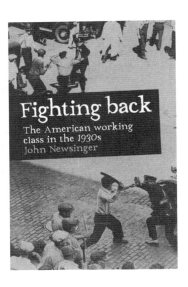

John Newsinger provides fresh insights into these turbulent years with this fascinating and detailed account, based on extensive research and primary sources.

From the private police state of the 1920s to the socialist-led struggles of 1934 and the sit-down strikes of 1937, no working class movement in the West has fought harder for its rights. Newsinger tells the story not just as history, but as a lesson for workers today facing our own Great Depression.

John Newsinger is the author of ten books including *The Blood Never Dried: A People's History of the British Empire* (Bookmarks 2007) and *British Counterinsurgency: From Palestine to Northern Ireland* (Palgrave 2002).

BOOKMARKS
PUBLICATIONS

Bookmarks the socialist bookshop
1 Bloomsbury Street, London WC1B 3QE
020 7637 1848 www.bookmarksbookshop.co.uk

Back to "normality"?
US foreign policy under Obama

Alexander Anievas, Adam Fabry and Robert Knox

"Change we can believe in".[1] We all remember the hope-laden slogans of the brilliantly executed Obama 2008 presidential campaign. This was much less a promise of change than a return to "normality" after the deviant years of the Bush-Cheney regime. Or so many on the liberal left believed. What a difference three years make. Not since John F Kennedy's inauguration has a presidency been so symbolically significant and yet so vacuous—if not damaging—in substantive foreign policy terms. With US military power engaged on multiple fronts, Obama's 2008 campaign mantra has become a painfully ironic reminder of the pitiful state of US politics and democracy. So what has changed in US foreign policy since Obama's coming to power?

The truth is not a hell of a lot. Abroad the "war on terror" continues unabated, if under new surreptitious labels. Under Obama, the US military has not only intensified the drone bombings in Afghanistan and Pakistan (Af-Pak) that began under Bush Jr, but has now expanded targeted strikes into Yemen and Somalia. US military forces remain 80,000 strong in Afghanistan, providing support to the crony regime of the Karzai clan, whose rule is not even guaranteed within the heavily fortified

---

1:    The authors would like to thank the *International Socialism* editors, and particularly Alex Callinicos, for their comments on an earlier draft of this article.

Green Zone of Kabul.[2] The prison camp in Guantanamo, which Obama promised to close down before 2009, persists under increasingly and dangerously legalistic pretences. The drawdown of US troops from Iraq over 2011 occurred on the schedule set by the Bush Jr presidency, breaking a central promise of the Obama campaign.[3] What is more, the Obama administration actually proposed to leave US military bases in Iraq. It was only after negotiations with the Maliki cabinet in which US plans were rejected, and all remaining US forces were forced to withdraw in late December 2011.[4]

In the Middle East, Obama's attempts to charm the Muslim world with his hyped-up rhetoric of "a new beginning", declared in a speech at Cairo University on 4 June 2009, has turned out to be just that: a gimmick. While condemning "rogue states" (such as Iran and Syria), the US continues to provide financial, military and political support to its allies in the region (including such "bastions of liberalism" as Israel and Saudi Arabia). More recently, we have seen the Obama administration attempting to rebuild the previously discredited idea of "humanitarian intervention" in toppling the Gaddafi regime in Libya, in order to steer the revolutionary tide unleashed by the Arab revolutions in the region. And it doesn't stop here. As recent dispatches from Washington have revealed, the Obama administration is recalibrating its attention towards the Asia-Pacific theatre in a Faustian bid to revitalise the faltering US economy, manage the rise of Chinese power and rebuild US "leadership" internationally.

In the light of these dire developments, readers of this journal might easily feel themselves as being timewarped to the 1990s, when discourses of "liberal interventionism" and "just wars" were common parlance on both sides of the Atlantic. This then begs the question as to how we arrived here. What are the changes and continuities in the Obama administration's foreign policies? And is there any larger "grand strategy" lurking behind this?

2:   Earlier this year Taliban forces carried out massive coordinated guerrilla attacks across Afghanistan, including an 18-hour siege of the capital, Kabul, and simultaneous attacks in three eastern provinces.

3:   As Megan Trudell pointed out in this journal, "During his presidential campaign Obama pledged to withdraw the 142,000 troops from Iraq within 16 months of taking office [ie by May 2010]"—Trudell, 2009. The confetti from Obama's inaugural speech had barely been cleaned from streets of Washington, when he announced the postponement of US withdrawal to September 2010, and said the "residual" 50,000 troops could continue to engage in combat operations to "protect our ongoing civilian and military efforts"—Obama, 2009a.

4:   MacAskill, 2011.

US imperialism in historical perspective

To understand the Obama administration's foreign policies, we need to first frame them within a broader historical perspective tracing how deeply embedded they are within US strategic thinking of the 20th century. The guiding thread of this thought is usually referred to as "Wilsonianism".[5] This is defined as a combination of putatively universal ideals with US economic self-interest in an uneasy but potent mix of unilateral *and* multilateral tactics ("multilateralism when possible, unilateralism when needed") geared towards the construction of a "liberal–capitalist international order"[6] under US hegemony. In other words, when possible US policymakers will attempt to work through international organisations (such as the UN or NATO) or robust allied coalitions. However, when such coalitions are not forthcoming, US foreign policymakers (from Clinton to Bush Jr to Obama) are perfectly willing to go it alone (ie unilaterally) as exemplified with the Bush Jr's administration's rejection of NATO's evocation of the collective security principle in response to the 9/11 attacks.[7] As Obama made clear in 2007 during the Democratic primary elections: "I will not hesitate to use force, unilaterally if necessary, to protect the American people or our vital interests whenever we are attacked or imminently threatened".[8]

Most basically stated, the aim of US foreign policy strategy is to facilitate the ceaseless accumulation of capital buttressed through an "open" world economic system. Though immediately identified with President Woodrow Wilson (1913-21), the central characteristics associated with Wilsonianism as an operational baseline for conducting US foreign relations pre–date its namesake.

A significant point that needs emphasising is that Wilsonianism has *always* entailed a combination of multilateral *and* unilateral tactics. In mainstream popular and academic discussions, the tendency is to counterpose multilateralism and unilateralism, the former seen as a defining feature

5:   See, for example, Ninkovich, 1999.
6:   As termed by the historian N Gordon Levin, 1968.
7:   This is further illustrated by the close strategic overlaps between the Bush administration and its Washington establishment critics (Republican and Democrat alike) in the run-up to the 2003 invasion of Iraq. As a study by Vivek Chibber well demonstrates, "On the basic matter of regime change...there was no objection from either wing of the foreign policy establishment. The debate was over how Bush should organise the campaign to depose Hussein, and what the appropriate timing ought to be"—Chibber, 2009, p37.
8:   Obama, 2007, p7. It is worth noting that the article, audaciously entitled "Renewing American Leadership", appeared in the July/August 2007 issue of *Foreign Affairs* (published by the ultra-establishment Council on Foreign Relations), which is the chief organ through which the US foreign policy elite talks to itself.

of the liberal democratic cosmopolitan vision of world order.[9] In contrast, self-proclaimed realist critics of Wilsonianism identify it with the "idealist" or "utopian" tradition in US foreign policymaking; that is to say, a tradition associated with a naive, legalistic liberalism which eschews power politics in the pursuit of morally virtuous aims.[10] Now, if realists have been correct in highlighting some of the deficiencies and contradictions of Wilsonianism as a strategy and ideology of US foreign policymaking, they have been less successful in explaining its origins. As the historian Lloyd C Gardner writes, while radicals "may criticise his [Wilson's] naive moralism and idealism along with the realists…a full account of the development of that outlook is a much more difficult problem". According to Gardner, this was an "outlook" which had "developed from a much keener insight into the nature of his [Wilson's] society (and its needs) than would appear from the realist critique".[11]

There is, then, something much more *structural* to Wilsonianism that escapes realism, which fails to grasp the role of ideology in foreign policymaking. The significance of Wilsonianism to President Obama's foreign policy agenda is not that it sets him apart from his predecessors but that it demonstrates the clear lines of continuity with them. But fully to understand these continuities demands a Marxist analysis of the dynamic interaction of social forces animating the Wilsonian project with its changing international and world economic environments. In what follows we briefly sketch the originating socio-historical context from which Wilsonianism emerged before moving on to consider its relevance as a project for the continuation of US Empire under the current administration.

The "Open Door" strategy in the era of classical imperialism
The period of "classical imperialism" (1896-1945) was characterised by a fundamental contradiction between the simultaneous internationalisation and statisation of capitalist productive powers whereby the abstract logic of the world market came to increasingly dominate the fates of each and every state. This was driven by intensified geopolitical competition ensuing from the synchronised collective outward thrust of rapidly industrialising and newly emergent capitalist states of the time. With the *quantitative* multiplication of "autonomous" centres of capital accumulation, politically rooted in

---

9:   This is perhaps best represented within disciplinary International Relations. See, for example, Ruggie, 1996, and Mandelbaum, 2002.

10: For the classic realist critique of Wilsonianism, see Kennan, 1951, and Morgenthau, 1951.

11: Gardner, 1967, pp205-206.

national-state spaces, came the *qualitative* transformation of the rhythms and dictates of geopolitical rivalry.[12] Different states pursued different foreign policy strategies to compete effectively in this changing international milieu. These differences were bound to specific trajectories of capitalist development and processes of class formation related (in time and space) to the overall history of world capitalism. It is with this in mind that one can understand the emerging "Open Door" strategy of US foreign policymaking.

Under the strains of heightened economic competition on the world market typical of the period, a coalescence of US finance-industrial and political interests concluded that the marketing of America's increasing manufacturing surpluses was necessary both to (1) maintain economic growth and domestic prosperity and (2) circumvent radical sociopolitical and economic reforms at home. In other words, to avoid a substantive redistribution of the *relative* shares of national income, there had to be an *absolute* increase in its overall volume. This was only possible if US state managers and segments of the capitalist class could develop foreign outlets for US goods and services which were perceived as having developed in surplus of what could be *profitably* absorbed by the domestic market.[13] Wilsonianism was a response to these dilemmas.

In essence, then, Wilsonianism represented the steady globalisation of the "Open Door" model of "non-territorial" expansionism[14] originally formulated by secretary of state John Hay in the McKinley administration's (1897-1901) attempts to pry open the great Chinese market at the turn of the 20th century. The Open Door stipulated an equality of opportunity for the commerce of all nations. For Wilson and others, it was viewed as both a key means of promoting US interests and creating a so-called world community of power and interests, the two being viewed as mutually complementary. Given the massive economies of scale, enormous domestic

---

12:    Here we leave aside the much-debated question of the precise theoretical standing of the international system in Marxist theories of imperialism. On this very important issue see the contributions in Anievas, 2010.

13:    Best illustrated in the historical works of LaFeber, 1993; 1998; Sklar, 1988; and Parrini, 1969. As President Woodrow Wilson continually reiterated, "Our domestic market no longer suffices. We need foreign markets"—quoted in Wilson and Link, 1966, volume 25, p16.

14:    It must not be forgotten that the non-territorial form taken by US expansionism both presupposed a long and violent history of internal colonisation on the North American continent and continuing military interventions in perceived US "spheres of interest". For these reasons, among others, one must *not* think of the Open Door as the only purely capitalist model of expansionism as do, for example, Wood, 2003; and Gindin and Panitch, 2004. For a useful corrective see Callinicos, 2009.

market, and advanced mass production techniques characterising the US political economy, state managers and corporate capitalists viewed this global equalisation of trade and investment conditions as necessarily favourable to US-based capitals. This ensured, as President Wilson put it, that "the skill of American workmen would dominate the markets of all the globe".[15] Indeed, "the brilliance of liberal US internationalists in this period, with Woodrow Wilson as their flag-bearer", Neil Smith writes, "lay in the implicit realisation that the wedding of geography and economics undergirding European capital accumulation was not inevitable; that the coming era could be organised differently; and that economic expansion divorced from territorial aggrandisement dovetailed superbly with US national interests". In these ways, Smith continues, "US internationalism pioneered a historic unhinging of economic expansion from direct political and military control over the new markets".[16]

However, it is necessary to be cautious here. There is a strong sense in which the "non-territoriality" of the US Open Door model of expansionism is misleading. The Wilsonian strategy always entailed the remaking of sovereign territoriality in ways amenable to US capitalism and thus entailing its necessary violation through both formal and informal means. Witness the administration's record in enforcing the Monroe Doctrine in Central and South America, where Wilson would set out, as he put it, "to teach the South American Republics to elect good men".[17] Wilson ordered more military interventions without declarations of war than any other US president in the 20th century save Clinton (a path that the Obama administration is fast following).[18] Yet, at the same time, Wilson is best known in popular and academic debates for his doctrine of self-determination, which envisages the transformation of the empire-state system into a plurality of formally sovereign territorial units.

Following Wilson's "American exceptionalism" line of reasoning, the US "leads" the world, because it should and must. One can see this quintessentially Wilsonian motif at work in Obama's pompous declaration of the "end" of military operations in Iraq in December 2011: "Unlike the old empires, we don't make these sacrifices for territory or for resources—we do

15: Wilson, quoted in Kennedy, 1980, p299.

16: Smith, 2003, pp141-142. The British Empire's "imperialism of free trade" (Gallagher and Robinson, 1953) during the 19th century was, in many ways, the real pioneer. However, the Open Door is *not* synonymous with Victorian free trade imperialism: the latter denoted low tariffs and the maintenance of special spheres of interests and the former demanded equality of commercial opportunities.

17: Wilson, quoted in Knock, 1992, p27.

18: Hoff, 2008, p36.

it because it's right. There can be no fuller expression of America's support for self-determination than our leaving Iraq to its people. That says something about who we are".[19] Reading such remarks justifying US intervention in the country as "doing the right thing" ("just war"), one could easily mistake Obama for his predecessor. The important point here is not simply to register the stark hypocrisy in all of this, but to illustrate the overwhelming *continuities* in the ideological discourse of US imperialism and the social antagonisms they seek to displace. Here we find a second dimension of territoriality underlying the Wilsonian form of US imperialism.

Much like the Whig history of the origins of capitalism Marx demolished in the chapter on "So-Called Primitive Accumulation" in volume one of *Capital*, US narratives of "American exceptionalism" delete the long and brutal history of US expansionism: first over the Native Americans on the North American continent, and then throughout the world. Between 1815 and 1870 the US state acquired land (through conquest, fraud or robbery) approximately doubling the country's original size. As Gareth Stedman Jones notes, "the whole *internal* history of US imperialism was one vast process of territorial seizure and occupation. The absence of territorialism 'abroad' was founded on an unprecedented territorialism 'at home'".[20] In a similar way, contemporary US policymakers work from a freeze-frame of the contemporary world and America's role within it abstracted from any historical view.

No matter who occupies the White House, Wilson's model of keeping the "world safe for democracy" (read: US-style capitalism) has remained something of a constant. While the forms of US foreign policy *tactics* have varied with the interconnected changes in the world economy, international system and domestic configurations of class forces, the overriding *strategic objectives* have not.

US foreign policy and world economic crisis

The Obama administration came into power at a moment of profound economic and geopolitical turmoil. The bursting of a speculative bubble in the US housing market—the alleged subprime mortgage crisis—was already unspooling into a global "credit crunch", which at the time was estimated to cause the global economy losses of at least US$1 trillion.[21] Concomitantly, US military power projection abroad was experiencing a relative decline as epitomised by the Russia-Georgia conflict of August 2008. Bogged down in

19: Obama, 2011.
20: Stedman Jones, 1972, p66.
21: IMF, 2008.

the wars in Afghanistan and Iraq, and freshly reeling from the first jolts of the global financial crisis, the "lame duck" administration of Bush Jr found itself with few cards to play in dealing with the conflict. The episode represented the most concrete strain between Russia and the US since the end of the Cold War. It also brought to the fore simmering tensions within the NATO camp. But despite some sabre-rattling from Washington, little of substance was actually achieved, as key Western European governments (France, Germany and Italy in particular), heavily dependent on Russian energy supplies and quick to avoid any action that might endanger these, diplomatically deferred on the issue. The post Cold War manifestation of the Open Door international order, founded upon the twin pillars of "neoliberalism at home and globalisation abroad" under US economic and political dominance, was showing severe signs of weakening. The task set out by the Obama administration itself, and the hopes of its allies, was that the newly elected "reformist" president in Washington was going to reinvigorate this order.

Faced with the twin challenges of a new great recession and the corresponding geopolitical shifts, the initial response of the Obama administration was to pursue modest fiscal expansionary policies at home, while engaging in a multilateralist charm offensive abroad. In February 2009 Obama signed the American Recovery and Reinvestment Act (ARRA), which provided the US economy with a fiscal stimulus of US$787 billion through a combination of tax breaks and government spending on infrastructure, welfare and education programmes.[22] This was accompanied by successive programmes of quantitative easing by the US Federal Reserve—effectively meaning the central bank sought to stimulate the economy by printing money and pumping it into the financial system.[23] Concomitantly, vice-president Joe Biden travelled to Europe, where he promised to "reset" tarnished US-Russian relations at the Munich Security Conference. At the G20 summit in April, Obama personally negotiated a compromise between France and China, and, at the Summit of the Americas later in the month, promised a "new beginning" with Cuba, a gesture also aimed at the hemisphere's other "radical-leftist" governments. The Obama charm campaign reached its zenith in June 2009,

22: By comparison, Chinese leaders announced a fiscal stimulus package of RMB¥4 trillion (US$586 billion) in November 2008. As Jane Hardy and Adrian Budd, 2012, point out in an earlier issue of this journal, this represents "the largest economic stimulus package in history, equivalent to 14 percent of gross domestic product (GDP)".
23: Since the onset of the crisis the Fed has spent a whopping US$ 1.8 trillion on quantitative easing programmes. The limitations of government responses to the crisis, in the US and elsewhere, have been covered thoroughly by this journal since the onset of the crisis.

when the president, in a speech at Cairo University, reached out to the Muslim world, in attempting to mend US–Muslim relations, which had been "severely damaged" under the Bush Jr presidency.

Within the US foreign policy community, as well as the Obama administration itself, this was often referred to as the new administration's strategy of "multilateral retrenchment". This was music to the ears of the liberal press, who saw this as a confirmation of Obama's healing power of transforming America's image abroad.[24] Less diplomatically, we can see this recalibration of US foreign relations as an attempt to reconsolidate and maintain US "hegemony on the cheap"[25]—a redistribution of imperial burden sharing. Indeed, as Daniel Drezdner notes, this was how allies even interpreted "the Obama administration's supposed modesty".[26]

Yet by the time Obama was due to give his first State of the Union address in 2010, the concrete results of his administration's efforts of rebuilding American "leadership" were few and far between. Efforts of orchestrating an internationally coordinated response to the global slump had largely failed as demonstrated by the empty resolutions of various G20 summits, the continued stalemate in the Doha trade negotiations, and the currency war with China between 2009 and 2011. Following this series of failures the Obama administration very rapidly shifted its foreign policy tactics.

Tactics of American empire

The particular form that these tactics took bears a great deal of resemblance to those of the Bush-Cheney regime that Obama supposedly had broken with. Nowhere is this more evident than in the continued US intervention in Afghanistan, Pakistan and other states under the aegis of the war on terror. The Obama administration very pointedly disowned the label "global war on terror" in an effort to distance itself from the legacy of George W Bush. Yet at the same time, it massively increased the number of operations conducted in Afghanistan and Pakistan.

The most spectacular example of this was, of course, the killing of Osama bin Laden in April 2011. This operation was conducted without the express permission of the Pakistani government and—allegedly—pursuant to a secret agreement with the Musharraf regime.[27] However, the most

24: Neoconservatives in the Murdoch-dominated US press snidely referred to this as the "Obama apology tour". See, for example, Rove, 2009.
25: The term "hegemony on the cheap" is here taken from Colin Dueck's 2003/2004 analysis of the Bush Jr administration's foreign policy.
26: Drezner, 2011.
27: Walsh, 2011.

far-reaching policy choice here has been the escalation in drone bombings of Afghanistan and Pakistan. Of particular note have been the innovative operational methods deployed, which include killing secondary "members" of Al Qaeda and then bombing their funerals or rescuers so as to eliminate other, more important, members.

All but the most diehard Obama supporters have struggled with the fact that this policy has encompassed the killing of US citizens, as with Anwar al-Awlaki in Yemen. The fact that al-Awlaki's killing occurred inside of Yemen points to the high level of convergence between the policies of the Obama and Bush administrations. While some case can be made that Afghanistan is a conventional war, and so does not need the justification of a war on terror (which could stretch to the border regions with Pakistan), the same can hardly be said of Yemen. Indeed, the only argument that could be raised here is that of a global war on terrorism, and this is precisely what the Obama administration has done. In a series of speeches by top legal representatives of the US government the political and legal case for these strikes has been made.[28] For example, in a speech on 5 March 2012 Attorney General Eric Holder argued that the US deployed military force "in response to the attacks perpetrated—and the continuing threat posed—by Al Qaeda, the Taliban, and associated forces". [29] As a result:

> Our legal authority is not limited to the battlefields in Afghanistan. Indeed, neither Congress nor our federal courts has limited the geographic scope of our ability to use force to the current conflict in Afghanistan. We are at war with a stateless enemy, prone to shifting operations from country to country. Over the last three years alone, Al Qaeda and its associates have directed several attacks—fortunately, unsuccessful—against us from countries other than Afghanistan.[30]

If all this sounds familiar, it is because it is almost the exact same justification used by the Bush administration in the infamous 2002 National Security Strategy (NSS). The absence of a fundamental break in foreign policy between the Bush Jr administrations and the Obama regime can, on one level, be explained by the noticeable level of personal overlap between the two administrations. Names that come to mind here include ex secretary of defence Robert Gates (2006-11), Timothy Geithner, who

---

28: Koh, 2010; Brennan, 2011; and Holder, 2012.
29: Holder, 2012.
30: Holder, 2012.

after serving as president of the Federal Reserve of New York under Bush Jr became Obama's secretary of the treasury, and Generals Eikenberry, McChrystal and Petraeus, who all held high-ranking positions under both administrations.[31] However, the similarities run deeper than this.

One of the more controversial aspects of the 2002 NSS was in its argument that the US government would "make no distinction between terrorists and those who knowingly harbour or provide aid to them".[32] Yet this argument was again replicated by Holder, who argued force could be deployed within a state without its consent "after a determination that the nation is unable or unwilling to deal effectively with a threat to the United States".[33]

Finally, perhaps the *most* controversial aspect of the 2002 NSS was its doctrine of pre-emptive self-defence, which argued that the threats posed by stateless terrorists with nuclear weapons meant that the US could no longer "solely rely on a reactive posture".[34] Accordingly, so the argument went, the understanding of an "imminent" threat would need to be transformed, meaning the US could intervene (unilaterally) to prevent emerging threats. This justification has been reproduced almost word for word by the Obama administration's representatives, with John O Brennan bluntly arguing a "more flexible understanding of 'imminence' may be appropriate when dealing with terrorist groups",[35] and Holder relying on similar reasoning.[36]

One difference that *might* exist on this front has been the Obama administration's shift away from a military model based on ground troops to one based on unmanned vehicles. Hence there has been the "withdrawal" from Iraq, completed in December 2011, and the planned gradual decrease in troop numbers in Afghanistan. Immediately though it should be remembered that in practice the former was considered a rational relocation of military power to Afghanistan, where the Obama administration asserted the "real" threat was. Furthermore the Obama administration continued the Bush policy of the "troop surge" in Afghanistan, vastly increasing the number of ground troops. Finally, as Andrew Cockburn pointed out in a recent issue of the *London Review of Books,* the Obama administration's posture of moving to a leaner military, concentrated around technology,

---

31: A more detailed study of the continuities in personnel between the Bush Jr and Obama administrations can be found in de Graff and Apeldoorn, 2011.
32: NSS, 2002.
33: Holder, 2012.
34: NSS, 2002.
35: Brennan, 2011.
36: Holder, 2012.

is hardly new; indeed it has distinct echoes of Bush Jr's rhetoric and the "shock and awe" tactics initially deployed in the invasion of Iraq.[37]

Defusing the Arab revolutions

Thus with Obama's policy shift things seem to have remained very much the same. Of course, as noted above, this fundamental unity is not simply with the Bush administration, but is characteristic of the Wilsonian strategy that has characterised the US imperial position. When the Obama administration's initial attempt to engage in multilateral tactics largely failed, it shifted back to unilateral methods, yet these were naturally shaped by the relative decline in the US's economic and military position on the global stage as well as domestic exhaustion and opposition to foreign wars.

The return to the war on terror rhetoric has also marked a more explicit revival of the language of American exceptionalism that is central to Wilsonianism, and also lay at the heart of the Bush administration.[38] While initially the Obama administration was quite modest on America's exceptional character,[39] leading to outraged sputtering on the part of many conservative commentators,[40] the expanded justifications for the war on terror have seen the language of exceptionalism return with a vengeance. Hence discussions of terrorism are framed by discussions of American values and the importance of the rule of law and democracy.[41] Nowhere has this strange mix of American exceptionalism and the vacillation between unilateralism and multilateralism been more visible than in the response of the Obama administration to the revolutionary processes in the Middle East and North Africa.

The initial events—particularly in Tunisia and Egypt—caught the Obama administration by surprise. At the beginning of the Egyptian uprising, various members of the Obama administration—including Hillary Clinton and Joe Biden—stressed Mubarak's historical role as friend of the US.[42] As the uprising progressed, this position began to shift somewhat,

---

37: Cockburn, 2012.
38: Tariq Ali makes a similar point in his excellent analysis of the Obama presidency at its mid-term, pointing out that "historically, the model for the current variant of imperial presidency is Woodrow Wilson, no less a pious Christian, whose every second word was peace, democracy or self-determination, while his armies invaded Mexico, occupied Haiti and attacked Russia, and his treaties handed one colony after another to his partners in war. Obama is a hand-me-down version of the same, without even Fourteen Points to betray"—Ali, 2010, p73.
39: Obama, 2009b.
40: Krauthammer, 2010.
41: NSS, 2002.
42: Murphy, 2011; Reuters, 2011.

with increasing emphasis placed on the universality of "American" values of democracy and the rule of law.[43] Of course, this fact was contradicted by the cans of tear gas and mortar used to suppress the uprising that had "Made in America" stamped on them. As events moved towards a decisive confrontation—with a geopolitically uncertain outcome—the Obama administration attempted to find a halfway house that would enable support for the uprising, while guaranteeing a regime friendly to its interests. Hence Hillary Clinton argued that the US supported an "orderly transition",[44] a position that was soon rendered inoperative by the demands on the street.

The response to Egypt—which can be seen as a microcosm of the whole Arab revolutionary process—was indicative of the real problems the Obama administration faced geopolitically. The ousting of the various dictators (most of whom were at least favourable to US interests) would have serious geopolitical consequences. This was reinforced by the genuinely popular character of the uprisings against the regimes, which remained largely free of "outside influences". At the same time the geopolitical climate rendered the US relatively unable to intervene in these revolutionary processes. Despite Obama's "reconciliation" tour, the thought of the US meddling in Arab affairs was still a problem, there was little ability to craft a "multilateral" response to the uprisings (owing to the relative decline of the US internationally) and the US was too invested in these regimes simply to abandon them. These structural constraints created a vacillating position on the uprisings, whereby the Obama administration was essentially led by the "Arab street", but tried to dampen its revolutionary potential at every turn.[45]

However, these tactics proved much more successful in the case of Libya. Here the Obama administration, with a coalition of other imperialist powers, was able to intervene directly in the revolutionary process and allow Libya to remain open to the interests of the US (and its allies). Once again this particular outcome showcases the potent mix of multilateral and unilateral tactics that characterise US foreign policy.

In terms of multilateralism, the US together with France and the UK was able to operate through the Security Council so as to guarantee the result. This was firstly done through the imposition of an arms embargo under Resolution 1970,[46] while ostensibly this was to prevent further arms

43: BBC News, 2011.
44: Landler, 2011.
45: More recently we have seen Washington working with the Muslim Brotherhood and the Supreme Command of the Armed Forces in Egypt in an attempt to restabilise the situation. See, for example, Schmitt and Cooper, 2012, and Charara, 2012.
46: UN Security Council Resolution 1970, 2011, paragraph 9.

reaching the Gaddafi regime, but it also guaranteed that no support for the Libyan rebels would be forthcoming from Arab revolutionary movements. This created a situation in which the "international community"—led by the US, the UK and France—was the only possible "agent" that could intervene in the process. This was duly realised under Resolution 1973, which authorised a no-fly zone for humanitarian purposes. Russia and China, which have historically vetoed such resolutions—and have been stressing their rivalry with the US—merely abstained from the vote. This is partly explained by the fact that, when the Libyan uprising first began, it was in the interests of *all* of the advanced capitalist countries that the revolutionary process be brought under control, given the unpredictable geopolitical consequences that could ensue.

Yet this also gives an insight into the ways in which the Obama administration deployed "unilateral" tactics as well. One reason that Russia and China merely abstained from the Security Council vote is that they understood the intervention permitted under Resolution 1973 to be a limited one, focusing purely on humanitarian concerns—with no mandate for regime change or a ground invasion. Evidently the Obama administration thought differently. But aside from the way in which the facts played out on the ground, the Libyan intervention was also very explicitly perceived as a way of re-legitimating US military power. Thus proponents of "humanitarian intervention" inside the White House saw this as a way of "rescuing" that doctrine from its use by the Bush administration.[47] This outcome was precisely the one opposed by Russia and China, which is one of the reasons for the continuing Syrian deadlock.

Although the Libyan situation has become largely chaotic, the intervention was relatively successful on the US's terms. There was little popular opposition to the campaign; indeed, most opposition came from within the military itself, and the way in which the Syrian events have played out shows the way in which the debate has been transformed. Thus, in this instance, the mixture of the exceptionalism of American "humanitarian" values, together with different tactics—the key features of Wilsonianism—does seem to have been relatively successful in securing US interests in the region. It is clear, however, that this has come up against determined opposition from Russia and China, and that the particular multilateral option in Libya may have been a result of the extraordinary conjuncture represented by the insurgent Arab revolutionary process.

47: Calabresi, 2011.

Containing China

By the time Obama was taking power in the White House, the credit crunch was spreading to the "real" economy, marked by falling levels of economic output globally. However, the effects of the global slump were uneven: while the US and German economies contracted by 2.4 and 5.0 percent respectively in 2009, China and India were continuing to project robust growth rates of 8.7 and 5.7 percent respectively.[48] The relative transfer of economic power and wealth from what some have described as the "liberal-capitalist heartlands"[49] of the US and Western Europe to South East Asia has recently spawned something of a "status anxiety" among US foreign policy makers. Indeed, this "global shift" from West to East, potentially rendering the international system constructed after the Second World War "almost unrecognisable by 2025", was already a major theme of the National Intelligence Council's (NIC) 2008 "Global Trends 2025: A Transformed World" report. Although, as the study points out, "'international system' is a misnomer, as it is likely to be more ramshackle than orderly, its composition hybrid and heterogeneous, as befits a transition that will still be a work in progress in 2025". At the centre of this global shift is the rapid yet contradiction-ridden rise of states like Brazil, Russia, India and particularly China (the BRICs). As the report states:

> In terms of size, speed, and directional flow, the transfer of global wealth and economic power now under way—roughly from West to East—is without precedent in modern history. This shift derives from two sources. First, increases in oil and commodity prices have generated windfall profits for the Gulf States and Russia. Second, lower costs combined with government policies have shifted the locus of manufacturing and some service industries to Asia.

Growth projections for the BRICs indicate they will collectively match the original G7's share of global GDP by 2040-50. China is poised to have more impact on the world over the next 20 years than any other country. If current trends persist, by 2025 China will have the world's second largest economy and will be a leading military power.

These projections strike a familiar chord with the claims of those pundits who have recently argued that the ascent of leading emerging market economies heralds the future of global capitalism. Hence, while the NIC

48: IMF, 2010.
49: Van der Pijl, 1998.

report states that "the US is likely to remain the single most powerful actor", it warns that "the US's relative strength—even in the military realm—will decline and US leverage will become more constrained".[50]

Policymakers in Washington have clearly been taking such claims seriously. Indeed, these arguments can clearly be traced in the foreign policy strategy of the Obama administration. In a recent article in *Foreign Policy*, Hillary Clinton, writing in a style reminiscent of Woodrow Wilson himself, laid down the future foreign policy priorities for the administration:

> Harnessing Asia's growth and dynamism is central to American economic and strategic interests and a key priority for President Obama. Open markets in Asia provide the United States with unprecedented opportunities for investment, trade, and access to cutting-edge technology. Our economic recovery at home will depend on exports and the ability of American firms to tap into the vast and growing consumer base of Asia. Strategically, maintaining peace and security across the Asia-Pacific is increasingly crucial to global progress, whether through defending freedom of navigation in the South China Sea, countering the proliferation efforts of North Korea, or ensuring transparency in the military activities of the region's key players.[51]

Clinton's words, along with her recent nearly two-week long diplomatic tour of South East Asia and the Middle East (including visits to Japan, Mongolia, Vietnam, Laos, Cambodia, Egypt and Israel) form part of the Obama administration's self-described "strategic pivot" towards Asia where the Pentagon is now set to send 60 percent of the US fleet by 2020. The new strategy aims, on the one hand, to reassert US hegemony over the oil-rich regions of the Middle East and Central Asia, and on the other, to contain China's growing economic, political and military influence in the region. This strategy entails a substantial increase of US military presence in the region, which, despite defence secretary Panetta's claims to the contrary, appears directly aimed at checking China's rise as a global power.[52]

Critical in all of this is maintaining an "Open Door" in the South China Sea. A recent report for the Center for a New American Security (CNAS)[53] arguing for increased US naval defence spending emphasised that:

50: Quotes above are from NIC, 2008, ppvi; 1.

51: Clinton, 2011.

52: Perlez, 2012.

53: Founded in 2007, CNAS exerts significant influence on the foreign policy thinking of the Obama administration. According to Carlos Lozada of the *Washington Post*, "In the era of Obama... CNAS may emerge as Washington's go-to think tank on military affairs"—Lozada, 2009.

The geostrategic significance of the South China Sea is difficult to overstate. The South China Sea functions as the throat of the Western Pacific and Indian Oceans—a mass of connective economic tissue where global sea routes coalesce, accounting for $1.2 trillion in US trade annually. It is the demographic hub of the 21st century global economy, where 1.5 billion Chinese, nearly 600 million South East Asians and 1.3 billion inhabitants of the Indian subcontinent move vital resources and exchange goods across the region and around the globe. It is an area where more than a half-dozen countries have overlapping territorial claims over a seabed with proven oil reserves of 7 billion barrels as well as an estimated 900 trillion cubic feet of natural gas.[54]

Further, as Cronin and Kaplan go on to note:

The South China Sea is where a militarily rising China is increasingly challenging American naval pre-eminence—a trend that, if left on its present trajectory, could upset the balance of power that has existed since the end of the Second World War and threaten these sea lines of communication (SLOCs). As the principal guarantor of global freedom of navigation, the United States has a deep and abiding interest in ensuring that SLOCs remain open to all, not only for commerce but also for peaceful military activity, such as humanitarian interventions and coastal defence.[55]

And although "the recent upsurge in diplomatic theatrics over who owns what in the South China Sea does not appear to be intense enough to heighten the risk of major interstate conflict in the near term", Cronin and Kaplan maintain that "the South China Sea has also become the epicentre of what appears to be a long-term geopolitical struggle in which classical power politics and nationalism are intensifying alongside the rise of China".[56] This seems about right,[57] even though the US-Chinese rivalry goes beyond just the South China Sea.

Indeed, classified diplomatic documents released by Wikileaks further confirm this picture of simmering geopolitical and economic tensions between China and the US. In a 7 February 2010 meeting with representatives of the major international oil corporations in Lagos, a senior US official detailed China's expanding economic investments and influence

---

54: Cronin and Kaplan, 2012, p5.
55: Cronin and Kaplan, 2012, p7.
56: Cronin and Kaplan, 2012, p9.
57: For the latest incident of escalation in this long-standing dispute see Branigan, 2012.

on the African continent. The US Assistant Secretary for African Affairs described China as a "very aggressive and pernicious economic competitor with no morals", which involved itself in Africa for primarily selfish motives including the securing of "votes in the United Nations from African countries". While denying that Washington viewed China as "a military, security or intelligence threat", the assistant secretary cautioned:

> There are trip wires for the United States when it comes to China. Is China developing a blue water navy? Have they signed military base agreements? Are they training armies? Have they developed intelligence operations? Once these areas start developing then the United States will start worrying. The United States will continue to push democracy and capitalism while Chinese authoritarian capitalism is politically challenging.[58]

The terms of the US-Chinese rivalry could hardly be more clearly stated. The stakes of the conflict are not only about which power dominates the markets and raw materials of those countries, but also which "variety of capitalism" (authoritarian versus democratic) will act as the model to be emulated. Geopolitical and economic competition thus continues to form two sides of the same coin. Meantime, since at least January 2007 there has emerged a "star wars" arms race between the countries. This was supposedly sparked off when the Chinese government shot down its own weather satellite thus "shocking" Washington by demonstrating its capability to fight a space war.[59]

During the standoff over the weather satellite incident US officials privately threatened to take military action if Beijing did not desist. As classified documents show, Washington responded in February 2008 when it shot down a malfunctioning US satellite to prove that it too could fight a space war, though US officials denied that this was a military exercise. More recent cables sent from secretary Clinton's office in January 2010 detail new anti-satellite missile tests conducted by the Chinese military and emphasise that the Obama administration "has retained the Bush-era concerns over space weapon plans".[60] In particular, Mrs Clinton reiterated that the "military option" threatened in the 2008 demarches to China was "still valid and reflects the policy of the United States". As stipulated in the 2008 demarches:

58: *Guardian*, 2011.
59: *Telegraph*, 2011.
60: *Telegraph*, 2011.

Unfettered access to space and the capabilities provided by satellites in orbit are vital to United States national and economic security... Any purposeful interference with US space systems will be interpreted by the United States as an infringement of its rights and considered an escalation in a crisis or conflict... The United States reserves the right, consistent with the UN Charter and international law, to defend and protect its space systems with a wide range of options, from diplomatic to military.[61]

In an election year one can expect jingoistic rhetoric to be pitched a tone higher than usual (recall Obama's "Sputnik moment" in his State of the Union 2011 speech). Yet clearly something deeper is going on here. But perhaps even more worrying for the immediate future is the state of US-Iranian relations.

Intimidating Iran

If the Obama administration has so far been relatively successful in defusing the revolutionary fervour in the Middle East, it has largely been ineffective when dealing with Iran. The question of how to best deal with Iran represents, as Tariq Ali points out, a lingering conundrum to American elites: on the one hand, the regime in Tehran is publicly posing itself as an anti-imperialist "Islamic Republic" breathing fire against the "Great Satan", while on the other, it quietly collaborates with it when most needed, whether it came to conspiring with the counter-revolution in Nicaragua, invading Afghanistan or, more recently, in the rebuilding of post-war Iraq.[62] However, for Israel the benefits of all this have been few and far between, leading its rulers to take a much more downbeat view of Tehran's rhetorical posturing, directed with greater ferociousness at it, than at its patrons in Washington. In particular, since the prospect of Iran developing a nuclear programme of its own began to loom on the horizon in the mid-1990s (which, if realised, would effectively bring Israel's monopoly on weapons of mass destruction in the Middle East to an end), Tel Aviv has exploited its assets in Washington, London and elsewhere, in order to galvanise political support for decisive military action against Iranian nuclear facilities. While the Republicans still ruled in the White House, Washington proved more than amenable to the idea, matching Tehran's rhetorical attacks (for example, by including Iran in the administration's "axis of evil") and tightening economic sanctions against the regime.

61: *Aftenposten*, 2011.
62: Ali, 2010, p48.

Obama's initial response was tacitly to reject the "cowboy diplomacy" of his predecessor, favouring diplomatic dialogue instead, seeking to reach a settlement in the interest of all parties: stripping Iran of nuclear capability in exchange for economic and political embrace from the US and its allies. This message was candidly delivered by Obama's *Nowruz* [Iranian New Year] message on 20 March 2009, in which the president ensured "the people and leaders of the Islamic Republic" that his administration was "committed to diplomacy that addresses the full range of issues before us". Speaking in classical Wilsonian parlance, Obama went on to outline his hopes for a "new day" in US-Iranian relations, based on "renewed exchanges among our people, and greater opportunities for partnership and commerce. It's a future where the old divisions are overcome, where you and all of your neighbours and the wider world can live in greater security and greater peace".[63] But the timing was unfortunate and the calculations were upset by political ruptures inside Iran following the fraudulent presidential elections in June 2009 and the suppression of popular dissent by militia violence.[64] As a result, Obama's plans for a historic reconciliation between the two states were soon set aside for traditional *Realpolitik*.

Since then the Obama administration has reverted to the tactics of its predecessor, seeking to lock in China and Russia—the consent of its European allies can be taken for granted—to impose ever stricter economic sanctions on Iran, in the hope that it will strangle the country and thereby either oust the neoconservative Supreme Leader Ali Khamenei and his puppet President Ahmadinejad or force them to come to terms. Should these pressures fail, the use of military force by US and/or Israeli fighter jets remains a distinct possibility. As Alex Callinicos notes:

> There seems no enthusiasm for an attack on Iran in Washington. Obama, busy realigning US global strategy to meet the geopolitical challenge represented by China, has no desire to step into another Middle Eastern quagmire (and is speeding up withdrawal from Afghanistan, where recent events have underlined how the West's grip is slipping). But Netanyahu will no doubt seek to exploit the US presidential contest, where the rival Republicans are outdoing themselves in their protestations of loyalty to Israel, to pressure him into supporting an attack on Iran. So there may be another war in the Middle East this year.[65]

63: Quoted in Black, 2009.
64: On the Iranian revolt, see Jafari, 2009
65: Callinicos, 2012, pp6-7.

Indeed, while the option of a US-Israel led war against Iran sounds like political lunacy and a human catastrophe in the making, the possibility of war cannot altogether be ruled out. There are three reasons for this. Firstly, the Western powers at large—not only Obama, but also Cameron and Merkel—have made it very clear that they will not tolerate any Iranian nuclear capability, leaving very little room for diplomatic manoeuvring if this should materialise. While the Obama administration still opposes a pre-emptive attack on Iran, secretary of state Hillary Clinton recently warned Tehran during her latest visit to Israel that Washington and Tel Aviv are "on the same page" and that the US is prepared to employ "all elements of American power to prevent Iran developing a nuclear weapon". [66] However, US support for Israel does, of course, not stop at mere rhetorical assurances, but also includes a deepening of financial and military aid to Tel Aviv. On 27 July 2012 Obama reiterated Washington's "unshakable commitment to Israel" by signing the US-Israel Enhanced Security Act, which pledges an additional US$70 million in military aid to Israel in order to help it expand its short-range rocket defence system.[67] Moreover, the US has recently beefed up its military presence in the Persian Gulf, in order to counter Iran. For example, it has deployed one of the navy's oldest transport ships, the *Ponce*, which has been thoroughly redesigned as a mobile forward base capable of carrying out important military operations, such as reconnaissance, sabotage and direct strikes across the region.[68] Secondly, Tehran's threat of retaliation should not be discounted, especially in the light of the Iranian military's downing of an unarmed US spy plane in late 2011 or its bullish stance during the standoff in the strategically important Strait of Hormuz in early 2012. [69]

Finally, there are also Washington's allies in the Middle East to be considered.[70] Here recent reports suggest that Israeli leaders, led by the trigger-happy troika of prime minister Benjamin Netanyahu, defence minister Ehud Barak and minister of strategic affairs Moshe Ya'alon, seem to have

66: BBC News, 2012.

67: Al Jazeera, 2012.

68: Shanker, 2012.

69: The Strait of Hormuz is of major geopolitical significance. Located between the Gulf of Oman in the south east and the Persian Gulf, with Iran controlling the northern coast and the United Arab Emirates and Oman controlling the southern coast of the strait, it is the only sea passage to the open ocean for large areas of the oil-exporting Persian Gulf and is one of the world's most strategically important "choke points". Approximately 15 million barrels of oil, one fifth of the world's total, passes through the strait every day in tankers—US Energy Information Administration, 2011.

70: Here, we focus only on Israel, as it remains the key agent of US imperialism in the region.

succumbed to, even welcomed, the prospect of "going it alone" and "demonstrating their resolve" at a time when their security is threatened both from abroad, not only by the prospect of Iran developing nuclear weapons, but also by the convulsions of the Arab revolutions, and from within, by simmering public discontent against social inequality. Tel Aviv's increasing disposition towards a unilateralist stance vis-à-vis Iran was bluntly described by Ya'alon in a *New York Times Magazine* interview in early 2012, where he stated:

> Our policy is that in one way or another, Iran's nuclear programme must be stopped… It is a matter of months before the Iranians will be able to attain military nuclear capability. Israel should not have to lead the struggle against Iran. It is up to the international community to confront the regime, but nevertheless Israel has to be ready to defend itself. And we are prepared to defend ourselves…*in any way and anywhere that we see fit.*[71]

The aim of Israeli leaders seems to be clear: stopping Iran's nuclear project by *all* means necessary. As a result, Tel Aviv is now engaged in a bloody, covert and ongoing war with Tehran in order to remove "important brains" from the nuclear programme. Since 2010 a number of high-ranking members in the Iranian nuclear project have been killed in attacks, which are widely presumed to have been carried out either directly by Mossad, the Israeli intelligence agency, or with tacit support from the Israelis (through recruited operatives, such as the Jundallah, a Pakistan-based Sunni group, which is ranked as a terrorist organisation by both Iran and the US).[72] While Iran has so far refrained from using military force against these intimidations, the political temperature in the region is likely to remain hot in the autumn.

Conclusion

In rhetorical terms the current administration is much more in sync with President Woodrow Wilson's model of employing international law in the service of US force than the inconvenient truths of unbridled US unilateralism uttered by the swaggering cowboys of the Bush administration. Yet looking beyond this surface image a different picture emerges. The Obama administration has continued and even expanded many of the Bush Jr administration's "unilateral" policies, often adopting wholesale the

---

71: Cited in Bergman, 2012 (emphasis added by authors).

72: The US has condemned these assassinations, while Israel has officially denied any involvement in them (although memos and field reports from the US intelligence services show that Mossad has run a programme for recruiting Jundallah members). See Bergman, 2012, and Perry, 2012.

legal arguments of its predecessor. Equally, the Bush Jr administration very frequently had recourse to international institutions—to legitimate its occupations, to coordinate "anti-terrorist" action and so on. On reflection then, there is a fundamental unity between the two administrations. This unity points us to the fact that "official multilateralism is not a *Weltanschauung* [worldview] but an imperialist strategy—which can coexist with its supposed opposite, unilateralism, without much difficulty".[73] The more principled elements of the liberal left have been quick to cry "Betrayal" over Obama's similarities with the Bush-Cheney regime. Yet to do so is fundamentally to misunderstand the nature of US foreign policy and the imperatives that drive it. As we argue, US foreign policy has been structured by an essentially "Wilsonian" orientation produced by the insertion of the US in the global social relations of capitalism. Consequently, the only way radically to transform this foreign policy is to transcend capitalism itself. *This* is the only change we can believe in.

References

Aftenposten, 2011, "Second Demarche for China Regarding China's January 2007 Anti-Satellite Test", *Aftenposten* (4 January), www.aftenposten.no/spesial/wikileaksdokumenter/article3971894.ece

Al Jazeera, 2012, "Obama signs bill for Israel missile defence" (27 July), www.aljazeera.com/news/americas/2012/07/201272718113852794.html.

Ali, Tariq, 2010, *The Obama Syndrome: Surrender at Home, War Abroad* (Verso).

Anievas, Alexander (ed), 2010, *Marxism and World Politics: Contesting Global Capitalism* (Routledge).

BBC News, 2011, "In quotes: Reaction to Egypt protests" (30 January), www.bbc.co.uk/news/world-middle-east-12316019

BBC News, 2012, "Hillary Clinton issues new warning to Iran on Israel visit" (16 July), www.bbc.co.uk/news/world-middle-east-18852286

Bergman, Ronen, 2012, "Will Israel attack Iran?", *New York Times Magazine* (25 January).

Black, Ian, 2009, "Barack Obama offers Iran 'new beginning' with video message", *Guardian* (20 March), www.guardian.co.uk/world/2009/mar/20/barack-obama-video-iran

Branigan, Tania, 2012, "China Lambasts US over South China Sea Row", *Guardian* (6 August), www.guardian.co.uk/world/2012/aug/06/china-us-south-china-sea

Brennan, John O, 2011, "Strengthening our Security by Adhering to our Values and Laws", www.whitehouse.gov/the-press-office/2011/09/16/remarks-john-o-brennan-strengthening-our-security-adhering-our-values-an

Calabresi, Massimo, 2011, "Why the US Went to War: Inside the White House Debate on Libya", *Time* (20 March), http://swampland.time.com/2011/03/20/why-the-u-s-went-to-war-inside-the-white-house-debate-on-libya

---

73: Miéville, 2008, p83.

Callinicos, Alex, 2009, *Imperialism and Global Political Economy* (Polity).

Callinicos, Alex, 2012, "Rumours of Crisis, Revolution and War", *International Socialism 134* (spring), www.isj.org.uk/?id=792

Charara, Nasser, 2012, "Brotherhood, SCAF, and US: The Three Way Tango", *Alakhbar English* (27 June), http://english.al-akhbar.com/node/8982

Chibber, Vivek, 2008, "American Militarism and the US Political Establishment: The Real Lessons of Iraq", in Leo Panitch and Colin Leys (eds), *Socialist Register 2009: Violence Today-Actually Existing Barbarism?* (Merlin Press).

Clinton, Hillary, 2011, "America's Pacific Century", *Foreign Policy* (November).

Cockburn, Andrew, 2012, "Drones, Baby, Drones", *London Review of Books*, volume 34, number 5 (8 March).

Cronin, Patrick M and Robert D Kaplan, 2012, "Cooperation from Strength: US Strategy and the South China Sea" in Patrick M Cronin (ed), *Cooperation from Strength: The United States, China and the South China Sea* (Center for a New American Security), www.cnas.org/files/documents/publications/CNAS_CooperationFromStrength_Cronin_1.pdf

Drezner, Daniel W, 2011, "Does Obama Have a Grand Strategy?", *Foreign Affairs*, volume 90, number 4 (July/August).

Dueck, Colin, 2003/2004, "Hegemony on the Cheap: Liberal Internationalism from Wilson to Bush", *World Policy Journal*, volume 20, number 4 (winter), www.worldpolicy.org/journal/articles/wpj03-4/dueck.html

Gallagher, John, and Ronald Robinson, 1953, "The Imperialism of Free Trade", *The Economic History Review*, volume 6, number 1.

Gardner, Lloyd C, 1967, "American Foreign Policy 1900-1921: A Second Look at the Realist Critique of American Diplomacy", in Barton J Bernstein (ed), 1968, *Towards a New Past: Dissenting Essays in American History* (Pantheon).

Gindin, Sam, and Leo Panitch, 2004, *Global Capitalism and American Empire* (Merlin).

de Graff, Nana, and Bastian van Apeldoorn, 2011, "Varieties of US Post-Cold War Imperialism: Anatomy of a Failed Hegemonic Project and the Future of US Geopolitics", *Critical Sociology*, volume 37, number 4 (July).

Guardian, 2011, "US Embassy Cables: US Monitors China and Its Expanding Role in Africa" (8 December), www.guardian.co.uk/world/us-embassy-cables-documents/250144

Hardy, Jane, and Adrian Budd, 2012, "China's Capitalism and the Crisis", *International Socialism 133* (winter), www.isj.org.uk/?id=777

Hoff, Joan, 2008, *A Faustian Foreign Policy from Woodrow Wilson to George W Bush: Dreams of Perfectibility* (Cambridge University Press).

Holder, Eric, 2012, "Attorney General Eric Holder Speaks at Northwestern University School of Law", www.justice.gov/iso/opa/ag/speeches/2012/ag-speech-1203051.html

IMF, 2008, *World Economic Outlook, April 2008*, www.imf.org/external/pubs/ft/weo/2008/01/

IMF, 2010, *World Economic Outlook, April 2010*, www.imf.org/external/pubs/ft/weo/2010/01/

Jafari, Peyman, 2009, "Rupture and revolt in Iran", *International Socialism 124* (autumn), www.isj.org.uk/?id=585

Kennan, George F, 1951, *American Diplomacy, 1900-1950* (University of Chicago Press).

Kennedy, David M, 1980, *Over Here: The First World War and American Society* (Oxford University Press).

Knock, Thomas J, 1992, *To End All Wars: Woodrow Wilson and the Quest for a New World Order* (Oxford University Press).

Koh, Harold, 2010, "The Obama Administration and International Law", www.state.gov/s/l/releases/remarks/139119.htm

Krauthammer, Charles, 2010, "Obama only believes in his own exceptionalism", http://fullcomment.nationalpost.com/2010/07/10/charles-krauthammer-obama-only-believes-in-his-own-exceptionalism

LaFeber, Walter, 1993, *The American Search for Opportunity, 1865-1913* (Cambridge University Press).

LaFeber, Walter, 1998, *The New Empire: An Interpretation of American Expansion, 1860-1898*, 35th anniversary edition (Cornell University Press).

Landler, Mark, 2011, "Clinton Calls for 'Orderly Transition' in Egypt", *New York Times* (30 January), www.nytimes.com/2011/01/31/world/middleeast/31diplo.html

Levin, Gordon N, 1968, *Woodrow Wilson and World Politics* (Oxford University Press).

Lozada, Carlos, 2009, "Setting Priorities for the Afghan War", *Washington Post* (7 June), www.washingtonpost.com/wp-dyn/content/article/2009/06/05/AR2009060501967.html.

MacAskill, Ewen, 2011, "Iraq rejects US request to maintain bases after troop withdrawal", *Guardian* (21 October), www.guardian.co.uk/world/2011/oct/21/iraq-rejects-us-plea-bases

Mandelbaum, Michael, 2002, *The Ideas that Conquered the World: Peace, Democracy, and Free Markets in the Twenty-First Century* (Public Affairs).

Miéville, China, 2008, "Multilateralism as Terror: International Law, Haiti and Imperialism", *Finnish Yearbook of International Law*, volume 19, http://eprints.bbk.ac.uk/783

Morgenthau, Hans J, 1951, *In Defense of the National Interest: A Critical Examination of American Foreign Policy* (Knopf).

Murphy, Dan, 2011, "Joe Biden says Egypt's Mubarak No Dictator, He Shouldn't Step Down...", *Christian Science Monitor* (27 January), www.csmonitor.com/World/Backchannels/2011/0127/Joe-Biden-says-Egypt-s-Mubarak-no-dictator-he-shouldn-t-step-down

National Intelligence Council, 2008, "Global Trends 2025: A Transformed World", www.dni.gov/nic/NIC_2025_project.html

National Security Strategy, 2002, http://georgewbush-whitehouse.archives.gov/nsc/nss/2002/

Ninkovich, Frank A, 1999, *The Wilsonian Century: US Foreign Policy Since 1900* (University of Chicago Press).

Obama, Barack, 2007, "Renewing American Leadership", *Foreign Affairs*, volume 86, number 4 (July/August).

Obama, Barack, 2009a, "Responsibly Ending the War", speech at Camp Lejeune, North Carolina (27 February), www.whitehouse.gov/the_press_office/Remarks-of-President-Barack-Obama-Responsibly-Ending-the-War-in-Iraq

Obama, Barack, 2009b, "News Conference by President Obama" (4 April), www.whitehouse.gov/the_press_office/News-Conference-By-President-Obama-4-04-2009

Obama, Barack, 2011, "Remarks by the President and the First Lady on the End of the War in Iraq" (14 December), www.whitehouse.gov/the-press-office/2011/12/14/remarks-president-and-first-lady-end-war-iraq

Parrini, Carl P, 1969, *Heir to Empire: United States Economic Diplomacy, 1916-1923* (University of Pittsburg Press).

Perlez, Jane, 2012, "Panetta Outlines New Weaponry for Pacific", *New York Times* (1 June), www.nytimes.com/2012/06/02/world/asia/leon-panetta-outlines-new-weaponry-for-pacific.html

Perry, Mark, 2012, "False Flag", *Foreign Policy* (January).

Reuters, 2011, "US urges restraint in Egypt, says government stable" (25 January).

Rove, Karl, 2009, "The President's Apology Tour", *Wall Street Journal* (23 April).

Ruggie, John G, 1996, *Winning the Peace: America and World Order in the New Era* (Columbia University Press).

Schmitt, Eric, and Helene Cooper, 2012, "Egypt Results Leave White House Relieved but Watchful", *New York Times* (24 June), www.nytimes.com/2012/06/25/world/white-house-relieved-over-egypt-announcement.html

Shanker, Thom, 2012, "Floating Base Gives US New Footing in the Persian Gulf", *New York Times* (11 July), www.nytimes.com/2012/07/12/world/middleeast/the-navy-ship-ponce-reflects-the-new-united-states-way-of-war.html

Sklar, Martin J, 1988, *The Corporate Reconstruction of American Capitalism, 1890-1916: The Market, the Law, and Politics* (Cambridge University Press).

Smith, Neil, 2003, *American Empire: Roosevelt's Geographer and the Prelude to Globalization* (University of California Press).

Stedman Jones, Gareth, 1972, "The History of American Imperialism", in Robin Blackburn (ed), *Ideology in Social Science* (Fontana).

Telegraph, 2011, "Wikileaks: US and China in Military Standoff in Space" (2 February), www.telegraph.co.uk/news/worldnews/wikileaks/8299495/WikiLeaks-US-and-China-in-military-standoff-over-space-missiles.html

Trudell, Megan, 2009, "Obama's 100 Days", *International Socialism* 123 (summer), www.isj.org.uk/?id=553

United Nations Security Council Resolution 1970, 2011, "Peace and Security in Africa", www.un.org/Docs/sc/unsc_resolutions11.htm

United States Energy Information Administration, 2011, "Strait of Hormuz", *World Oil Transit Chokepoints*, 30 December), www.eia.gov/countries/regions-topics.cfm?fips=WOTC#hormuz

van der Pijl, Kees, 1998, *Transnational Classes and International Relations* (Routledge).

Walsh, Declan, 2011, "Osama bin Laden mission agreed in secret 10 years ago by US and Pakistan", *Guardian* (9 May), www.guardian.co.uk/world/2011/may/09/osama-bin-laden-us-pakistan-deal

Wilson, Woodrow, and Arthur S Link, 1966, *The Papers of Woodrow Wilson*, 69 volumes, (Princeton University Press).

Wood, Ellen Meiksins, 2003, *Empire of Capital* (Verso).

In perspective: John Holloway

Paul Blackledge

John Holloway's *Change the World Without Taking Power* (2002), like that other key text of autonomist post-Marxism, Michael Hardt and Toni Negri's *Empire* (2000), cut with the grain of the global anti-capitalist mood at the beginning of the millennium.[1] More than this, Holloway's book was the focus for important debates on the international left[2] and deserves praise both for emphasising the link between socialism and human self-activity and for criticising the idea that the capitalist state can be used to bring about socialist change.

Nevertheless, *Change the World Without Taking Power* was also a very flawed book. This is perhaps most evident in its central idea of the "scream". This concept is much more problematic than Holloway initially allowed. He argued that screams are the elemental way we react to capitalism—a system we create but which we experience as an alien and oppressive power over us.[3] If this approach allowed him to focus on the self-activity of ordinary people, this strength was undermined by his reluctance, at least in the first edition of his book, to differentiate between various forms of scream. It might be true, for example, that the student riots at Millbank in 2010 expressed screams of anger against the system,

1:   Bensaïd, 2005, p170.
2:   See, for instance, the symposia in *Capital & Class* 85, 2005, *Historical Materialism* 13.4, 2005, and the essays collected at www.herramienta.com.ar. See also Gonzalez, 2003; Callinicos, 2003; Callinicos, 2004; and Harman, 2004
3:   Holloway, 2010a, p1.

but so too does the demand for "British jobs for British workers". More generally, as Michael Löwy argues, screams can often take a destructive form: he points out that it's hard to imagine how screams taking the form of "suicide, going mad, terrorism, and other sorts of anti-human responses to the system" could act as the "starting point for emancipation".[4] This simple yet profound point suggests that we need some positive standpoint by which we might judge individual acts. Unfortunately, though Holloway has come to accept the claim that screams can take reactionary forms and that this creates a problem for any approach that starts from the scream, he has little to say about the concrete mechanisms by which this problem might be overcome beyond writing that "an anti-authoritarian form of articulation will tend to filter out authoritarian expressions of the scream".[5]

If this claim is palpably inadequate in the face, for instance, of the struggle against fascism, this weakness reflects Holloway's general refusal of any positive criterion for emancipation. Indeed, he goes beyond a denial of any such criterion to suggest that those who argue otherwise reproduce the kind of hierarchical institutional forms against which the anti-capitalist movement should be fighting. It is on the basis of this claim that he makes a distinction between what he calls "traditional Marxism" and his own interpretation of Marxism which he roots in Marx's suggestion that communism is not an ideal but rather "the *real* movement which abolishes the present state of things".[6]

Holloway argues that the logic of Marx's position is that "we do not know" how to change the world.[7] At one level this is a perfectly reasonable claim—clearly there is no idiot's guide to revolution that can lead us to the Promised Land. The problem is that Holloway means much more than that the left must feel its way out of the political ghetto. For him, not knowing has become something of a shibboleth by which he delineates his interpretation of Marxism from "traditional Marxism". However, Holloway's category of "traditional Marxism" involves a caricatured presentation of, especially, Lenin's thought as an ideology of "knowers" who seek to impart revolutionary consciousness into the working class from without.[8] What is more, he performs a contradiction of his own by playing down the way his interpretation of Marxism depends upon him "knowing" the truth of a whole series of propositions, for instance about

4:    Löwy, 2005, p24.
5:    Holloway, 2010a, pp227-228.
6:    Holloway, 2010a, p219; see Marx and Engels, 1976, p49.
7:    Holloway, 2010a, p215.
8:    Holloway, 2010a, p225.

the nature of alienation, the state and traditional Marxism, which are, to say the least, highly contentious.

These problems are evident in his latest book, *Crack Capitalism*—a work best understood as an attempt to complement and go beyond the limits of *Change the World Without Taking Power*. *Crack Capitalism* opens with an analogy. Though capitalism appears to be a closed room with no doors or windows through which we might escape, the room is in fact riddled with a myriad of tiny "cracks". These cracks reflect the multiple ways in which people resist the alienation of modern life. The examples he cites are eclectic, but far from exhaustive. They include gardening, composing, reading, striking, occupying, spending time with children, etc. If the list could be endless because there are endless ways that we say no to the system, Holloway's enticing answer to the question "What can we do?" involves trying to "expand and multiply" these cracks to break capitalism.[9] This argument follows directly from the thesis of *Change the World Without Taking Power*—Holloway believes that each of these cracks is a concrete manifestation of practices based upon particular examples of the scream, and that they all, in their various ways, begin to prefigure alternative ways of life that point beyond our alienated existence.[10]

At one level Holloway's cracks point to something real in our lives. When I play with my children, for instance, we experience a joy that suggests an escape from the instrumentalism of modern life. However, it takes only a moment's consideration to recognise that although my play might be one example among many of the ways in which people cannot be reduced to the neoliberal fantasy of *homo economicus*,[11] it is also the case that this behaviour poses no threat to the system. On the contrary, as a father I can easily be addressed as a consumer either to buy toys for my children or to buy a house in the catchment area of the "best" school, and I certainly feel the pressure of "pester power" by which advertisers aim to commodify all aspects of leisure time. It is because similar pressures are brought to bear on gardeners, readers and composers, etc that we should be very cautious about placing too much faith in many of the practices listed by Holloway as pointing beyond our alienated existence: each of these is, in one way or another, an aspect of the system of alienation. One need only think, for instance, of the way that even playing with children

9:   Holloway, 2010b, pp4-5; 11.
10:   Holloway, 2010a, p221; 2010b, p29; 2012.
11:   For an excellent critique of fantasies about human nature that populate economics textbooks see Keen, 2011, pp38-73.

tends increasingly to be justified in instrumental terms: "It's good for their education, which will be good for their career etc."

This issue points to a fundamental weakness with the way Holloway makes use of Marx's concept of alienation. The great strength of his book lies in its reiteration of the claim that Marx's concept of "abstract labour" marks the deepening in *Capital* (1867) of the term alienation used most readily in the *Economic and Philosophical Manuscripts* (1844).[12] By alienation Marx meant something very different from the way this word is used in ordinary language. Typically, alienation is used in ordinary language to describe a vague feeling of angst or meaninglessness. For Marx, by contrast, alienation refers to something much more precise.[13] He argued that humans are essentially social animals who meet their needs by working together on nature. Our nature is thus simultaneously determined, we have a variety of biological and historical needs for food and warmth, etc, and free, we can choose among different strategies to meet these needs. Capitalism robs us of this freedom because production aimed at the market ensures that everyone loses control over (is alienated from) both what is produced and how we produce it. Moreover, though capitalism is an integrated social form of production, individual appropriation means that we are alienated from the social aspect of our nature: markets are unable to register anything but individual desires. Finally, we have an alienated relationship to nature: rather than feeling ourselves to be part of nature, consumers confront nature merely as a means of meeting individual needs.[14]

Marx's concept of alienation is thus a model of how we are dehumanised by capitalism, and by linking this idea with a central concept within *Capital* Holloway helps to remind us that Marx never dropped his youthful humanistic critique of capitalism in his more mature works. This is important because the concept of abstract labour sits at the core of Marx's mature critique of political economy. Indeed, it is by means of this concept that Marx overcame fundamental problems with the ways Adam Smith and David Ricardo conceived the labour theory of value.[15] Whereas neither Smith nor Ricardo fully grasped how distinct and very different types of labour could be compared, Marx was able to solve this problem through the argument that labour had a dual character: it was both "concrete labour"—the specific act of working to produce useful things—and "abstract labour"—the process

---

12:   Holloway, 2010b, p93.
13:   Sayers, 2011, px.
14:   Marx, 1975, pp322-334.
15:   Rubin, 1979, pp248-255.

of value creation through the equalisation of concrete acts of labour under the discipline of competition.[16] Because abstract labour is value realised in the marketplace, and because the production of things for sale as commodities in the marketplace creates a world that takes the form of an alien power over us, abstract labour is best understood as alienated labour.

Unfortunately, despite reiterating this important point, in his concrete analysis of capitalism Holloway simultaneously over- and underestimates the reality of alienation. The kernel of truth in his critique of "traditional Marxism" is that many 20th century Marxists downplayed the significance of the concept of abstract labour. Starting from weaknesses with Engels's popularisation of Marx's ideas, these writers tended to skirt over the discussion of value in the first chapter of *Capital*. This led many of them to conflate Marx's theory of value with Ricardo's, effectively reducing the concept of abstract labour to (an agglomeration of simplified acts of) concrete labour. This approach not only obscured the specifically capitalist character of value, it also opened the door to criticisms of the labour theory deployed by neo-Ricardians in the 1970s. By rejecting the labour theory of value, these critics tended to reduce socialism to a moral critique of exploitation.

This movement tended to reverse Marx's political evolution. Marx's comment about socialism being the "real movement of things" was intended to help move the left beyond the limitations of moralistic conceptions of politics. Whereas moralists imagined universal moral truths, for Marx capitalism was a historically specific system of alienation (unfreedom) and the concrete form taken by human freedom in the modern world was through those specific forms of solidarity by which workers struggled for real democracy against the reduction of their conditions of life to forms of abstract labour. In the 1970s those theorists—including Holloway and writers associated with this journal[17]—who sought to defend Marx from the criticisms made by the neo-Ricardians looked for inspiration to writers beyond the mainstream tradition of Marxist political economy. The most important writer they looked to was the Russian economist (and victim of Stalinism) Isaac Ilyich Rubin. In contrast to the dominant voices of 20th century Marxism, Rubin's articulation of the labour theory of value focused on the first chapter of *Capital* generally and Marx's concept of abstract labour more specifically.

Unfortunately, though Rubin's interpretation of Marx provided

---

16:   Saad-Filho, 2002, pp26-29; Rubin, 1973, pp131-158; Colletti, 1972, pp82-92.
17:   Green 1978; 1979.

socialists with powerful ammunition to counter the neo-Ricardian critique of value theory, it had weaknesses of its own. Because the commodity (rather than capitalism) is the focus of the first chapter of *Capital*, analysts who focus one-sidedly on this part of Marx's work have tended to invert rather than correct the errors associated with the traditional interpretation of the labour theory of value. Thus, as opposed to the dominant tendency to reduce abstract labour to concrete labour, theorists associated with the Rubin tradition have, by focusing on the realisation of the value of commodities in the process of exchange, tended to disassociate concrete and abstract labour.[18] This, in effect, is Holloway's position. He transforms Marx's *analytical* distinction between abstract and concrete labour into a division between non-alienated "doing" and alienated production for the market.[19] He argues that acts of concrete labour can be understood as acts of doing and that the cracks within capitalism reflect contradictions between doing and alienation: the focus of his book is therefore on "the conflict between concrete doing and abstract labour, on the struggle of doing *against* labour".[20]

But this distinction isn't tenable. Under capitalism labour is simultaneously abstract and concrete.[21] When I teach, for instance, while I can make an analytical distinction between the concrete way I teach and the way that my teaching is abstractly compared with other forms of labour in the marketplace, in practice I cannot separate out the concrete act of teaching from the way it exists within alienated relations. I might be able to imagine teaching in a way that isn't structured around tests and marks for reified chunks of knowledge, but the reality of my actual teaching is determined by the demands of the job: it is saturated by alienated relations. This is true of all forms of concrete labour within a capitalist economy—even those not oriented to the market. Thus even outside work, when we read, cook, decorate or whatever, the very fact that we live our lives around objectively determined and alienated divisions between work time and leisure time means that all our actions are overdetermined by alienated relations: one needs only think of the experiences either of vegetating exhaustedly in front of a TV after a day at work or "playing" a sport that is increasingly regimented along lines reminiscent of factory production to recognise that it would be a grave mistake to posit a simple distinction between work and leisure[22]—and this is before we take

---

18: This is a very condensed version of an argument made by Alfredo Saad-Filho (Saad-Filho 1997; see also Saad-Filho, 2002, pp21-34; and Weeks, 1981; 1990).
19: Holloway, 2010b, p89.
20: Holloway, 2010b, p156.
21: Saad-Filho, 1997, p465.
22: Braverman, 1974, p278; Brohm, 1978.

into consideration the ways new technologies help work colonise our leisure time. More generally it is impossible to be powerless before an alien world at work, and then magically to become autonomous self-determining agents when we read, play, socialise or have sex. Even more, it is wishful thinking to believe that somehow concrete acts of labour at work can prefigure non-alienated relations of the future: market relations do not just compare abstract labour—they shape the concrete ways we actually labour.

Holloway underestimates the consequence of this process because he one-sidedly focuses on the way that capitalism, by forcing us to compare concrete acts of labour in the marketplace so that we can sell our products for money to buy things we need to live, robs labour of its intrinsic value and replaces it with an instrumental logic. He gives the example of cake baking: a talent, he suggests, that might have emerged because someone enjoys baking, eating and sharing cakes, but which if expanded into market production becomes a mere means to the end of making money.[23] Unfortunately this example is very misleading, for though it illuminates the process by which market exchange forces production to become ever more efficient in ways that deprive it of any intrinsic value, it misses a deeper interrelationship between use values and exchange values under capitalism. Specifically, capitalism determines not only how we produce[24] but also what it is useful to produce in the first place. Tanks have the use value of being able to kill, nuclear power stations are useful for making nuclear bombs, bakers play a role in reproducing the labour force as cheaply as possible, and among the uses of teachers is an ability to fail an awful lot of people in ways that help justify the existing division of labour. As these examples suggest, doing is not only made more instrumental by commodity exchange, but is profoundly shaped by this process. Indeed, under capitalism the only use values that will be produced for the market are those that have an exchange value, and the "doings" that produce many of these things will have no place in a socialist society.

So while it is true, as Holloway points out, that "concrete labour exists...in any society",[25] it is far from the case that the forms of concrete labour as they exist in capitalist society can prefigure a non-alienated future. A massive amount of them will not exist, and those that continue to exist—house building and food production, for instance—will be transformed fundamentally.

This is not to say that alienation is absolute. It would be foolish to

23: Holloway, 2010b, p92.
24: Holloway, 2010b, pp94, 98.
25: Holloway, 2010b, p92.

imagine capitalist society simply as a form of social atomisation, for, along-side tendencies to reduce human interaction to a space of clashing individual wills, modern society is simultaneously characterised by forms of solidarity by which people rebel against alienation. These processes help maintain forms of sociality against the pressures of egoism and this helps explain how we are able to imagine types of sex or parenting, for instance, that are either more or less instrumental or through which we are more or less able to realise our social individuality. Nevertheless, because alienation is a social phenomenon—we are social beings who have lost control of the way that we *socially* interact with nature to meet our needs—it cannot be solved individually or even locally, and any solution will be a lot more complex than merely freeing doing from the rule of abstract labour.

One reason Holloway shies away from this obvious corollary of Marx's conception of alienation is that he imagines it permits no room from which to imagine an alternative to capitalism. Indeed, he believes that the alternative to his vision of doing against abstract labour involves choosing between either Theodor Adorno's extreme pessimism or Lenin's supposed elitism.[26] But this is a false dichotomy.

Adorno's *Negative Dialectics*, on which Holloway draws,[27] opens with a famous critique of the Hegelian notion of the "negation of the negation".[28] The aim of this criticism was not simply theoretical—to deny the positive content of the dialectic; more importantly it was practical—to deny that workers' solidarity was able to point beyond our alienated existence. Conversely, when Marx rescued this concept from its metaphysical baggage he deployed it (at least in one of his uses) to make sense of the way that capitalism not only dehumanises people (the negation) but also of how, in rebelling against this condition, these dehumanised people create networks of solidarity that point towards a *positive* alternative to capitalism (the negation of the negation).[29] How can we adjudicate this debate? The key point is to grasp, first, that recognising the importance of the concept of abstract labour does not entail dismissing labour movement struggles[30] and, second, that beneath the philosophical language there are competing interpretations of the nature of the workers' movement within capitalism. Whereas Marx thought that this movement pointed towards the possibility of socialism, Adorno believed that these struggles were trapped within alienated relations.

26: Holloway, 2010b, pp213, 217.
27: Holloway, 2009a; 2009b.
28: Adorno, 1973, pxix.
29: Marx, 1976, p929.
30: See Green, 1978.

The key weakness in Adorno's argument, according to Raya Dunayevskaya, was a failure to "listen to the voices from below". Adorno, she argues, overlooked the ways in which real workers developed forms of organisation that pointed beyond the struggle within capitalism towards a struggle against it.[31]

Insofar as Holloway justifies his own version of Adorno's critique of the labour movement he does so through reference to arguments put forward by Moshe Postone in his *Time, Labour, and Social Domination* (1996).[32] But just as Dunayevskaya criticised Adorno, Peter Hudis and David McNally have pointed to the fundamental weaknesses with Postone's reduction of the labour movement to the movement of abstract labour. Thus, in a critique of Postone that is directly relevant to Holloway's work, Hudis argues that "the struggle of the proletariat does not simply involve a struggle over the distribution of value. It involves a struggle over the very existence of value".[33]

If Holloway accepts Adorno's one-sided critique of the labour movement, he simultaneously assumes that a variant of this position was shared by Lenin. Indeed, he repeats a variant of what Lars Lih calls the "textbook interpretation" of Leninism.[34] According to this model, Lenin had a condescending attitude to workers who, he believed, were only able to attain "trade union consciousness". Socialist consciousness was therefore to be introduced by an elite of Marxists to the working class from without. These Marxists would use the workers as their stage army through which they would aim at winning state power. Once in power, their combined elitism and statism would, despite their best intentions, reproduce exactly the kind of alienated hierarchical relations against which they were supposed to be fighting.[35]

Unfortunately, because something like this interpretation of Russian history became a commonplace on both sides of the Cold War (in a neat symbiosis the idea that Lenin led to Stalin helped justify not only Stalinism in the East but also the liberal critique of Marxism in the West) and because it has become a lazy commonsense in the years since the collapse of the Soviet Union, casual readers of *Change the World Without Taking Power* have tended not to question Holloway's criticisms of Lenin. This is unfortunate, because these are among the weakest arguments in Holloway's books.

According to Holloway, one problem with "traditional Marxism" is its failure to see that because abstract labour is alienated labour, movements which start from abstract labour will remain trapped in alienated relations.

31: Dunayevskaya, 2002, p187.
32: Holloway, 2010b, pp172, 187.
33: Hudis, 2004, p155; McNally, 2004.
34: Lih, 2006.
35: Holloway, 2010b, p59.

From this perspective, the labour movement, and traditional Marxists who orient towards it, are doomed to remain trapped within alienated relations because labour movement struggles fundamentally concern the conditions of sale of labour power. The struggle for better terms and conditions at work may be justifiable in its own terms, but these struggles cannot point beyond capitalism: Holloway insists that "to take wage labour (or simply labour) as the basis of the anti-capitalist movement is quite simply to entrap that movement within capital".[36] His rejection of Leninism is therefore predicated upon his agreement with what he understands to be Lenin's (and Adorno's) critique of the limitations of working class consciousness!

It might seem strange that Holloway has come to this conclusion given the parallels between his work and Italian autonomism, for autonomism emerged as a political expression of the way that working class struggles in post-war Italy tended to push beyond the limits both of the Stalinist Communist Party and trade unionism.[37] Unfortunately, Holloway's political conclusions are less idiosyncratic than they at first appear. For one of the key problems with Italian autonomism was that its most important theorists reacted to the defeats suffered by the workers' movement in the 1970s by twisting the definition of the working class in a way that allowed them to dismiss organised workers as a new form of labour aristocracy while shifting their orientation towards the struggles of students and the unemployed.[38] While it was undoubtedly right to relate to these movements, autonomist criticisms of organised labour acted as a barrier to the kind of sober assessment of the defeats suffered by the labour movement which would have allowed them to maintain an orientation to the working class when the struggle was on the downturn.[39]

One problem with Holloway's caricatured critique of Leninism is that it obscures the parallels between Lenin's Marxism and the original insights of Italian autonomism. For instance, Lih shows that Lenin's entire orientation to the workers' movement was predicated on the fact that workers' struggles and workers' consciousness tend to spill over from the

36: Holloway, 2010b, pp104, 159.
37: On Holloway's relationship to autonomism see Holloway, 2010a, pp160-175; 2010b, p190. For a friendly overview of the emergence of autonomism see Cleaver, 2000, pp58-77, and for a more critical note see Fuller, 1980.
38: Callinicos, 2001, p38; more generally, see Wright, 2002.
39: Compare this approach with Cliff, 1979, and Harman, 1979. A similar tendency is apparent today among those who dismiss organised workers and fetishise the so-called precariat as a revolutionary alternative.

limits of mere trade unionism.[40] It is because Holloway, not Lenin, dismisses the socialist potential of the workers' movement that he is unable to conceive of revolutionary parties other than as elites that hand down commands to the working class from above. This is even true when he has insight enough to recognise that the "existence of what is sometimes called a 'vanguard' probably cannot be avoided".[41] Holloway is right about this: it is precisely because movements from below are fragmentary, sectional and uneven that they will generate leaders (vanguards) at any particular juncture. He is also right that left activists should not waste their time debating whether vanguards should or should not exist—they are simply a fact of struggle—but should instead discuss the nature of socialist leadership.

Unfortunately, his reification of labour movement struggles as struggles trapped within alienated relations means he is unable to see beyond the caricatured view of Leninists as those who insist on making the revolution for the working class.[42] Lenin, by contrast, was sharply critical of the model of socialist leadership that Holloway ascribes to him. Indeed, he argued that a revolutionary party must aim at organising the real leadership of the movement from below. Thus, in a comment on the British left in 1920, he said that "we categorically insist on the British communists serving as a link between the party—that is, the minority of the working class—and the rest of the workers. If the minority is unable to lead the masses and establish close links with them, then it is not a party and is worthless in general".[43] Ironically, because Lenin understood vanguards as the organised leadership of real movements from below, many of the practical implications of his conception of leadership are not a million miles away from Holloway's claim that revolutionary theory involves "feeling the way forward".[44]

It is not that Holloway's criticisms of the labour movement are without insight—it is clear that much of the leadership of the British labour movement has done its damndest to sabotage the recent pensions struggle, for instance. It is rather that his approach is one-dimensional.[45] The strength of Holloway's position comes from his understanding of how reformism, which is best understood as a strategy aimed at improving the condition of workers and other exploited and oppressed groups within the system of abstract labour

40: Lih, 2006; Blackledge, 2006.
41: Holloway, 2010a, p230.
42: Holloway, 2010a, pp230-231.
43: Lenin, 1991, p170.
44: Holloway, 2010a, p220.
45: Indeed, it involves a retreat from his earlier formulations about the nature of labour movement struggles—Holloway, 1995b, p178.

(capitalism), has its highest expression at the level of the state. If real reforms have been won at this level the great weakness of reformism is that it tends to view the state as a neutral arbiter between conflicting interests within civil society. This is mistaken: states are "structurally interdependent" with capital, and, as we shall see below, their apparent neutrality merely reflects the specific form in which capital exploits wage labour.[46] Because of this, Holloway is right to say that any social movement that aims to win state power will remain trapped within a broader capitalist framework, and this will limit possible reforms to those compatible with the demands of capital accumulation.

What Holloway's account of abstract labour misses is that labour movement struggles cannot be reduced to this limit. Whereas the hegemony of reformism within the workers' movement has roots both in the structural bargain over the price of labour power and reformism's historical ability to deliver real reforms in periods of economic expansion, there is always a tension between reformism and workers' self-activity and this tension tends to deepen as boom turns to bust. In such periods reformists tend to justify austerity as the only way to get capitalism back into good health. This approach exacerbates differences between ordinary workers and their leaders, and these differences become especially acute if and when workers begin to fight to maintain their standard of living. In situations such as these, because the real movement of workers effectively challenges the (capitalist) parameters of what reformists believe is possible, they create a space for revolutionaries to challenge the hegemony of reformism within the working class. Insofar as this approach is rooted in an orientation to forms of solidarity that prefigure socialism within capitalism, there is an overlap with Holloway's claim that each step of socialist activity should "prefigure" the goal of socialism itself.[47]

However, because this struggle involves both a conflict between classes and a conflict for hegemony between reformists and revolutionaries within the working class it cannot simply prefigure socialism. Though workers' solidarity is the basis for Marxism's wager on the possibility of socialism, because the victory of socialism is merely one possibility among many, it is incumbent upon socialists to struggle to win the leadership of the movement from below. While this struggle does not prefigure socialism, neither is it a hierarchical imposition on the workers' movement. Rather it involves attempts both to make workers self-conscious of the anti-capitalist implications of their own actions and to win them over from the reformist claim that these implications are impractical. To dismiss the socialist

46: Harman, 1991, p13.
47: Holloway, 2010a, p221.

potential of labour movement struggles is therefore not merely mistaken; it effectively means surrendering leadership of these movements to those reformists who would sacrifice them to the goal of capital accumulation.

It was Marx's great insight about the working class, made on the basis of involvement with socialist circles in Paris and through the experience of the Silesian weavers' revolt,[48] that the movement of this "new-fangled" class developed solidarities that tended to overflow the confines of alienation and point towards a new form of democracy. In contrast not simply to aristocratic rule but also to the limited political forms of bourgeois democracy, because workers' struggles tend to overcome the division between politics and economics they point to a deepening of the concept of freedom as real democracy. This linkage between workers' struggles and the idea of democracy is fundamentally important to Marx because it points to a real alternative to capitalism immanent within struggles against it.[49] Whereas bourgeois democracy reflects the capitalist separation between politics and economics, there is historical evidence aplenty that struggles rooted in the workplace tend towards a new form of democracy that overcomes this separation.[50] It is because this conception of democracy sits at the core of Marxism's positive alternative to capitalism that Holloway's division between "traditional Marxism" and Marx's conception of socialism as the "real movement of things" is unsustainable. Traditional Marxism, or at least the classical tradition from Marx and Engels through Lenin, Trotsky, Luxemburg, Gramsci and others,[51] is best understood as a developing tradition rooted in lessons drawn from the real movement of ordinary workers.

Far from being an invention of a vanguard, this positive alternative to capitalism is a real tendency within workers' struggles. And far from the vanguard acting as an "external force"[52] imposing its ideas on the movement, it is best understood as the most advanced sections of the movement for democracy. Interestingly, whereas the concept of democracy is immanent to Marx's model of workers' struggles, it is much less central to Holloway's work. This is not to say that he has nothing to say about democracy. Far from it: when he was pushed by Michael Löwy to explain the relative absence of the concept of democracy from *Change the World Without Taking Power*, he replied with a defence of workers' councils as the basis for real

48: Perkins, 1993, pp15-45.
49: Blackledge, 2008, p135; 2010a, pp114-117; 2012, pp56-59.
50: See the essays collected in Ness and Azzellini, 2011.
51: Molyneux, 1985.
52: Holloway, 2009b, p95.

democracy that (mistaken comments on the nature of Leninism to one side) could easily have come from the pages of *International Socialism*.[53]

However, whereas our conception of workers' democracy is rooted in the way that the real movement of workers against capitalism tends to overcome the division between politics and economics, Holloway's comments on this topic appear as a disjointed add-on to the rest of his work. This is unsurprising once we recognise that the cracks Holloway notices within capitalism originate in a myriad of "screams" based on a myriad of "doings". It is merely wishful thinking to suppose that these practices can come together in a democratic alternative to capitalism—and reference to the Zapatista slogan of a "world of many worlds" merely serves to rephrase the problem.[54] Conversely, because the workers' movement can only triumph on the basis of its unity, real democracy is immanent in the solidarities that must be forged by workers in their struggles to resist capitalism. Indeed, it is because these forms of solidarity challenge the idea of egoistic individualism that this movement within capitalism is also the basis of the movement against capitalism.

One key difference between this movement and Holloway's conception of a movement of a myriad of cracks is that whereas the former creates the basis for a systemic alternative to capitalism,[55] it is difficult to imagine the latter except, at best, as a variety of forms of resistance to capitalism. This explains a superficially curious characteristic of his work. Despite his ultraradical rhetoric, his practical suggestions are very close to the self-consciously statist reformism of writers such as Hilary Wainwright.[56] For instance, in a discussion of the relationship of social centres to local councils, Holloway dismisses the idea of a "golden rule" by which any contact with the state is forbidden.[57] The problem with this argument is not that it is wrong—in a slightly different context I've worked alongside socialist councillors in Leeds who have helped facilitate anti-cuts groups in opposition to their own local and national party leadership—but rather that Holloway fails to raise theory to the level of practice. Instead his comments merely operate as an ad hoc justification for work alongside more openly reformist elements. If

---

53: Holloway, 2011; 2010b, p40.
54: Holloway, 2010b, p210.
55: Blackledge, 2011.
56: Wainwright 2003; Wainwright and Holloway, 2011.
57: Holloway, 2010a, pp235, 262. The overlaps between Holloway's politics and left reformism go back a long way. See, for instance, the tension expressed in a book written by a group including Holloway and left reformists—CSE State Apparatus and Expenditure Group, 1979, p129.

this reflects an admirable lack of sectarianism on his part, it sits alongside a dogmatic refusal seriously to engage with Marx's arguments about the fundamental importance of a workers' state in the revolutionary process.[58]

According to Marx, the idea of a workers' state flows from the needs of this movement. This is what he argued in a famous letter to Joseph Weydemeyer:

> And now as to myself, no credit is due to me for discovering the existence of classes in modern society or the struggle between them. Long before me bourgeois historians had described the historical development of this class struggle and bourgeois economists the economic anatomy of the classes. What I did that was new was to prove: (1) that the existence of classes is only bound up with particular phases in the development of production, (2) that the class struggle necessarily leads to the dictatorship of the proletariat, (3) that this dictatorship itself only constitutes the transition to the abolition of all classes and to a classless society.[59]

Far from having a statist perspective, Marx explicitly distanced his position from state socialism by arguing that "freedom consists in converting the state from an organ superimposed on society into one thoroughly subordinated to it".[60] This is why Engels was able to equate the concept of the dictatorship of the proletariat with real democracy: "Our party and the working class can only come to power under the form of a democratic republic. This is even the specific form of the dictatorship of the proletariat".[61]

By contrast with Marx and Engels, Holloway professes an inability even to comprehend the idea of a workers' state. Thus he rejects Alex Callinicos's discussion of how the workers' state idea emerges out of the needs of the movement from below with the claim that the concept of a workers' state is "absolutely absurd".[62] This proposition explains Holloway's insistence that Lenin was a state socialist despite the latter's claim that socialism could only be won on the basis of "smashing" the existing state.[63] By dismissing the concept of a workers' state as an oxymoron, Holloway sidesteps any serious discussion of Lenin's contribution to thinking through how, because revolutions

---

58: Holloway, 2010a, p217.
59: Marx, 1983, pp62-65.
60: Marx, 1974, p354.
61: Engels, 1990b, p227.
62: Callinicos and Holloway, 2005, p122.
63: Holloway, 2010a, p11; 2010b, p83; Lenin, 1968.

involve working class people collectively taking control of their own destiny in a context still inherently marked by the defects of the old regime, their rule will involve state-like practices. Thus he nowhere engages with how democratic structures based upon workers' councils must decree, legislate, judge, punish and reward, distribute, organise, and take up arms against counter-revolution.[64] Moreover, this gap in his thought is no mere personal idiosyncrasy: it reflects real limitations with his theory of the state.

Holloway's approach to the problem of the state was framed by debates on the left in the 1960s and 1970s. He was one of a number of theorists associated with the journal *Capital & Class* who sought to move beyond the limitations of the debate between Ralph Miliband and Nicos Poulantzas about Marx's theory of the state. Despite their different approaches, both Miliband and Poulantzas theorised state autonomy in ways that opened the door to reformist reformulations of Marxism.[65] It was to help escape these limitations that Holloway and his co-thinkers looked to the German "state derivation" debate for answers.[66] The core insight Holloway took from these theorists was that the apparent autonomy of the state in capitalist societies was in fact a fetishised reflection of the way that capitalist relations of production assume separate economic and political forms. This mistake, made in different ways by both Miliband and Poulantzas, meant that their analyses became entrapped in the fetishised appearance of states in ways that obscured their capitalist essence.[67]

While this perspective marked a step forward beyond the Miliband-Poulantzas debate, Colin Barker pointed to a fundamental weakness with Holloway's approach. Because Holloway reduced capitalist relations of production to direct relations of exploitation his analysis of the relationship between state and capital operated at an inappropriate level of abstraction. Specifically, both the German debate and the exploration of this debate in the pages of *Capital & Class* failed to locate individual states within a system of states. Barker argued that this gap in the theory informed a misunderstanding of the state's role vis-à-vis competition with other states and thus a misunderstanding of the way that as capitalism aged there emerged a tendency for states to intervene in the production process itself to foster national competitiveness. As a consequence, Holloway and his co-thinkers

64: Thanks to Colin Barker for this point.
65: Harman, 1991, p4.
66: On the German debate, see Nachtwey and ten Brink, 2008.
67: Holloway and Picciotto, 1991, pp112-117; 1978, p19.

misconstrued the scale and nature of state intervention within both Eastern and Western economies in the 20th century.[68]

Holloway's criticism of the concept of a workers' state is best understood in relation to this weakness. Just as his understanding of capitalism blinded him to important aspects of the specific social content of modern states, his tendency to move too quickly from an analysis of the value form to conclusions about the state form underpins his rejection of the concept of a workers' state.[69] Specifically, his inability to conceive of workers' states as forms of power distinct from capitalism is a consequence of this tendency to reduce all states to fetishistic expressions of capitalist relations of production.

Somewhat ironically, Holloway combines his rejection of Marx's concept of a workers' state with praise for the one institution that Marx and Engels associated with this concept: the Paris Commune.[70] Engels wrote:

Of late, the Social-Democratic philistine has once more been filled with wholesome terror at the words: Dictatorship of the Proletariat. Well and good, gentlemen, do you want to know what this dictatorship looks like? Look at the Paris Commune. That was the Dictatorship of the Proletariat.[71]

By dismissing this argument, Holloway is able to conflate Lenin's revolutionary politics with reformism through the less than illuminating claim that they both aim at winning "state power".[72] Moreover, he combines this criticism of Lenin with the equally trite suggestion that "the council...is quite different from the party".[73] Of course it is, but this does not mean that it makes sense to posit party and council as alternatives.[74] It is far better to see the party as that section of the workers' movement that is most conscious of, and the best fighters for, the democratic goals immanent to the workers' movement.[75]

These weaknesses with Holloway's argument are not merely of academic interest; they undermine his pretensions to offer a theory of

---

68: Barker, 1978; 1991, p206. This continues to be the case even in the wake of Holloway's partial acceptance of Barker's arguments—see Holloway, 1995a, p137.

69: Bob Jessop rightly argues that Holloway's essentialist model of the relationship between state and capital informs a reductionism which obscures the specificity of the state form—Jessop, 1982, pp133-135. See also Bieler and Morton, 2003, p474.

70: Holloway, 2010b, p40.

71: Engels, 1990a, p191.

72: Holloway, 2010b, p83.

73: Holloway, 2010b, p40.

74: Holloway, 2010b, p60.

75: Harman, 2004, pp30-33, 39-44.

revolution. Indeed, he repeats the type of anarchistic criticisms both of revolutionary parties and the distinction between workers' and capitalist states that led Marx to write of Bakunin that "he understands absolutely nothing about the social revolution, only its political phrases".[76] Unfortunately, this seems an apt response to Holloway's comments on the problem of what to do when revolutionary movements are confronted with the institutions of the state. Caught between the practical necessities of the movement from below—one need only think of contemporary movements in Egypt and Syria, for example—and a theoretical model that acts as a barrier to him engaging adequately with this problem, Holloway is left paralysed: on the one hand he writes that "it is probably a mistake to think of arms as being key to self-defence", while on the other he admits, "I hum and I haw and I have no answer".[77] Though it would be foolhardy to counter this posture with the claim that classical Marxism has all the answers, it is nevertheless true that the history of the workers' movement does provide us with lessons that are relevant today.

Holloway's discussion of the link between abstract labour and alienation and his focus on human agency within the anti-capitalist movement are important counters to some of the more anti-humanistic voices within the movement. However, most evidently over the issue of state power, his theory falls short of the needs of the movement. To raise the level of his theory to the needs of revolutionary practice it is necessary that he moves beyond his one-sided conception of negativity, his overly abstract model of the state, his misunderstanding of the nature of alienation, and his caricatured interpretations of both the labour movement and classical Marxism. As it stands, his focus on "doing" against abstract labour means his politics remain unwittingly enmeshed within alienated relations that provide neither a basis for an adequate critique of capitalism nor a movement against it. In fact, insofar as he theorises a movement within capitalism that does not point beyond it, his approach resembles a variant of reformism.[78]

76: Marx, 1974, p334. See also Blackledge, 2010a; 2011.
77: Holloway, 2010b, p56; 2010a, p237.
78: See Callinicos, 2004; Harman, 2004.

References

Adorno, Theodor, 1973, *Negative Dialectics* (Continuum).

Barker, Colin, 1978, "The State as Capital", *International Socialism 1* (summer), www.marxists.de/theory/barker/stateascap.htm

Barker, Colin, 1991 (1978), "A Note on the Theory of the Capitalist State", in Simon Clarke (ed), *The State Debate* (Macmillan), www.marxists.de/theory/barker/capstates.htm

Bensaïd, Daniel, 2005, "On a Recent Book by John Holloway", *Historical Materialism*, 13.4.

Bieler, Andreas, and Adam David Morton, 2003, "Globalisation, the State and Class Struggle: a 'Critical Economy' Engagement with Open Marxism", *British Journal of Politics and International Relations*, 5.4.

Blackledge, Paul, 2006, "What was Done?", *International Socialism 111* (summer), www.isj.org.uk/?id=218

Blackledge, Paul, 2008, "Marxism and Ethics", *International Socialism 120* (autumn), www.isj.org.uk/?id=486

Blackledge, Paul, 2010a, "Marxism and Anarchism", *International Socialism 125* (winter), www.isj.org.uk/?id=616

Blackledge, Paul, 2010b, "Marxism, Nihilism and the Problem of Ethical Politics Today", *Socialism and Democracy*, 24.2, http://sdonline.org/53/marxism-nihilism-and-the-problem-of-ethical-politics-today/

Blackledge, Paul, 2011, "Anarchism, Syndicalism and Strategy: A Reply to Lucien van der Walt", *International Socialism 131* (summer), www.isj.org.uk/?id=746

Blackledge, Paul, 2012, *Marxism and Ethics* (SUNY).

Braverman, Harry, 1974, *Labour and Monopoly Capitalism* (Monthly Review).

Brohm, Jean-Marie, 1978, *Sport: A Prison of Measured Time* (Pluto).

Callinicos, Alex, 2001, "Toni Negri in Perspective", *International Socialism 92* (autumn), http://pubs.socialistreviewindex.org.uk/isj92/callinicos.htm

Callinicos, Alex, 2003, "State of Discontent", *Socialist Review*, 272 (March), www.socialistreview.org.uk/article.php?articlenumber=8349

Callinicos, Alex, 2004, "The future of the Anti-Capitalist Movement", in Hannah Dee (ed), *Anti-Capitalism: Where Now?* (Bookmarks).

Callinicos, Alex, 2005, "Sympathy for the Devil? John Holloway's Mephistophelian Marxism", *Capital & Class* 85 (spring).

Callinicos, Alex, and John Holloway, 2005, "Debate: Can We Change the World Without Taking Power?", *International Socialism 106* (spring), www.isj.org.uk/?id=98

Cleaver, Harry, 2000, *Reading Capital Politically*, second edition (AK).

Cliff, Tony, 1979, "The Balance of Class Forces in Recent Years", *International Socialism 6* (autumn), www.marxists.org/archive/cliff/works/1979/xx/balance1.htm

Colletti, Lucio, 1972, *From Rousseau to Lenin* (Monthly Review).

CSE State Apparatus and Expenditure Group, 1979, *Struggle over the State* (CSE Books).

Dunayevskaya, Raya, 2002, *The Power of Negativity* (Lexington).

Engels, Frederick, 1990a, "Introduction to K Marx's *The Civil War in France*", in Karl Marx and Frederick Engels, *Collected Works*, volume 27 (Lawrence and Wishart) www.marxists.org/archive/marx/works/1871/civil-war-france/intro.htm

Engels, Frederick, 1990b, "A Critique of the Draft Social Democratic Programme of 1891", in Karl Marx and Frederick Engels, *Collected Works*, volume 27 (Lawrence and Wishart), www.marxists.org/archive/marx/works/1891/06/29.htm

Fuller, Jack, 1980, "The New Workerism: The Politics of Italian Autonomism", *International Socialism 8* (autumn), www.marxists.org/history/etol/newspape/isj2/1980/no2-008/fuller.htm

Gonzalez, Mike, 2003, "Crying out for Revolution", *International Socialism* 99 (summer), http://pubs.socialistreviewindex.org.uk/isj99/gonzalez.htm

Green, Peter, 1978, "The Necessity of Value: I", *International Socialism* 3 (winter), www.marxists.org/history/etol/writers/green-p/1978/xx/value.html

Green, Peter, 1979, "The Necessity of Value: II", *International Socialism* 4 (spring), www.marxists.org/history/etol/writers/green-p/1979/xx/value2.html

Harman, Chris, 1979, "Crisis of the European Revolutionary Left", *International Socialism* 4 (spring), www.marxists.org/archive/harman/1979/xx/eurevleft.html

Harman, Chris, 1991, "The State and Capitalism Today", *International Socialism* 51 (summer), www.isj.org.uk/?id=234

Harman, Chris, 2004, "Spontaneity, Strategy and Politics", *International Socialism* 104 (autumn), www.isj.org.uk/?id=12

Holloway, John, 1979, "Introduction to Pannekoek on Organisation", *Capital & Class*, 9 (autumn 1979).

Holloway, John, 1991 (1980), "The State and Everyday Struggle", in Simon Clarke (ed), *The State Debate* (Macmillan).

Holloway, John, 1995a (1994), "Global Capital and the National State", in Werner Bonefeld and John Holloway (eds), *Global Capital, National State and the Politics of Money* (Macmillan).

Holloway, John, 1995b, "From scream of refusal to scream of power", in Werner Bonefeld and others (eds), *Open Marxism Volume 3: Emancipating Marx* (Pluto).

Holloway, John, 2005a, "Change the World Without Taking Power", *Capital & Class*, 85 (spring).

Holloway, John, 2005b, "No", *Historical Materialism*, 13.4.

Holloway, John, 2009a, "Why Adorno?", in John Holloway and others (eds), *Negativity and Revolution* (Pluto).

Holloway, John, 2009b, "Negative and Positive Autonomism: Or Why Adorno? Part Two", in John Holloway and others (eds), *Negativity and Revolution* (Pluto).

Holloway, John, 2010a, *Change the World Without Taking Power*, third edition (Pluto).

Holloway, John, 2010b, *Crack Capitalism* (Pluto).

Holloway, John, 2011, *Power and Democracy*, www.johnholloway.com.mx/2011/07/30/power-and-democracy/

Holloway, John, 2012, "Preoccupy: John Holloway", *Occupied Times* (3 July), http://theoccupiedtimes.co.uk/?p=5752

Holloway, John, and Sol Picciotto, 1978, "Introduction: Towards a Materialist Theory of the State", in John Holloway and Sol Picciotto (eds), *State and Capital* (Edward Arnold).

Holloway, John, and Sol Picciotto 1991 (1977), "Capital, Crisis and State", in Simon Clarke (ed), *The State Debate* (Macmillan).

Hudis, Peter, 2004, "The Death of the Death of the Subject", *Historical Materialism*, 12.3.

Jessop, Bob, 1982, *The Capitalist State* (New York University Press).

Keen, Steve, 2011, *Debunking Economics* (Zed).

Lebowitz, Michael, 2005, "Holloway's Scream", *Historical Materialism*, 13.4.

Lenin, VI, 1968 (1917), "The State and Revolution", in *Lenin's Selected Works* (Progress), www.marxists.org/archive/lenin/works/1917/staterev/

Lenin, VI, 1991 (1920), "Speech on the Role and Structure of the Communist Party", in John Riddell (ed), *Workers of the World and Oppressed Peoples, Unite! Proceedings and Documents of the Second Congress, 1920* (Pathfinder), www.marxists.org/archive/lenin/works/1920/jul/x03.htm#fw2

Lih, Lars, 2006, *Lenin Rediscovered* (Brill).

Löwy, Michael, 2005, "To change the world we need revolutionary democracy", *Capital & Class*, 85 (spring).

Marx, Karl, 1974 (1874), "Conspectus of Bakunin's 'Statism and Anarchy'", in Marx, *The First International and After* (Penguin), www.marxists.org/archive/marx/works/1874/04/bakunin-notes.htm

Marx, Karl, 1974 (1875), "Critique of the Gotha Programme", in Marx, *The First International and After* (Penguin), www.marxists.org/archive/marx/works/1875/gotha/

Marx, Karl, 1975 (1844), "Economic and Philosophical Manuscripts" in Marx, *Early Writings* (Penguin), www.marxists.org/archive/marx/works/1844/manuscripts/labour.htm

Marx, Karl, 1976 (1867), *Capital*, volume I (Penguin), www.marxists.org/archive/marx/works/1867-c1/

Marx, Karl, 1983 (1852), "Letter to Joseph Weydemeyer", in Marx and Engels, *Collected Works*, volume 39 (Lawrence and Wishart), www.marxists.org/archive/marx/works/1852/letters/52_03_05-ab.htm

Marx, Karl, and Frederick Engels, 1976 (1845), "The German Ideology", in Marx and Engels, *Collected Works*, volume 5 (Lawrence and Wishart), www.marxists.org/archive/marx/works/1845/german-ideology/

McNally, David, 2004, "The Dual Form of Labour in Capitalist Society and the Struggle over Meaning", *Historical Materialism*, 12.3.

Molyneux, John, 1985, *What is the Real Marxist Tradition?* (Bookmarks), www.marxisme.dk/arkiv/molyneux/realmarx/index.htm

Nachtwey, Oliver, and Tobias ten Brink, 2008, "Lost in Translation: The German World Market Debate in the 1970s", *Historical Materialism*, 16.1.

Ness, Immanuel, and Dario Azzellini, 2011, *Ours to Master and to Own* (Haymarket).

Perkins, Stephen, 1993, *Marxism and the Proletariat* (Pluto Press).

Rubin, Isaac Ilyich, 1973, *Essays on Marx's Theory of Value* (Black Rose), www.marxists.org/archive/rubin/value/index.htm

Rubin, Isaac Ilyich, 1979, *A History of Economic Thought* (Ink Links).

Saad-Filho, Alfredo, 1997, "Concrete and Abstract Labour in Marx's Theory of Value", *Review of Political Economy*, volume 9, number 4.

Saad-Filho, Alfredo, 2002, *The Value of Marx* (Routledge).

Sayers, Sean, 2011, *Marx and Alienation* (Palgrave).

Wainwright, Hilary, 2003, *Reclaim the State* (Verso).

Wainwright, Hilary, and John Holloway, 2011, "Crack Capitalism or Reclaim the State" (Transnational Institute), www.tni.org/article/crack-capitalism-or-reclaim-state

Weeks, John, 1981, *Capital and Exploitation* (Princeton University Press).

Weeks, John, 1990, "Abstract Labour and Commodity Production", *Research in Political Economy*, volume 12, http://jweeks.org/1990%20Abstract%20labor.pdf

Wright, Steve, 2002, *Storming Heaven* (Pluto).

The Vote:
How it was won and how it was undermined

Paul Foot

£13.99 out now

Paul Foot's last book is a searing account of the fight for democracy from the 17th century to the 21st, and how the limited democracy that has been won has failed to deliver on its promise. Telling the inspiring stories of the radicals in the English Revolution, the Suffragettes and many others, he shows that the struggle for real democracy must continue today.

"Superb. Foot at the height of his powers" John Pilger

"Exhilarating, passionate, energetic and invincibly cheerful" Francis Wheen, Guardian

"Paul Foot was one of the most powerful advocates of social justice and democracy and his last book brings them to the forefront of our political debate" Tony Benn

"Chavs", class and representation

Nicola Ginsburgh

A review of Owen Jones, **Chavs: The Demonisation of the Working Class** *(Verso, 2011), £9.99*

Owen Jones's best-selling *Chavs: The Demonisation of the Working Class* has deservedly been praised as an accessible and refreshing engagement with the issues of class in modern Britain. Since its publication last year Jones has achieved celebrity status as the unofficial figurehead of a re-emergent young left. His popularity is significant testimony to a resurgent interest in left wing politics, and indicative of a mood of both struggle and discontent with Tory and New Labour thinking.

    Chavs traces the rise of an offensive caricature of the working class: a racist hooligan, an alcoholic thug; women unable to control their vaginas, men unable to control their fists; brainless, feckless scroungers—working class people, as represented by the term *chav*, are nothing more than parasitic growths on society. Jones demonstrates how the figure of the chav is used to deflect blame away from the structures that create inequality onto individuals. The chav caricature implies poverty is the result of personal choices and moral deficiencies—laziness, pure unadulterated barbarity and primitive atavism—rather than the system itself. Consequently, such representations not only shroud the real causes of inequality, but also act to justify further attacks upon the welfare system. After all, why should taxpayers' money go towards sustaining the gross lifestyles of indolent plebs?

    Jones argues that derogatory working class caricatures gained currency because the working class has relatively little power over how it is represented. The proportion of people from working class backgrounds in journalism and politics has significantly dwindled, while the middle class edges further and further towards monopolising positions of power, replicating society in its own image to serve its own needs. Put simply, there is a class bias in the dominant representations of society. Even genuine attempts to give the working class a fair representation or voice inevitably reproduce unrealistic stereotypes due to the middle class's detachment from the actualities of working class life.

Alongside growing contempt for the working class, class itself has been increasingly ignored and disavowed by politicians and the media. Jones argues that Thatcherism's all-out assault on trade unions and the welfare state crippled the working class, allowing for the subsequent airbrushing of the working class out of public life. He lambasts the disingenuous claim made by Thatcherites that we live in a classless society, pointing to the fact that those who made such statements were ruthlessly pursuing their own class agenda. Jones is also disdainful of New Labour's capitulation to this logic, with their feeble response that "we are all middle class now". This idea, or the notion that we live in a meritocracy in which all can, regardless of background, achieve unlimited wealth and success, denies the fact that class affects people's lives in any real meaningful way and entrenches the belief people are responsible for their own poverty.

Jones wants to reveal the real working class behind these representations. He dismisses the idea that class is about how much you earn, home ownership or lifestyle, instead defining the working class as "people who have no means of sustenance other than the sale of labour" and who lack autonomy or control over that labour.[1] He describes an increasingly female workforce, based in service industries, working in poor conditions for low pay. He criticises the drive to create a flexible workforce of temporary and part-time employees working under terrible conditions, and explores the social cost of unemployment within communities destroyed by the closure of industries during the 1980s.

Like Jones, Marxism sees class as "the collective social expression of the fact of exploitation, the way in which exploitation is embodied in a social structure".[2] Class is essentially a social relationship: "Class society arises when a minority establishes sufficient control over the means of production to compel the direct producers—slaves, peasants or workers—to

---

1:   Jones, 2011, p144.
2:   Ste Croix, 1984, p100.

labour not simply for themselves but also for the exploiting minority".[3] Class position is objective and exists with or without class consciousness. A person may consider themselves to be middle class because they have a university degree, work in a white collar industry or display what are regarded as middle class consumption patterns and tastes, but it is their relationship to the means of production and to other classes in society that determines their class. Although it is tempting define class by occupation, this mystifies more than it reveals. For example, identifying the working class with manual workers overlooks the fact that "manual workers" can be shop-floor workers, supervisors and small businesspeople, just as the term "white collar" can bunch together the CEO of a large corporation and the low-paid office worker in the same category.[4] Class is not about identifying static social groups within a predefined hierarchy; classes are better "defined as *common positions within the social relations of production*, where production is analysed above all as a system of exploitation".[5]

Culture and class

Despite *Chavs* being about the working class, the opinions of journalists and politicians take precedence throughout the book. The middle class, who are the main focus of Jones's anger and criticism, simultaneously provide his main sources, while those who own and control the means of production—the capitalists—escape largely unscathed.

Nevertheless, there is much of worth in Jones's discussion of the realities of working class life today and his acknowledgement that "ultimately it is not the prejudice we need to tackle, but is the fountain from which it springs".[6] This is a refreshing departure from much recent scholarship of class identity, which analyses class through looking at culture and perceptions, and ideas of hierarchy and status in which class position is not only determined through the relationship to the means of production, but is also formed through consumption patterns and lifestyle choices.[7] Thus Floya Anthias argues for a definition of class that "is not so much concerned with resource distribution and allocation but rather with inferiorisation at the cultural or ascriptive level, as well as the level of identity and access to cultural or symbolic resources".[8]

3:   Callinicos and Harman, 1987, p6.
4:   Callinicos and Harman, 1987, p4.
5:   Wright, 1979, p17.
6:   Jones, 2011, p12.
7:   Much of this culturalist approach is influenced by French sociologist Pierre Bourdieu.
8:   Anthias, 2004, p25.

Similarly, Andy Medhurst has argued that "class is not just an objective entity, but also (and mostly?), a question of identifications, perceptions, feelings".[9] This approach is more interested in the "linguistic condescension" levelled at those with working class accents, than that those who own such accents are working for the minimum wage with no job security. For these writers, Marxist analysis suffers from an "obsession" with economics. Medhurst argues "class privilege and class prejudice are not reducible to dispassionate debate or the algebras of abstraction".[10] They see the need to address cross-class cultural differentiation and the ways in which the middle class sneer at working class culture because this is fundamental to their idea of how class is constituted. However, this ultimately drags them further and further away from the material social relations at the heart of class.

If we focus on the prejudices attached to status, the key to transforming society becomes an appreciation of chav stereotypes and tropes—a perverse donning of Burberry and gold earrings as a route to emancipation and tolerance. The answer to changing society does not lie in eradicating "status snobbery" which ultimately elevates the importance of people's subjective attitudes towards one another above the unequal distribution of wealth and property. Jones's strength lies in his concise articulation of the need for class struggle rather than status parity in *Chavs*, emphasising the need for strong unions and an international labour movement as the means through which real equality can be achieved.

However, although the idea that we need to tackle issues of status rather than distribution and ownership has enjoyed a resurgence in recent times, it is not particularly new, and the failure to recognise this is a weakness of *Chavs*. In the 1950s Labour revisionists sought to shed the rhetoric of class, believing it alienated the electorate and attributing their 1951 defeat to their characterisation as a party of the working class. Leading revisionist Anthony Crosland claimed the material inequalities in society had been largely overcome, increased state planning had protected people against ravages of capitalism and the real problem of society was the importance attached to status—that people did not feel like they were equal. People were apparently living in an age of affluence in which discontent was not a result of actual material deprivation or class antagonism, but "status anguish".[11] Concurrently, "embourgeoisement" theorists

9:   Medhurst, 2000, p20.
10: Medhurst, 2000, p21.
11: Callaghan, 1990, pp174-180.

of the 1950s and 1960s claimed the working class had benefited from capitalism; content with their material lot, the real issue at stake for the working class was *cultural* acceptance.[12]

A history of class demonisation

The tendency to underplay such continuities emanates from Jones's stress upon Thatcherism as the decisive turning point in class relations. Although he has rebutted claims that he romanticises the pre-Thatcherite working class, he maintains that:

> There was a time when working class people had been patronised rather than openly despised. Disraeli had called working class people "angels in marble". "Salt of the earth" was another phrase once associated with them. Today, they are more likely than not to be called chavs. From salt of the earth to scum of the earth. This is the legacy of Thatcherism—the demonisation of everything associated with the working class.[13]

This claim that Thatcherism saw the birth of contempt for the working class leads Jones to underplay the historical antecedents of class demonisation. The "undeserving poor", the Victorian "social residuum", the 1960s "culture of poverty"—class demonisation is not simply a product of Thatcherite neoliberal ideology and policies, and neither was it absent during Labour's post-war period. Broadly speaking, these ideas can be traced back to the 17th century Poor Law, which sought to differentiate between "deserving" and "undeserving" claimants.[14] Similarly at the turn of the 20th century, debates raged regarding proposals to segregate the very poor into detention centres, to remove children from "degenerate" parents and even to send the "residuum" overseas.[15]

Descriptions of the self-inflicted poverty of sections of the working class have been used to justify attacks upon social provisions for the poor for centuries. Just as Thomas Malthus argued at the end of the 18th century that Poor Laws "diminished the will to save, and weakened incentives to sobriety, industry and happiness",[16] today David Cameron argues that welfare has created a "culture of entitlement" and has remarked that "the benefit system has created a benefit culture. It

12: See, for example, Zweig, 1961.
13: Jones, 2011, pp71-72.
14: Welshman, 2006, p4.
15: Stedman Jones, 1976, p314.
16: Welshman, 2006, p5.

doesn't just allow people to act irresponsibly, but often actively encourages them to do so".[17]

The unemployed have a particularly long history of demonisation. John Harrison has shown how people receiving benefits have been criminalised since the inception of unemployment benefits:

> Stigmatised as the "dole"...granted only after a household means test carried out by the local Public Assistance Committee... No aspect of the 1930s was more hated and remembered more bitterly than the means test. It often involved officials coming into the home; it penalised thrift and encouraged tale-telling and petty tyranny...smelled strongly of the Board of Guardians and the workhouse.[18]

This proves strikingly similar to contemporary government campaigns on "benefit thieves", which encourage individuals to ring a confidential hotline to report suspicious behaviour of others and the constant media denunciations of benefit scroungers and fraudsters.[19] To acknowledge that people are unemployed because of the economic system would require questioning capitalism; it is easy to see why blaming the poor for their own poverty has always appealed to the ruling class. It is also convenient for these people to deflect questions of theft and fraud onto the poorest in society: MPs' "overclaimed" expenses, on average 31 times the amount claimed by "benefit thieves", banking scandals and corporate corruption draw attention to who the real criminals of society are.[20]

Race and the "underclass"

One frequent criticism levelled at Jones concerns his treatment of race in *Chavs*. The language of race has long been used to emphasise the supposedly deep foundations of immoral behaviour which invites poverty. Jose Harris notes that "from 1870 down to 1914 popular discussion of the problems of the very poor frequently referred to them in biological and anthropological

---

17: Cameron, 2011.
18: Harrison, 1984, p371.
19: Although a crude gauge, a quick online search for "benefit fraud" on newspaper websites has the following results. The *Sun*: 585 articles, the *Daily Mail*: 1,311 articles, the *Telegraph*: 5,640 articles.
20: "Benefit Fraud Average Cost 31 Times Lower Than MP Expense Overclaims", *Political Scrapbook*, 30 May 2011, http://politicalscrapbook.net/2011/05/mps-expenses-vs-benefit-fraud/

terms as 'a backward people' and 'a race apart'".[21] During this period, which witnessed the rise of biological racial determinism, some social Darwinists argued not only that there was a hierarchy of races, but that the poor, criminals and prostitutes were themselves evolutionary throwbacks, evidence of racial degeneration of the "white race".

Likewise, in modern discussions of poverty, culturalist approaches tend to talk about the supposed criminal traits and behaviours of the poor as if they were part of a fixed culture, a hereditary disease—effectively to describe sections of the working class in racial terms. One of the most famous propagators of the culturalist approach to poverty is Charles Murray who has written extensively on the "underclass":[22]

> The underclass does not refer to degree of poverty, but to a type of poverty. It is not a new concept. I grew up knowing what the underclass was; we just didn't call it that in those days. In the small Iowa town where I lived, I was taught by my middle class parents that there were two kinds of poor people. One class of poor people was never even called "poor". I came to understand that they simply lived with low incomes, as my own parents had done when they were young. Then there was another set of poor people, just a handful of them. These poor people didn't lack just money. They were defined by their behaviour. Their homes were littered and unkempt. The men in the family were unable to hold a job for more than a few weeks at a time. Drunkenness was common. The children grew up ill-schooled and ill-behaved and contributed a disproportionate share of the local juvenile delinquents.[23]

The underclass concept itself is incontrovertibly tied up with ideas of race. First appearing in America, the disproportionate concentration of African Americans living in poverty led policymakers and academics to describe "underclass behaviours" as predominantly belonging to the African American community. The idea of a specifically black underclass entrenches the imagined dichotomy between a respectable white working class and a black "sub-class", existing outside of working class struggle and with distinct interests. Moreover, it denies the role of racism and capitalism

21: Harris, 1993, pp235-236.
22: The notion of the underclass has numerous contested conceptualisations and has both right and left wing adherents. Here I focus only on those who stress cultural and behavioural determinants, rather than those who see the underclass as created primarily by structural causes, while recognising that these approaches are not completely distinct as there is often considerable overlap between the two.
23: Murray, 2006, p24.

in the concentration of poverty in black communities, instead blaming black culture and behaviour. Consequently, whites who fall into similar levels of poverty are described in similar racialised terms.[24]

An apt example of how class inequalities are sometimes treated as racial issues is Jones's infamous debate with right wing historian David Starkey immediately after the 2011 British riots. Starkey claimed that "the substantial section of the chavs...have become black. The whites have become black. A particular sort of violent, destructive, nihilistic, gangster culture has become *the* fashion." Jones lambasted Starkey for equating economic and social power, and respectability, with whiteness.[25] Deploying the language of race functions to ascribe to poor whites static cultural and genetic characteristics, and simultaneously reinforces racist ideas—that whiteness is normal and superior, and blackness alien and inferior with the potential to "infect" white people.

Gareth Stedman Jones has detailed how the "social residuum" of the 19th century "was considered dangerous not only because of its degenerate nature but also because its very existence served to contaminate the classes immediately above it".[26] Yet, although racial ideas have certainly been applied to the domestic white working class, we cannot collapse class into race. Talking about class as if it were race confuses the specifics of both; racial oppression exists to justify unequal relationships in society, whereas class is the relationship of exploitation embodied in the structure of society. Racism may be ideological, but has tangible effects; oppression is lived and is real, but race itself is a historically specific category with no objective basis. Acknowledging that certain sections of society are described in racial language which assigns people particular criminal and poverty-inducing cultures and behaviours helps to uncover how their poverty is legitimised and individualised, but does not explain why that poverty exists.

The working class whitewashed

Furthermore, using the language of race to describe sections of the working class potentially reinforces the propensity to describe the white working class as a specifically dispossessed racial group. In *Chavs* Jones states that inequality has been racialised, that "the promotion of multiculturalism in an era when the concept of class was being abandoned meant that inequality

---

24: Although Murray denies race plays a significant role in the British context (Murray, 2006) the ideological underpinnings and assumptions remain.

25: *Newsnight*, BBC, 12 August 2011.

26: Stedman Jones, 1976, p289.

became almost exclusively understood through the prism of race and ethnic identity".[27] Jones is referring to a liberal multiculturalism that conceives of a set of pre-defined, homogeneous cultures assigned to distinct ethnic groups, living side by side with completely different needs and attitudes, struggling to tolerate the innate differences between them. Within this understanding of multiculturalism the portrayal of the working class as exclusively "white", with a monocultural British identity, has been used to claim that poverty and inequality are direct results of the presence of ethnic minorities. Alongside the portrayal of the white working class as an endangered cultural relic under attack from distinct "ethnic cultures",[28] it is argued that ethnic minorities receive preferential treatment by the state in the allocation of resources and that the immigration involved puts unnecessary pressure on taxpayers.[29]

Therefore the white working class are not always portrayed as "chavs", but can also be represented as victims—particularly as victims of immigration. The *Daily Mail* frequently prints stories featuring headlines such as "Nine Out Of Ten Jobs Created Last Year Went To Foreign Nationals" and "Mass Immigration Has Made The UK's Poor Even Poorer".[30] In the 2011 elections Tory candidate Maureen Pearce stood on a patriotic, virulently xenophobic platform which fed off notions of a white British identity under siege. Her manifesto stated a dedication to:

(1) Flying the Union Jack and Cross of St George all year round.
(2) Stopping mass immigration into Britain.
(3) Putting "political correctness" into the dustbin of history.[31]

Jones rightfully expresses the need to recognise the multiracial nature of the British working class to counter this inaccurate portrayal of a racially homogeneous working class under attack. In his new preface he states,

27: Jones, 2011, pp101-102.
28: This is problematic for several reasons. The notion that ethnic groups have distinct, uncomplicated cultures ignores cultural variation *within* nationalities and ethnicities. It also ignores the mixing that has gone on for thousands of years between people from different backgrounds to such a degree that to speak of any distinct national or ethnic culture is meaningless. It also denies the ideological role static and fixed conceptions of culture play, and fails to see the various and diverse interpretations and meanings cultures can have to different social groups within different circumstances and contexts, or see culture as a process rooted within material practice and the struggle between social groups. For a more detailed discussion, see Rosen, 2011; Barker, 1981; Jenkins, 2011.
29: For a rebuttal of such claims see Barker, 1981; Kimber, 2010.
30: *Daily Mail*, 13 May 2011; 31 August 2011.
31: "Labour Slam Tories Over Attempts To 'Woo the BNP Vote'", *Your Thurrock*, 3 May 2011.

"*Chavs* was sometimes referred to as a book solely about the white working class. One of the purposes of the book was to take on this narrow, exclusive image of the working class".[32] Although Jones understands that the chav is a representation that does not encompass the reality or diversity of the working class, his focus on this representation only allows him to show how the white working class has been demonised. To demonstrate the demonisation of a multiracial working class, the specific ways in which different sections of the working class have been represented must be recognised. Much could be gained from looking at the similarities in the ways in which chavs, immigrants and people of colour have been represented: derogatory stereotypes serve an ideological function in dismissing the structural causes of inequality, and reinforce the idea that particular groups of people have inherent immutable cultures prone to criminality and sloth. These categories are by no means identical, in either their development or their effects—but it is worth noting their similarities nonetheless.

Jones's argument that the criminality of working class individuals is used as a template for the entire working class resonates with the way the media and politicians present crimes by particular immigrants and ethnic minorities. In his study of race and the press Teun A Van Dijk found that "crime is not covered [in the press] as involving black individuals, but as a form of 'group crime', for which the whole black community tends to be blamed".[33] Immigrants, like chavs, are portrayed as benefit thieves, fraudsters and scroungers. Many politicians are keen to emphasise the supposed inherent degeneracy of immigrants, who are regularly depicted as self-ostracising, with values and interests antithetical to the imagined white national community.

The working class has certainly been demonised, but it has been demonised in many different ways through numerous prisms that veil the commonalities and shared position of exploitation of people from different backgrounds. The chav figure must be placed alongside these other forms of demonisation to show how the multiracial working class is attacked and divided.

Working class racism

One of the most interesting sections in *Chavs* is the exploration of how the white working class has been portrayed as a racist rabble. The working class is regularly depicted as actively choosing to live in ignorance: ignorance of manners, ignorance of other cultures and a fervent anti-intellectualism.

32: Jones, 2011, p xiv.
33: Van Dijk, 1991, p100.

This portrayal of working class racism has been used to justify attacks upon the welfare state. The odious 2006 report *The New East End* uses the idea of racial competition over resources precisely for these ends.[34] Welfare, it claims, is a "faceless bureaucracy", an "impersonal force" based on taking "out" of the system, encouraging competition over resources that creates racial tensions, whereas "when competition is channelled into serving national goals, and putting something *into* the community, then its effect is likely to be increased solidarity, as happened during the war".[35]

Yet there is another function in projecting all issues of racism onto the working class. When racism is seen as the product of morally and socially sick individuals who embrace their self-inflicted ignorance it becomes "a problem involving those on the outer edge of society which [does] not threaten the core of present mainstream society, culture, or the state",[36] a problem which can be ignored. The image of the chav is a convenient canvas onto which all problems of racism and crime can be projected by a media and state eager to protect their liberal and tolerant self-characterisation; each denunciation of the racist chav minority a ritual purification to cleanse and absolve themselves from their roles in the development and propagation of racism. Within this climate, where the working class is demonised as a racist underclass, the BNP and far-right groups attempt to align themselves in an empathetic position, claiming they are also wrongly victimised and accused of racism by a hypocritical ruling class.

Jones shows how the typical BNP supporter is likely to be portrayed as a working class lout. This view is also pervasive in much of academia; in a study of the National Front in east London Christopher Husbands has argued that the working class East End has an "unusual local culture" that encourages its inhabitants to be predisposed to politics of racial exclusionism.[37] Much of this thinking centres on the presumption that the working class are more likely to be racist than other sections of society. Jones demonstrates how liberal commentators use the apparent racism of the working class to berate and mock them,[38] but highlights that it is the working class who are most likely to live and work with, marry and befriend immigrants. Yet he maintains that "attitudes towards immigration are liable to depend

34: Indeed, it argues that not only has welfare increased racism, it has been detrimental to women and disproportionately benefits the middle and upper classes.
35: Dench, Gavron and Young, 2006, p7. For a debunking of the myth of cross-class solidarity during the war, see Calder, 1992.
36: Witte, 1996, p174.
37: Husbands, 2007, pp55, 26.
38: Jones, 2011, pp117-118.

on the class of the person who holds them. Indeed, prospective employers stand to gain from cheaper foreign workers".[39]

The implication of this is that anti-immigration feeling is stronger within the working class, because it is they who suffer most from an influx of competitive foreign labour. Jones argues that "the average BNP voter is likely to be working class... The BNP has thrived in traditionally white working class areas with a long history of returning Labour candidates," without acknowledging the real class basis of fascist organisations.[40] For example, one prominent former BNP donor is millionaire Charles Wentworth; EDL strategist and funder Alan Lake, or Alan Ayling, is a rich director of a City investment fund; while successive leaked BNP membership lists point to a petty bourgeois core of supporters.[41] Additionally, there is no strict correlation between votes for the BNP and levels of deprivation. One report found that the BNP's election results were negatively correlated with the highest levels of poverty and greatest numbers claiming state benefits, concluding, "Overall it seems the poorer the ward the less likely the BNP are to do well".[42]

Furthermore, working class people, black and white, have repeatedly organised and fought against oppression. There is a long history of working class anti-racist struggles, from Cable Street in 1933 to Lewisham in 1977 and contemporary mobilisations against fascist organisations, which complicate the image of a liberal, tolerant middle class desperately trying to hose down the frothing racism of the working class hordes.

While Jones argues that we should direct anger at the bosses rather than immigrants, he nevertheless reduces the causes of racism to the material concerns of the working class. Jones may give some anecdotal evidence of some middle class racists, but this is an inadequate substitute for considering where racist ideas actually come from and the role of capitalism in developing racial categories.[43] Working class people do not instinctively turn to racist ideas to explain their material deprivation—the state and media play a fundamental role in shifting the blame for inequality onto immigrants.

Representations of the working class

Even if we accept that there was a time when the working class had an easily identifiable and largely positive representation, problems remain.

39: Jones, 2011, p240.
40: Jones, 2011, p223.
41: Basketter, 2008. For a more detailed analysis of the BNP see Smith, 2009.
42: John, Margetts, Rowland and Weir, 2006, p15.
43: See Callinicos, 1993.

Peter Hitchcock has argued that the difficulties involved in working class representation start with the fundamental abstractness of class itself:

> Representations of class are active negotiations on the meaning of class as it is lived but do not constitute the real proletarian Being as an abstraction for capital. This certainly explains why cultural representations in themselves do not encompass social change, but it also goes a long way towards explaining the tenuousness of working class expression in general.[44]

The working class has never possessed a unique, homogeneous culture and identity that can be given a singular representation. Representation can provide insights into how class is lived in specific contexts, but cannot fully *explain* class or social change. In *Capital* Marx contrasts class in its "pure" abstract form with its historically specific manifestations, remarking:

> In England, modern society is indisputably more highly and classically developed in economic structure. Nevertheless, even here the stratification of classes does not appear in its pure form. Middle and intermediate strata even here obliterate lines of demarcation everywhere.[45]

While this stratification can exist within a class, the fundamental characteristic of the working class remains intact—the fact of its own exploitation. Therefore this recognition of diversity within the working class does not rid the working class of its collective role or suggest these strata are in antagonistic relations with one another, but rather points to varying degrees of heterogeneity within a shared social position.

As Savage and Miles have explained:

> The British working class has always been heterogeneous...no single sector of employment ever accounted for more than 40 percent of the workforce throughout the period [1840-1940]. Even at the peak of Britain's industrial primacy the majority of workers were not employed in manufacturing. The British working class was never purely an industrial working class.[46]

As well as being diverse, the working class is also dynamic. Under

44: Hitchcock, 2000, p29.
45: Marx, 1959, p885.
46: Miles and Savage, 1994, p22.

capitalism, the means of production are continually revolutionised as new industries appear and once-profitable ones go into decline. As the needs of capital change, the working class is reshaped.

Despite this, a certain section of the working class is sometimes treated as representative of the class in its entirety. So the "traditional" white, male manual worker has often been used as shorthand for the working class. But anchoring definitions of class to this historically specific manifestation ignores the diversity of the working class in terms of employment, prioritises a static representation over the dynamism of class, tends to exclude women and ethnic minorities, and undermines understanding of the contemporary working class.

The decline of traditional manufacturing industries, which saw the destruction of many mining and industrial communities that for many had come to represent and embody what it meant to be working class, has led some to claim we are living in a post-class world or that the nature of class has been fundamentally transformed.[47] At the end of the 1980s a group associated with the publication *Marxism Today*, including cultural theorist Stuart Hall, produced a "Manifesto for the New Times":

> The "New Times" argument is that the world has changed, not just incrementally but qualitatively, that Britain and other advanced capitalist societies are increasingly characterised by diversity, differentiation and fragmentation, rather than homogeneity, standardisation and the economics and organisations of scale which characterised modern mass society.[48]

They argued this meant we were living in a "post-Fordist" world in which social life, culture and politics were no longer primarily based around class, but local decentred identities. Class seemed irrelevant to explaining the new wave of struggles rising in the second half of the 20th century around issues of gender, race and sexuality, and was increasingly regarded as simply one more facet of people's identities.

While Jones largely avoids such lines of reasoning and vehemently argues that class is still important today, his comments sometimes seem to reflect an understanding of class centred upon representation. This is the case, for instance, when he laments the dearth of working class bands in

47: For notable examples of the argument that the working class no longer has a revolutionary role, see Gorz, 1982, and Hobsbawm, 1978, or for a more recent example, Pakulski and Waters, 1996.
48: Hall and Jacques, 1989, p11.

popular music. This might seem like a pedantic point, but it is important to highlight how easily we can mistake a changed working class for its complete absence. In arguing that there have been no prominent working class bands since Oasis in the 1990s,[49] not only does Jones overlook arguably the most successful band in the past ten years, the Arctic Monkeys, who sing in an unmistakably working class Sheffield accent, he also fails to acknowledge that many current artists, such as Cheryl Cole, Tulisa Contostavlos and Emeli Sande, are from working class backgrounds. His examples of The Beatles and Happy Mondays as the heyday of working class prominence in popular music expressed a historically specific working class identity—just as these female artists do today. Of course these artists do not fit into the traditional representations of the working class male manual labourer—but as ethnically diverse women from urban areas they do reflect a changing and variegated working class.

Similarly, while adopting a broad definition of the working class, Jones's focus is on part-time, agency and short-term workers, employed in supermarkets or call centres. It is easy to see why, as he wants to explore those who are most likely to be demonised as chavs, but it leads to a tendency to see those in the worst paid jobs under the worst conditions as the most representative of the working class. These workers have been described as "precarious", characterised by insecurity at the hands of a flexible free market, an argument that often goes hand in hand with the idea that globalisation has fundamentally undermined job stability. Jones's argument that industry can "simply relocate" to countries with less expensive workforces[50] misunderstands the selective and uneven character of global industrial relocation: capital mobility is restricted by the expense of relocation and the particular requirements for productivity, such as a skilled workforce and developed infrastructure.[51]

In the UK the number of part-time workers was 7.9 million at the end of 2011, a rise of 2 million since 1992, and agency work currently accounts for somewhere between 1.1 and 1.5 million workers. Yet part-time work should not be unquestioningly understood as non-permanent and unstable, and agency work cannot be seen as unremittingly enveloping the permanent workforce.[52] Despite a trend towards flexibility, significant countervailing tendencies exist.[53] One in seven

49: Jones, 2011, p133.
50: Jones, 2011, p157.
51: See Harman, 1996.
52: Choonara, 2011.
53: See Dunn, 2004.

people still work in manufacturing in the UK, while most people still have permanent jobs.[54]

The chav is certainly unrepresentative of the working class, but we must be wary of suggesting the working class ever had a straightforward uncomplicated image, or that this representation, in itself, was necessary for the existence of class or for social change.

Although the underclass and chavs do not exist as a distinct class or social layer, these representations can have a real impact upon how people understand class. The chav is an attempt to win over sections of the working class to a ruling class idea—that there exists a minority who are responsible for their own poverty and from whom the problems of society ultimately stem.

However, these dominant representations are not simply unquestioningly repeated. For instance, people in council housing or in receipt of benefits can differentiate themselves from the *other* unworthy and lazy poor. But such representations can also be challenged and wholly rejected. As Jones notes, since the 1960s around half of the population have consistently seen themselves as working class, despite the lack of working class representation.[55] Representation, in itself, cannot fully explain class, either as an objective relationship of exploitation, or as a definitive indicator to gauge class consciousness or how people understand their class position. The meanings people take from representations are not static and fixed, existing in a vacuum outside of class struggle and the material world. While the ruling class presents its own vision of society and attaches derogatory characteristics to sections within it, social being—our lived experience of class in the socioeconomic structure—challenges and undermines this common sense ideology.

We should not doggedly fixate on older identities or engage in a top-down process of creating an ideal representation that the working class should strive to embody; collective interests and working class identity are transformed and given expression *through* struggle, rather than workers being passive bearers of imagined idealisations of class identity.

Conclusion

In his conclusion Jones attempts to set out a loose agenda for left politics in the 21st century, which reflects his belief in a predominantly fragmented and deskilled workforce. Therefore, while acknowledging that the workplace is still important, Jones nevertheless underestimates its continuing significance.

54: Smith, 2007.
55: Jones, 2011, p33.

Additionally, while Jones is right to argue against politics of rugged individualism and "aspiration" that focuses upon *escaping* the working class, and for the centrality of class rather than identity politics, some of his criticisms of the left are largely unwarranted. He complains that the current left are "more likely to be manning a stall about Gaza outside a university campus" than tending to the "bread and butter" concerns of the working class.[56] But such international issues *are class issues*. Not only do they have significance for particular oppressed sections of the working class who are Muslim or Arab, but the working class needlessly fight and die in imperialist wars, wasting lives and billions of pounds that could be better used upon housing and welfare. Moreover, support for imperialism is one method the ruling class uses to try to bind a section of the working class to itself, making it essential that the left challenges it.

Although Jones argues that "the biggest issue of British politics today is the crisis of working class representation",[57] the reality is that at the high point of "old" Labour and trade unionism working class parliamentary representation did not translate into unfettered equality. If, as Jones states, "Old Labour remained committed to raising the conditions of the working class as a class, even if this sometimes amounted to mere lip service",[58] we should also recognise that Labour remained committed to upholding a system that exploited those it claimed to represent. The reforms enacted under extra-parliamentary pressure should be seen as bringing significant improvements for the working class, but ultimately, as Tony Cliff noted, "in office, the Labour Party has always ensured the continuity of the capitalist state and guarded its harshest, most anti working class plans".[59]

The key to eradicating class inequality does not lie in giving the working class better representation within a system which maintains exploitative relations. Although this may bring improvements under particular conditions, it is the actions of the working class in collective struggles against capital that carry the potential to transcend that system.

Overall, Jones has made a welcome contribution to discussion of class in modern Britain during a period of economic turmoil in which working class people are being attacked. The chav may well mock a class reeling from the defeats under Thatcherism, and the power and influence of the ruling class to make its representations of society the most pervasive certainly impact

---

56: Jones, 2011, p257.
57: Jones, 2011, p258.
58: Jones, 2011, p88.
59: Cliff, 1975, p166. See also Coates, 1975, and Miliband, 1972.

upon the ways in which people understand society—but this is by no means the end of the story. The experience of growing unemployment and worsening living standards, while the rich visibly increase their wealth and push through policies that attack the poorest in society, undermines notions of classlessness, while social movements such as those based around the 99 percent reveal the common interests among the majority at the bottom of society and point to where the real divisions in society lie.

References

Anthias, Floya, 2004, "Social Stratification and Social Inequality: Models of Intersectionality and Identity", in Fiona Devine, Mike Savage, John Scott and Rosemary Crompton (eds), *Rethinking Class: Culture, Identities and Lifestyle* (Palgrave Macmillan).

Barker, Martin, 1981, *The New Racism: Conservatives and the Ideology of the Tribe* (Junction Books).

Basketter, Simon, 2008, "Leaked Membership List Reveals Middle Class Base of the Fascist BNP", *Socialist Worker* (25 November), www.socialistworker.co.uk/art.php?id=16518

Calder, Angus, 1992, *The Myth of the Blitz* (Pimlico).

Callaghan, John, 1990, *Socialism in Britain Since 1884* (Basil Blackwell).

Callinicos, Alex, 1993, *Race and Class* (Bookmarks).

Callinicos, Alex, and Chris Harman, 1987, *The Changing Working Class: Essays on Class Structure Today* (Bookmarks).

Cameron, David, 2011, "David Cameron Welfare Speech in Full" (17 February), www.politics.co.uk/comment-analysis/2011/2/17/david-cameron-welfare-speech-in-full

Choonara, Esme, 2011, "Is There a Precariat?", *Socialist Review* (October), www.socialistreview.org.uk/article.php?articlenumber=11781

Cliff, Tony, 1975, *Social Contract or Socialism* (Pluto).

Coates, David, 1975, *The Labour Party and the Struggle for Socialism* (Cambridge University Press).

Dench, Geoff, Kate Gavron and Michael Young, 2006, *The New East End: Kinship, Race and Conflict* (Profile).

Dunn, Bill, 2004, *Global Restructuring and the Power of Labour* (Palgrave).

Gorz, Andre, 1982, *Farewell to the Working Class: An Essay on Post-Industrial Socialism* (Pluto).

Hall, Stuart, and Martin Jacques, 1989, "Introduction", in *New Times: The Changing Face of Politics in the 1990s* (Lawrence & Wishart).

Harman, Chris, 1996, "Globalisation: A Critique of the New Orthodoxy", *International Socialism* 73 (winter), www.marxists.org/archive/harman/1996/xx/global.htm

Harris, Jose, 1993, *Private Lives, Public Spirit: A Social History of Britain, 1870-1914* (Oxford University Press).

Harrison, John FC, 1984, *The Common People: A History from the Norman Conquest to the Present* (Fontana).

Hitchcock, Peter, 2000, "They Must Be Represented? Problems in Theories of Working Class Representation", *Publications of the Modern Language Association of America*, volume 115, number 1.

Hobsbawm, Eric, 1978, "The Forward March of Labour Halted?", *Marxism Today* (September), www.amielandmelburn.org.uk/collections/mt/pdf/78_09_hobsbawm.pdf

Husbands, Christopher, 2007, *Racial Exclusionism and the City: The Urban Support of the National Front* (Routledge).

Jenkins, Gareth, 2011, "Culture and Multiculturalism", *International Socialism* 131 (summer), www.isj.org.uk/?id=742

John, Peter, Helen Margetts, David Rowland and Stuart Weir, 2006, *The BNP: The Roots of its Appeal* (Democratic Audit Human Rights Centre).

Jones, Owen, 2011, *Chavs: The Demonisation of the Working Class* (Verso).

Kimber, Charlie, 2010, *Immigration: The Myths They Spread to Divide Us* (Socialist Workers Party).

Marx, Karl, 1959 (1894), *Capital*, volume 3 (Progress), www.marxists.org/archive/marx/works/1894-c3/

Medhurst, Andy, 2000, "If Anywhere: Class Identifications and Cultural Studies Academics", in Sally Munt (ed), *Cultural Studies and the Working Class: Subject to Change* (Continuum).

Miles, Andrew, and Mike Savage, 1994, *The Remaking of the British Working Class, 1840-1940* (Routledge).

Miliband, Ralph, 1972, *Parliamentary Socialism: A Study in the Politics of Labour* (Merlin Press).

Murray, Charles, 2006, "The Emerging British Underclass", in Ruth Lister (ed), *Charles Murray and the Underclass: The Developing Debate* (IEA Health and Welfare Unit).

Pakulski, Jan, and Malcolm Waters, 1996, *The Death of Class* (Sage).

Rosen, Michael, 2011, "Culture: It's All in the Mix!", in Hassam Mahamdallie (ed), *Defending Multiculturalism* (Bookmarks).

Smith, Martin, 2007, "The Shape of the Working Class", *International Socialism* 113 (winter), www.isj.org.uk/?id=293

Smith, Martin, 2009, "How Do We Stop the BNP?", *International Socialism* 123 (summer), www.isj.org.uk/?id=556

Stedman Jones, Gareth, 1976, *Outcast London: A Study in the Relationship Between Classes in Victorian Society* (Penguin).

Ste Croix, Geoffrey de, 1984, "Class in Marx's Conception of History, Ancient and Modern", *New Left Review 146* (first series).

Van Dijk, Teun A, 1991, *Racism and the Press* (Routledge).

Welshman, John, 2006, *Underclass: A History of the Excluded, 1880-2000* (Hambledon Continuum).

Witte, Rob, 1996, *Racist Violence and the State: A Comparative Analysis of Britain, France and the Netherlands* (Longman).

Wright, Erik Olin, 1979, *Class Structure and Income Determination* (Academic Press).

Zweig, Ferdynand, 1961, *The Worker in an Affluent Society: Family Life and Industry* (Heinemann).

Could Keynes end the slump? Introducing the Marxist multiplier

Guglielmo Carchedi

For Marx, the proximate cause of crises is the fall in the average rate of profit (ARP).[1] An increasing number of studies has shown that this thesis not only is logically consistent but is also supported by a robust and growing empirical material.[2] If falling profitability is the cause of the slump, the slump will end only if the economy's profitability sets off on a path of sustained growth. Then the relevant question is: can Keynesian policies restore the economy's profitability? Can they end the slump?

To begin with, what are Keynesian policies? *First*, they are *state-induced* economic policies. *Second*, they can be *redistribution* policies or *investments* policies. *Third*, they should be *capital financed* and not *labour financed*. If labour-financed, they are neoliberal policies. *Fourth*, in the case of state-induced investment policies, they can be either *civilian* (mainly in public works like highways, schools, hospitals, etc, in order to avoid

---

1: The fall in the ARP is the proximate cause because it itself is caused by technological competition, ie by the introduction of labour-"saving" but efficiency-increasing new technologies.

2: See Carchedi, 2011a; Carchedi, 2011b; Roberts, 2012, as well as the literature in these works. Marx defines the rate of profit as $s/(c+v)$, where s stands for surplus value, c for constant capital (ie capital invested in means of production) and v for variable capital (ie capital invested in labour power, roughly equivalent to wages). Thus s is the numerator and $(c+v)$ the denominator of the rate of profit equation. The rate of profit depends on the rate of surplus value (s/v) and the organic composition of capital $(c:v)$.

competition with those private sectors already experiencing economic difficulties) or *military*. I shall not deal with "military Keynesianism" because presently this is not what Keynesian economists propose to end the crisis. Some might think that a major war might be the only way out of the depression. This is an open admission of the monstrosity of this system. But then why save it? Then what follows refers only to civilian Keynesian policies.

State-induced redistribution

Suppose the state brings about a redistribution of value from capital to labour through pro-labour legislation, progressive taxation, etc. Of course, it is the net outcome of these policies that counts. If the state cuts taxes for labour but also reduces public expenditure on services like health or education, either labour pays for those services, thus neutralising the effect of the wage rise on consumption, or its greater consumption is neutralised by the state's lower expenditure on pro-labour services.

Then let us assume that net wages (direct, indirect and deferred) rise. More consumer goods are sold and labour consumes more. This is why these policies are supposed to be pro-labour. Supposedly the sale of unsold consumer goods spurs the production of means of consumption. This would generate the demand for means of production. An upward cycle would start. And this is why these policies are supposed to be pro-capital as well. Both capital and labour would gain. This is the basis of Keynesian reformism, of class collaboration.

But does labour's greater consumption really cause a greater production of consumer goods and then of production goods and thus greater employment and economic growth? Suppose that some consumer goods are unsold. This is the hypothesis behind Keynesian interventionism (lack of demand). In this case, higher wages cause the *sale* of unsold consumer goods and not a greater *production* of these goods. Keynesian redistribution fails in its own terms, in terms of demand-induced production and thus employment and recovery.

But capitalism prospers not if production rises but if profitability rises. Once we introduce profitability, everything changes. If a capitalist cannot sell her output, she suffers a loss. If later, due to higher wages, those commodities are sold, she realises that unrealised profit. Profit and loss cancel out. But profitability falls. The proof requires three steps.

(a) Take the sector producing means of consumption. Under the most favourable hypothesis for the Keynesian argument, the whole of the wage increase is spent (on consumer goods). This sector on the one hand suffers a loss due to higher wages but on the other can sell unsold means of consumption for an equal price. The numerator of the rate of profit is unchanged. However, the denominator rises due to the higher investment in variable capital. Labour's consumption increases but the rate of profit falls.

(b) Next take the sector producing means of production. Its numerator decreases (because of higher wages and thus lower profits) and the denominator rises (because of higher investment in labour power). In this sector too labour's consumption increases but the rate of profit falls.

(c) Finally, the higher wages in the sector producing means of production lead to increased demand and consumption by the labourers in that sector and thus an extra profit for the sector that produces those means of consumption. But they are also equal to the loss for capital in the first sector. The loss in sector I and the profit in sector II cancel out.

The numerators of the two sectors return to the original value. However, the denominators have increased. The average rate of profit (ARP) for the two sectors falls. Two points follow. First, wages and thus consumption can increase without profits (not the ARP) falling. Second, production does not increase. What increases is the realisation of previously produced commodities. In sum, labour's consumption rises but production remains the same and the ARP falls. Keynesian redistribution fails not only on its own grounds, production, but also on grounds of profitability; the increase in labour's consumption and the worsening of the crisis are two sides of the same coin.

Suppose now that wages keep rising up to the point where all consumer goods are sold. Given that there is sufficient demand, there is no need for Keynesian intervention. Nevertheless, would not a further rise in wages spur the extra production of consumer goods? No. *Production increases both if profitability rises and if there is demand for the extra output, ie if the extra surplus value can be both produced and realised.* Production does not rise if one of these two conditions is not satisfied.

Higher wages increase the demand for consumer goods but at the same time lower the profit rate. Some capitalists might decide to increase production even at lower levels of profitability. But eventually, in spite of their efforts, the economy's production decreases. In fact, if profits fall, (a) less surplus value can be generated and thus reinvested and reserves are not invested in activities whose profitability keeps decreasing and, (b) due to higher wages, the weaker capitalists go bankrupt and cease production. *It follows that capitalists as a whole reduce their output in spite of higher demand* and in spite of their efforts to meet that demand. Thus the equation

higher wages = more consumption

is correct. However, the equation

more consumption = more production

is wrong because (a) in case of remnant sales, higher wages do not affect production (only the realisation of already produced commodities is fostered) while profitability falls and (b) from the point at which all output has been sold on, higher wages decrease profitability and thus production. Production is either unchanged or falls but profitability falls in both cases. Higher wages *cannot end the slump but worsen it*. The Keynesian medicine is worse than the illness.

The above has shed light on the essential difference between the Keynesian and the Marxist approach. Contrary to the latter, for the former *profitability* is not the essential *determinant* of production. The Keynesian approach inverts the order of causation. In it profitability is a *consequence* of greater demand-induced production, a consequence of greater physical production induced by higher consumption. In the Marxist approach, higher production is the consequence of higher profitability. The theoretical, political and ideological consequences are far reaching.

If a greater demand (induced by higher wages) spurred production, the economy would tend towards a point at which, given pro-labour redistribution, higher demand and higher supply would meet. This is the point at which growth and equilibrium join. This is conventional economics' illusion. But if the greater demand induced by higher wages does not spur production but actually causes its fall because of falling profitability, demand and supply cannot meet and *no point of equilibrium can be reached*. To counter falling profitability, wages would have to increase again. The result is a downward sequence of non-equilibrium points between demand and supply that are so many stations towards the crisis. Contrary to the Keynesian approach, higher wages at the cost of capital contribute not to the movement towards equilibrium and growth but to the movement towards depression and crises.

This conclusion is important for economic policy because it shows that policies aimed at stimulating growth through pro-labour redistribution are doomed to fail. But this conclusion is also important from a theoretical and political point of view because, by denying that the system, given the appropriate redistribution policies, can tend towards equilibrium and growth, we deny that this system is (or can be made to be) rational. Bourgeois economics, on the other hand, holds that the system is in or tends towards equilibrium at higher levels of production and consumption and that therefore it is rational. If this were the case, the consequences for labour's struggle would be devastating because the struggle against this system would become a struggle against a rational system and thus an irrational, spontaneistic struggle. But if the system is irrational because it tends towards crises in spite of Keynesian (or other) policies, labour's struggle is the conscious manifestation of the economy's objective movement towards crises.

Alternatively, the state can induce a redistribution of value *from labour to capital* through falling wages and other measures. These are neoliberal (the opposite of Keynesian) policies. Nevertheless, they should be briefly considered. A wage cut increases profitability. But at the same time it reduces the demand for consumer goods. In this case, capitalists reduce their output not because profits fall but because demand falls. But should the increased profitability not revive the economy in spite of lower demand and production? Could not more profits relative to the capital invested be made on a lower level of production?

In a crisis, if the demand for consumer goods falls due to lower wages, the extra profits from lower wages are not reinvested in that sector and thus cannot spur investment in the production of means of consumption. Moreover, capital does not disinvest in sector II and invest in sector I because profitability also falls in sector I. The extra profits are either set aside as reserves or invested in the unproductive sectors (commerce, finance and speculation) where profitability is higher (but only as long as the bubble does not burst) or can be moved to countries where they can be reinvested more profitably. For some countries more than others, they can feed corruption, criminality and inefficiencies (Italy is a typical case). In any case, these extra profits cannot get the economy going again.

The state too contributes to diverting value away from the productive sectors. In the present conjuncture, given the high levels of state debt, the (surplus) value appropriated by the state (for example, through higher taxation) is used to decrease state losses or financial capital's losses. Keynesian economists perceive state-induced "austerity" (an ideologically loaded word that should be carefully avoided) as the cause of (the deepening of) the crisis. In reality, the depression of consumption (lower wages) is the consequence of falling profitability, an attempt by private capital through the state to restore the ARP.

In sum, neoliberal policies are not the cause of the slump (they are the consequence of the slump, one of the factors counteracting the fall in the ARP) and fail to end the slump because profits are diverted away from productive investments and not, as held by Keynesian authors, because wage cuts reduce consumption. The dilemma "austerity" versus growth (policy measures paid by labour or by capital) as a remedy against the slump is a false one. Neither pro-labour nor pro-capital redistribution policies can end the slump. This can be empirically substantiated. Consider the following.

Figure 1: Wage share and ARP in the US productive sectors

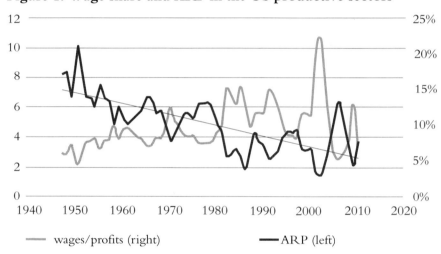

This chart shows that up to 1986 wages rose relative to profits and the ARP fell, conforming to Marx but not to Keynesian underconsumptionism. From 1987 to 2009 wages fell relative to profits and the ARP rose, again conforming to Marx but not to Keynesian underconsumptionism. But the trend in the ARP kept falling throughout the whole period. Both pro-labour and pro-capital redistribution did not prevent the ARP from falling tendentially.

State-induced investments

The strongest case for Keynesian policies is not state-induced redistribution but state-induced investment. As a rule, those authors (also Marxists) advocating state-induced investment policies as a way to end the slump omit a fundamental point, namely who is supposed to finance these investments (see footnote 4 below). There are two possibilities: *capital-financed* and *labour-financed* state-induced investment policies. I shall consider only capital-financed investment because labour-financed investments are not what Keynesian authors propose to end the slump.

Let us distinguish between sector I, the producer of public works, and sector II, the rest of the economy. Surplus value, **S**, is appropriated (eg taxed) by the state from sector II and channelled into sector I for the production of public works.[3] Rather than taxing surplus value, the state can appropriate unused reserves. But as far as capital is concerned, this is a loss and thus a deduction from surplus value. Having appropriated **S** from sector II, the state pays sector I a certain profit, **p**, and advances the rest, **S−p**, to sector I for the production of public works.

Consider first the effects for the state. The state receives public works from sector I to the value of **S−p+p★**, where **p★** is the surplus value generated in sector I (whether **p★** is equal to **p** or not). Sector I realises its profits because it has received **p** from the state, while **p★** belongs to the state. How does the state realise **S−p+p★**, the total value incorporated in public works? Under capitalism value is realised only if and when it is metamorphosed into money through the sale of the use value in which it is incorporated. Since the state does not sell public works (unless it privatises them, but privatisation falls outside our present scope), it would seem that that value remains potential, trapped in an unsold use value. However, public works can realise their value in a different way. Their use value is consumed by the users of those facilities who, in exchange for this use, must pay in principle for the share of the value contained in the public works they consume. Once the public works are totally consumed, the state receives **S−p+p★**. The state has realised the potential value of public works by charging capital and labour for their use. These fees are an indirect reduction of wages and profits. The state has gained **S−p+p★**, sector I has gained **p**, sector II has lost **S**, and the private sector has lost **S−p**.

Consider the effects on the ARP. Sector II loses **S** but sector I gains **p**. In sum, private capital loses **S−p** to the state. The numerator of the ARP decreases by that much. The ARP falls. But this is not the end of the story. The capitalised surplus value advanced by the state, **S−p**, is invested by sector I. To determine the effect of this investment on profitability, we must introduce what I shall call the Marxist multiplier.

3:    This is a simplification. The state appropriates surplus value from, eg taxes, both sectors. The point is that sector I receives more surplus value to invest than it loses to the state.

To produce public works, Sector I purchases labour power and means of production from other firms in both sectors. In their turn, these firms engage in further purchases of means of production and labour power. This multiple effect cascades throughout the economy. Under the most favourable hypothesis for the Keynesian argument, the state-induced investments are sufficiently large to first absorb the unsold goods and then stimulate new production. Given that the firms involved in the cascade effect have different organic compositions, three cases are possible.

(a) **S-p**, the initial investment by sector I, plus the ripple effect throughout the economy, is such that it forms a representative section of the whole economy. Then the rate of profit generated by it is equal to the economy's average. The ARP after these investments does not change. Neither does employment. The policy fails.

(b) Alternatively, the chain of investment stops at a point at which the organic composition of all the invested capitals (including the initial ones) is higher than the average. Then the ARP falls. Employment falls too. Again the policy fails. The reason why the higher organic composition of this aggregate worsens the crisis is that the extra investments have gone predominantly to the most efficient firms (those with higher organic composition). By selling their higher output at the same price as that of the lower output of the laggards, they appropriate value from these latter and eventually push them out of the market, thus worsening the crisis.

(c) In the opposite case, where the average organic composition falls as a result of these investments, the ARP and employment rise. But then the Keynesian policy has helped the *less* efficient capitals, those with lower organic composition and thus lower efficiency, to survive. In this case, this policy *postpones* the slump instead of ending it.

Notice that the three possible outcomes are not policy options that can be influenced by the state's policy. Once the initial state-induced capital has been invested, the final result in terms of organic composition and ARP depends on the spontaneous working of the system, ie on which capitals receive commissions by other capitals. The state can influence only the first step, by commissioning public investments to low organic composition capitals. But then, as in case (c) above, it helps to increase profitability but also to keep the less efficient capitals afloat.

But aside from this, the most likely outcome is a rise in the combined organic composition and thus a fall in the ARP because each capital in the cascade will tend to purchase the material it needs from the cheapest bidders. These are usually the most efficient ones, those whose organic composition is high relative to the average. The further investment induced by the state's initial investment will go mainly to these producers. The organic composition rises and the ARP falls. In short, as a result of state-induced investment, either average profitability falls or, if it rises, the less efficient capitals are artificially kept alive. The crisis is either worsened or postponed. And if it is postponed, capital cannot self-destruct and the recovery is further delayed. In neither case can the economy restart.

Beside the limits underlined by the Marxist multiplier, state-induced redistribution and/or investment policies meet a further obstacle. They are possible when private capital can bear the loss of surplus value (or of reserves). But when capital sinks into crisis, when profitability falls, their financing becomes increasingly problematic. These policies can be applied where they are least needed and cannot be used where they are most needed. This shows how unrealistic is the call also by prominent Marxists for a massive wave of state-induced capital-financed redistribution and/or investment in the present economic predicament as a way out of the crisis.[4]

Some Keynesian authors propose to stimulate demand neither through redistribution nor through investments but by increasing the quantity of money. The assumption is that the ultimate cause of crises is lack of demand so that a higher quantity of money in circulation would stimulate demand. The argument against this view is not so much whether these policies are inflationary (as Austrian economists hold) or not.

Rather the objection is that by printing money one increases

4: For example, as Alan Freeman holds, "if the state makes available, to as many people as possible on an equal basis, the capabilities that capitalism has brought into existence, stepping in wherever private capital will not, the crisis will end"—Freeman, 2009. On the contrary, the crisis will either deepen or be postponed. Anwar Shaikh too thinks that direct government investment can pull the economy out of the crisis. This would stimulate "demand provided that the people so employed do not save the income or use it to pay down debt"—Shaikh, 2011. Aside from the unrealistic nature of the assumption that people do not save and do not pay back debts, given that banks need labour's savings and that the default on debts means principally default on banks' debt, this is a sure recipe for a financial crisis. Similarly, Foster argues, "Theoretically, any increase in government spending at this time can help soften the downturn and even contribute to the eventual restoration of economic growth"—Foster, 2009. These and other similar proposals have a characteristic in common: they do not concern themselves with who should finance these policies. But, aside from this macroscopic defect, given that the economy exits the crisis through capital destruction, these policies delay rather than prevent the onset of the crisis.

the *representation* of value rather than value itself. The economy cannot restart if the surplus value produced relative to the capital invested is unchanged. Moreover, by printing and distributing money, one redistributes purchasing power. But we have seen that neither pro-labour nor pro-capital redistribution is the way out of the slump. But usually, by "printing money" one understands granting credit. The notion that credit is money is almost universally accepted and yet fundamentally wrong. By creating credit, one does not "create money out of nothing", an absurd proposition. Out of nothing, one can create nothing. Simply by creating credit one creates debt. So the crisis is postponed to the moment of debt repayment.

This is one of the reasons why the state may decide to *borrow* the capital needed for public works rather than expropriating it from capital. But eventually debts must be repaid. The Keynesian argument is that debts can be repaid when, due to these policies, the economy restarts and the appropriation of the surplus value needed for debt repayment does not threaten the recovery. But this is wishful thinking.

In fact, we have seen that state-induced capital-financed investment cannot restart the economy. At most, it can postpone the explosion of the crisis. Then, if either pro-labour or pro-capital anti-crisis policies are impotent against the slump, the crisis must run its course until it itself creates the condition of its own solution. This is the *destruction of capital*. Only when sufficient (backward) capitals have been destroyed (have gone bankrupt) can the more efficient productive units start producing again on an enlarged scale. It follows that, if these policies at best postpone the explosion of the crisis, they also postpone the recovery. By postponing the recovery, these policies are an *obstacle* to, rather than being a condition for, *the repayment by the state of its debt.*[5]

The thesis that state-induced redistribution and investment policies, possibly through state borrowing, could start a sustained recovery, provided the scale is sufficiently large, is not only theoretically invalid (see above) but also empirically unsubstantiated. The example usually mentioned is the long period of prosperity that followed the Second World War, the so-called Golden Age of capitalism. Supposedly, government borrowing made it possible for the US state to finance Keynesian policies and

5:   There is no affinity between this conclusion and the Austrian school. The differences are unfathomable. Just to mention two out of the many: for the Austrian school the economy, if not tampered with, tends towards equilibrium (rather than towards crises, as in Marx) and government intervention is the cause of crises (rather than being one of the many countertendencies, as in Marx).

thus to start the long period of prosperity. In reality, the US gross federal debt as a percentage of GDP *decreased* constantly during the Golden Age, from 121.7 percent in 1946 to 37.6 percent in 1970. The long spell of prosperity was due to reconversion, ie to the reconstitution of civilian capital, and to the liberation of pent-up purchasing power after the war.[6]

The lessons for labour

The above should not be construed as if labour should be indifferent to state-induced capital-financed redistribution and/or investment policies. On the contrary, labour should strongly struggle for such policies. But this struggle should be carried out not from a Keynesian perspective but from the proper, Marxist, perspective.

The Keynesian approach considers Keynesian policies as a way to improve *both* labour's conditions *and* capital's condition, a way to counter or exit the slump. From the Marxist perspective, state-induced capital-financed distribution and/or investment policies need not be Keynesian, ie need not carry the ideological content attached to the word, the community of interests between the two fundamental classes. The Marxist perspective stresses (a) that these policies may improve labour's lot but are impotent against the crisis—they can at most postpone it, and (b) the *political potential* of these policies. Through the struggle of labour for better living and working conditions, consciousness can arise and grow among workers that each time these policies are paid for by capital, capital is weakened both economically and politically, and that labour can exploit this to weaken the yoke of capital.

From the Marxist perspective, the struggle for the improvement of labour's lot and the sedimentation and accumulation of labour's antagonistic consciousness and power through this struggle should be two sides of the same coin. This is their real importance. They cannot end the slump but they can surely improve labour's conditions and, *given the proper perspective*, foster the end of capitalism.

6:    See Carchedi, 2011b.

References

Carchedi, Guglielmo, 2011a, *Behind the Crisis: Marx's Dialectics of Value and Knowledge* (Brill).

Carchedi, Guglielmo, 2011b, "Behind and Beyond the Crisis", *International Socialism 132*, (autumn), www.isj.org.uk/?id=761

Foster, John Bellamy, 2009, "Keynes, Capitalism and the Crisis", interview by Brian Ashley, www.zcommunications.org/keynes-capitalism-and-the-crisis-by-john-bellamy-foster

Freeman, Alan, 2009, "Investing in Civilization", MPRA, http://mpra.ub.uni-muenchen.de/26807/1/MPRA_paper_26807.pdf

Roberts, Michael, 2012, "A World Rate of Profit", http://thenextrecession.files.wordpress.com/2012/07/roberts_michael-a_world_rate_of_profit.pdf

Shaikh, Anwar, 2011, "The First Great Depression of the 21st Century", *Socialist Register 2011* (Merlin).

Germany's lost Bolshevik: Paul Levi revisited

Sebastian Zehetmair

A review of David Fernbach (ed), **In the Steps of Rosa Luxemburg: Selected Writings by Paul Levi** *(Brill, 2011), €99*

Introduction by John Rose

David Fernbach's selection of the writings of Paul Levi allows us not only to reassess the German Revolution's little known "lost" leader, but also to reassess the failure of the German Revolution itself.[1] This could hardly be more pertinent at the present time. We are in the middle of a full-scale capitalist crisis in a potentially dangerous combination with the widespread view that communist and socialist ideas are not relevant to it. The claim is that these ideas have been tried and failed.

That "Soviet Communism" failed is not in doubt. But this journal is associated with a tradition that rejects the view that the failure was inevitable—rooted in a misplaced utopian scheme to impose totalitarian perfectibility on an unwilling human nature. On the contrary, the prospects of transforming the stunted human nature that capitalism imposes—ruthlessly dividing society by social classes—was briefly offered by the successful socialist Bolshevik-led working class revolution in the mainly peasant country of Russia in October 1917. However, there was a vital precondition insisted upon by the Bolshevik leadership: the revolution must spread to the advanced industrial countries, otherwise the mainly peasant economy—and the surrounding capitalist states—would strangle it.

Germany was the country and the arena where this expectation was

---

1:    A cheaper edition was published by Haymarket in summer 2012.

most likely to be realised. But this most advanced industrial economy in Europe also had an advanced industrial working class with deeply rooted ideas about how to make progress. And these ideas rejected revolution in favour of reform even in the aftermath of the defeat of Germany in the First World War and the chaos, economic breakdown, impoverishment, demoralisation and, yes, revolutionary ferment that ensued.

It is true that workers' and soldiers' councils, or soviets, did emerge as an exciting and potentially plausible response to the crisis, raising prospects for an alliance with the struggling socialist republic of the soviets in Russia. But they were dominated by reformist ideas and mainly reformist leaders.

This allowed the Social Democratic Party (SPD), while mouthing revolutionary slogans when appropriate, to contain the revolutionary mood that was momentarily widespread in the working class. Large minorities of workers were ready to push for insurrection, but the majority was not. This complicated situation allowed established revolutionary socialist leaders such as Rosa Luxemburg and Karl Liebknecht to be outmanoeuvred. It was a problem that would recur time and again in Germany between 1918 and 1923 and it required innovative tactics and strategies. Tragically, the assassination of Luxemburg and Liebknecht prevented them from learning the lessons and the minority revolutionary wing of the movement was beheaded. German Social Democracy consolidated its position with majority support in the working class, even though at least some German SPD leaders had Luxemburg's and Liebknecht's blood on their hands.

We have here a particularly cruel and bitter warning that revolutionary socialist tactics and strategies do not automatically and mechanically transfer from one situation to the next. Did Bolshevik principles apply to the situation in Germany and similar countries in the rest of Europe? The answer was yes, but on condition that the effort of imaginative political thinking was made to understand fully the strengths of reformism and then how to train a cadre with the appropriate tactics and strategies.

As we will see, Paul Levi, Rosa Luxemburg's successor, understood this more than any other German revolutionary leader. But as a matter of fact the person who understood it most of all was Lenin.

"Politics", Lenin wrote in *"Left-Wing" Communism: An Infantile Disorder* in April-May 1920, "is a science and an art that does not fall from the skies... To overcome the bourgeoisie, the proletariat must train its own proletarian class politicians of a kind in no way inferior to bourgeois politicians".[2]

2:   Cliff, 1985, p30.

Tony Cliff described Lenin's pamphlet as of such importance that it could legitimately be compared to the *Communist Manifesto* of Marx and Engels.[3]

Its underlying principle called on revolutionary socialists to work wherever the masses are to be found.[4] Lenin was particularly concerned that the growing wave of emerging young communist parties across Europe and beyond learned simultaneously to relate to the revolutionary minorities and the reformist majorities in the working class movements at the same time. Above all this meant working within the reformist trade unions as well as taking parliamentary, regional and local elections very seriously. This included standing communist candidates where appropriate.

Lenin even called it "obligatory" on the party of the revolutionary proletariat to stand candidates.[5] Of course, there should be no illusions in the bourgeois democratic process but instead a sensitive recognition that most workers take such elections seriously and that they can provide a powerful public forum for revolutionary socialist ideas.[6]

Alas the KPD, the new Communist Party of Germany, had hardly had time fully to absorb Lenin's message before it was hit by a very different line of political argument. This sought to activate the revolutionary minority for a revolutionary offensive as a trigger for mass action—for what became known as the March Action of 1921—by the wider majority in the working class movement, irrespective of the mood of the majority. And the argument carried enormous weight—because it appeared authorised by the leadership of the recently established Communist International, or Comintern. The "theory of the offensive" as it was known had the catastrophic consequences of simultaneously destroying Paul Levi as a revolutionary socialist and derailing, arguably permanently, the German socialist revolution.

Sebastian Zehetmair, a young socialist historian from Germany, has done an excellent job in using the publication of Levi's writings to deepen our understanding of the processes involved here. He develops arguments used by Broué, Cliff and Harman among others to show how the "theory of the offensive" reflected the impasse reached by the Russian Revolution following the civil war, and symbolised by the Kronstadt sailors' uprising against the Bolsheviks and the introduction of the NEP,

---

3:    Cliff, 1985, p24.
4:    Cliff, 1985, p29.
5:    Cliff, 1985, p28.
6:    The principle is just as relevant today. For example, revolutionary socialists in the Egyptian Revolution have to relate to the widespread popularity of Islamist reformist ideas.

the New Economic Policy.[7] In a sense he demonstrates that the breakdown of the Russian Revolution was itself a key factor in the failure of the German Revolution.

By coincidence *International Socialism* editorial board member Gareth Jenkins is currently translating into English Pierre Broué's history of the Comintern from the French original.[8] Gareth draws conclusions which confirm the arguments used here:

> What comes through for me, I think, in Broué's account is how sections of the already degenerating Russian leadership (Zinoviev, in particular) translate the necessity for revolution in Germany. Its organic development (Open Letter,[9] patiently winning the majority of the masses from reformist and centrist leadership) is sacrificed to its forced development (building a centralised, militarised, disciplined party through Comintern envoys, directives from on high, etc) as a kind of short cut to help the Soviet state in its difficulties. The terrible irony is that this kind of forced development dovetailed with the impatience of leftists[10]—who thought that the new mass communist party (itself a qualitative breakthrough) could bring about the revolution irrespective of the actual state of the consciousness of the millions of workers outside it. Thus bureaucratic short-termism combined with voluntaristic short-termism made the theory of the offensive something that was deeply attractive to very different elements in the movement.

It would be a mistake to argue that the theory of the offensive sealed the Stalinist fate of the revolution. On the other hand its poisonous influence at a critical moment simultaneously in the evolution of Communism in Germany and the deepening crisis for Bolshevism in Russia significantly accelerated the degeneration towards Stalinism.

JR

7:    Cliff, 1985, pp132-134, 138-160.

8:    Broué, 1997.

9:    Levi's united front tactic in the reformist German trade unions—see below.

10:   Paul Levi's understandable hostility to ultra-leftism spilled over into a sectarianism that considerably weakened his position when he stood out against the "theory of the offensive". Lenin complained about his high-handed manner to Clara Zetkin: his "wholly negative criticism...indicated no sense of solidarity with the party"—quoted in Harman, 1997, p217. He showed no willingness to try to understand why considerable numbers of workers, employed as well as unemployed, could get drawn into lunatic ultra-left actions. On the other hand Levi's weakness here in no way justified the lies that were told about him at the Third Congress of the Comintern that frankly anticipated later Stalinist practices.

The fact remains that, during 1918-21, Levi was the only Communist leader outside Russia whose intransigent character and political penetration made him an interlocutor who could discuss with the Russian leaders on an equal basis, and that no one was able to fill the gap once he was expelled. He was the only person who posed in political terms the problem of Communism immediately after the victory of the revolution in Russia, how to graft on to the old solidly and deeply rooted tree of the Western workers' movement the living graft of the revolutionary advance of 1917 and of conciliar power.[11]

This is how Pierre Broué, one of the most authoritative socialist historians of the German Revolution, characterised the lawyer Paul Levi. Levi's name is almost unknown today outside a small community of specialised historians. But in the years 1919 and 1920 he was well known in Germany and abroad as the chair of the young Communist Party of Germany (KPD). He would become the most controversial figure in the German Communist movement. He was mainly responsible for building the KPD from a relatively small organisation in early 1918 into a truly mass party, but was then expelled in April 1921 after he publicly criticised the so-called "March Action", an ill-fated attempt at insurrection by the KPD. In 1922 he rejoined the Social Democratic Party (SPD), to which he had already belonged between 1912 and 1917. For this reason, social democrats have tried ever since to use him as a key witness against "Bolshevism". However, as an influential leader of the SPD's far-left wing he remained in constant opposition to the SPD leadership until his death in 1930.

It is good news that a collection of Levi's writings has finally been published in English, a valuable source for understanding some critical turning points in the history of German Communism. What follows is a short assessment of Levi's contribution to this history in its early years and an analysis of the crucial conflict that led to his expulsion.[12]

The inventor of the united front
Paul Levi became leader of the KPD in March 1919 following the murder of Rosa Luxemburg and Karl Liebknecht.[13]

11: Broué, 2006, p887. Conciliar power means workers' councils or soviets. Thanks to John Rose, Phil Butland and Kate Davison for ideas and comments on this article.

12: Fernbach's edition also includes important Levi writings from the later period, especially 1923, the year of the final attempt at revolution in Germany, which unfortunately cannot be covered in this journal for reasons of space.

13: The following is based on the general accounts given in Angress, 1972, Harman, 1997, and Broué, 2006. See also Riddell, 2011.

The KPD was founded amid a revolutionary mass movement after the downfall of Kaiser Wilhelm II at the end of 1918. In the first months of its existence it was far too small to have a decisive influence on the course of the revolutionary crisis in Germany, and only managed to assert broader political influence from 1920 onwards, when bourgeois rule in Germany had already begun to temporarily restabilise. This setting had a decisive impact on the development of the party. It had been formed by a small but experienced group of former left wing social democrats and initially attracted many newly politicised, often younger activists, who were excited by the first revolutionary wave of late 1918. The KPD's influence within the mass organisations of the workers' movement—the workers' councils in 1918-19 and the trade unions—initially remained very limited. The bulk of the organised working class still adhered to social democracy (by that time called majority social democracy, MSPD) or its "centrist" split-off, the Independent Socialist Party (USPD). Levi, who based his politics firmly on the principle of the self-emancipation of workers, saw the main task for the KPD in the struggle for the hearts and minds of the majority of workers. In doing so he laid the basis for what would in later years be called the "united front" approach.

This approach was first implemented in Communist politics in the winter of 1920-1 through a series of "open letters", with which the KPD addressed social democrats and the trade unions. These public letters made an offer of joint actions to defend workers' interests around a number of limited topics. It was a tactic that was consciously designed to strengthen working class self-activity on the one hand and to show in practice the limits of social democratic reformism on the other hand. Both social democracy and the trade union bureaucracy promised reforms but were unwilling to organise mass movements for them. The tactics behind the open letters were based on the assumption that a huge gap existed between expectation and reality inside social democracy, which could be used to strengthen Communist influence in mass organisations.

The open letters were not meant to be mere rhetorical demands. They were accompanied by massive campaigns for action in the lower ranks of workers' organisations, which allowed the KPD to directly approach social democratic workers with an appeal for common struggle. This showed the willingness of the KPD for unity in action—and thereby protected the Communists from the common accusation of acting in a divisive way. Levi wanted to avoid the well-known ideological differences between the two parties becoming an obstacle for joint practical initiatives as he was convinced that broader layers of social democratic workers could only be drawn towards the Communist movement through their own practical experience in the common struggle. The KPD became a mass party in Germany from late 1920 onwards by consistently applying these tactics.

The development of the tactical doctrine of the united front met considerable resistance from the left wing of the party. Part of the membership feared it would lead the young KPD back into the now despised political traditions of social democracy from which they had just broken. While the new approach helped to dispel workers' illusions about the reformism of the SPD and thereby strengthened the KPD in organisational terms, it still did not and could not spark real mass movements on a national scale by itself under the conditions of late 1920. This created considerable frustration among the left wing Communists who had expected a quick victory in 1918-19.

Levi and his close followers in the party leadership had to lead a sharp struggle against syndicalist and semi-anarchist currents that had dominated the KPD since its founding congress. The ultra-leftists argued for a principled denial of parliamentary involvement and a refusal to work in the existing unions. They could only resort to hopeless actions of radical minorities or a mere propagandistic approach. In order for the KPD to win over the left wing of the USPD Levi considered it to be necessary to push these currents out of the party—a decision that has proved controversial ever since.[14] Following the Heidelberg conference in autumn 1919, the leaders of the ultra-leftist tendency left the KPD to form the Communist Workers Party (KAP). The result was that in some regions the KAP—considerably smaller than the KPD numerically—exerted constant political pressure on the KPD, and Levi, who was never known for dealing with his inner-party opponents very diplomatically, became their main target. Nevertheless, in December 1920 the majority of the USPD decided to unite with the KPD and become part of the Communist International (CI). This can be attributed to a large degree to the cautious yet determined tactics Levi had helped to develop.

The Soviet regime and world revolution

Under the political leadership of Levi and close companions the KPD (among them Clara Zetkin) took a tremendous step forward. But his achievements have since been largely overlooked because of the conflict which developed in the winter of 1920-1 and finally resulted in his expulsion

---

14: Harman, 1997, considered this split a tactical mistake although he argued that Levi was correct in his principled opposition to the ultra-leftists. Marcel Bois and Florian Wilde concluded recently that in the end the split was hardly avoidable although the methods of Levi were disputable—Bois and Wilde, 2007.

in April 1921. This conflict, the Levi affair, was a major turning point in the history of the KPD and also had international consequences in the CI.

A crucial turning point in the Levi Affair lay in the conflict between the majority of the German party leadership around Levi and the Executive Committee of the Comintern (ECCI), the highest organ of the CI between its world congresses. The ECCI was heavily dominated by prominent members of the Russian Bolshevik Party, and therefore a number of historians have portrayed this conflict simply as a clash between supposedly "authoritarian Bolshevism" and democratic "Luxemburgism", that is, a conscious attempt to purge the KPD of any democratic traditions and bind it to the doctrines of Russian Bolshevism.[15]

Yet this portrayal rests on an ahistorical understanding of the concepts of "Leninism" and "Luxemburgism". Levi was undoubtedly critically influenced by both Lenin and Luxemburg and quoted them repeatedly in his writing in 1921. He can neither properly be called a "Luxemburgist" nor a "Leninist", simply because the notion of a distinct theoretical system of "Luxemburgism" didn't exist at the time.[16] Levi was well aware of a whole number of differences between Lenin and Luxemburg, yet he did not see them as representatives of two distinct "systems" but rather as fellow revolutionaries disagreeing on certain points and agreeing on others. Furthermore, the supposedly "monolithic" Bolshevik leadership was not at all united in the winter of 1920-1. On the contrary, the very fact that it was split over key questions contributed strongly to the unfortunate outcome of the conflict. Hence the "Levi affair" cannot be properly understood without understanding the dynamics of Bolshevik politics at the time.

In the years following the October Revolution, Bolshevik politics was based on the axiom that this initially successful revolution could ultimately only be secured if workers' power spread to other European countries. Since the First World War the Bolsheviks had been eager to support revolutionary movements in other countries and had initiated the founding of the CI in 1919. At the end of 1920 the Soviet government in Russia had just been through two and a half years of bitter civil war, which they had only won very narrowly, and which had caused an enormous death toll and severe economic devastation. This led to bitter conflicts inside Russia. The working class, which had been relatively small even in 1917, had been further reduced

---

15: This is true of Sigrid Koch-Baumgarten, 1986, and also Richard Löwenthal, 1960. However, despite this faulty assumption, both studies contain valuable source material about the conflict discussed here.
16: It was only coined during the process of Stalinisation in the Soviet Union after 1924.

by economic breakdown. The government relied on forced requisitions of food from the countryside to feed the starving towns, leading to repeated peasant uprisings that were repressed by force. Soviet Russia was in severe crisis—symbolised above all by the Kronstadt uprising in March 1921.

Throughout the years of civil war the problem of how to get out of this impasse had become very controversial within the Bolshevik leadership. In early 1921 two basic currents existed regarding the question of the international situation and the peasant question.[17] One, including Lenin and Trotsky, argued for concessions to the peasants in Russia and temporary peace with the bourgeois governments in Western Europe in order to win some breathing space for Russian society to recover. They finally won the argument in March 1921 with the implementation of the New Economic Policy, or NEP.

The other current argued for a continuation of the hard line towards the peasants in Russia, and hoped to get relief by launching a "revolutionary offensive" against the bourgeois governments in the West. The most prominent supporters of this "leftist" tactic in 1920-1 were Nikolai Bukharin and Grigori Zinoviev, both of whom held leading positions in the leadership of the CI. The fierce debate between these two camps peaked at the end of 1920 in a disagreement over the question of a feasible peace treaty with Poland (with which Soviet Russia had been at war for two years).

Bukharin had already demanded the right of "red intervention" by the Red Army in Europe at the Second World Congress of the CI in summer 1920, when the campaign in Poland was near its point of culmination and many (at that time including Lenin who would shortly afterwards change his mind) hoped that the Red Army would quickly reach the German border.[18] Bukharin declared the possibility of speeding up the revolution in Western Europe by military means. In winter 1920-1, when the momentum of the Red Army in Poland was lost, he kept publishing articles in which he explained his theory of the offensive. Zinoviev clearly sympathised with this theory although he articulated it in more cautious terms.[19]

17: It must be noted that the contemporary controversy inside the Bolshevik Party also covered other topics with different inner party alignments, eg on the trade union question Trotsky was closer to Bukharin and disagreed with Lenin, while he aligned with Lenin against Bukharin on the question of international perspectives. The inner-party controversies in Russia at the time were complex in general and the lines not always as clear cut as in regard to the international question touched here. For a detailed account of these controversies see Cliff, 1985, pp327-344, Carr, 1953, and Harman, 1997.

18: Broué, 2006, p461.

19: Reisberg, 1971, p91; Koch-Baumgarten, 1986, p78.

The ECCI recruited a group of Communists exiled in Russia (Kun, Rakosi and Pogany among others) who shared their impatience, but lacked their experience and theoretical understanding. A number of them had set up a journal called *Kommunismus* in 1920, in which they had developed their own version of the theory of the offensive. The ideas of the *Kommunismus* group were based on a philosophy which had little to do with Lenin or Marx: the concept of a determined minority that could initiate mass struggles by armed action. For the *Kommunismus* group any kind of defensive tactics were considered "social democratic", the "offensive" being the only approach permitted to Communists. Nevertheless Zinoviev and Bukharin expressly agreed with their views in late 1920 and integrated them into the "Small Bureau" of the ECCI.[20]

The ideas of the *Kommunismus* group obviously fitted their own desire quickly to open up a second front in Germany and by the spring they were operating in Germany with the authority of the ECCI. It was this group which gave the final impetus to the March Action in Germany.

There was almost certainly never a direct order for the March Action in the ECCI. But there was a group of irresponsible functionaries of the CI acting in Germany who were *believed* to act on the direct orders of the ECCI as their arguments echoed Zinoviev's and Bukharin's general arguments about the "revolutionary offensive". And there were left wing communists inside the KPD who were already impatiently waiting for an opportunity to "go on the offensive" and were now happy to take up the confused initiatives of Kun, Rakosi and their companions.

Open break

Levi had been on friendly terms with Bolshevik leaders during the world war, a number of whom he knew personally from his exile in Switzerland (amongst them Lenin, Bukharin and Karl Radek). As Lenin noted later, Levi had been a "Bolshevik" well before the Russian Revolution, supporting the attempts of the Bolshevik leaders to form a new international during the war.[21] But in late 1920 tensions between the ECCI and the group around Levi and Clara Zetkin in the KPD leadership grew over the contradiction between the united front approach of the KPD Zentrale (Central Committee) and the voluntarist tendencies described above that were gaining ground in the ECCI. A central factor in these conflicts was the fact that the bourgeois order in Western Europe had stabilised temporarily, while

---

20: Koch-Baumgarten, 1986, pp79-82.
21: Lenin, 1965.

in Russia internal tensions grew within the Bolshevik leadership, resulting in differing tactical approaches, although there was a shared understanding about the ultimate need to spread revolution to Western Europe.

The ECCI's increasing obsession with "speeding up the revolution" meant that the whole approach of the united front was put into question as it was a tactical doctrine designed for times of defensive struggles, not the moment of insurrection itself. Both Bukharin and Zinoviev were strongly opposed to the tactic of the "open letter" in January 1921, viewing this manoeuvre as a dangerous sign of "opportunism" and "passivity". The relationship between the KPD and the KAP became an additional source of conflict. [22] If revolutionary insurrection was possible in Germany in the short term, then it was imperative that the KPD set aside its quarrels with the most energetic and enthusiastic supporters of the "revolutionary offensive" in the KAP and link arms with them.

Radek, who was at the time working in the German party leadership as Bolshevik representative, vacillated for some months between the ECCI and the position of Levi and Zetkin, arguing for the united front approach in Germany and rejecting the idea of military export of the revolution. But Radek also called for a "more active" attitude by the KPD and for close collaboration with the KAP. In January 1921 he joined Levi in defending the "open letter" initiative and was narrowly able to prevent the ECCI from officially condemning it (also thanks to political support by Lenin).[23] However by the beginning of February 1921 Radek had made up his mind: he decided to support Zinoviev and Bukharin and told Levi frankly that he would be crushed if he thought about attacking them publicly.[24]

The growing alienation between the ECCI and the Levi-Zetkin group in the KPD finally became public in the debate about the tactics of the CI towards the Italian Socialist Party (PSI). This concerned the fundamental question of how the parties of the International should be built in the West. The left had stood their ground in the PSI more successfully than in the SPD. In 1920 there was no organised revolutionary force to the left of the PSI in Italy, which contained both reformists and revolutionaries alike. The mass of its members had opted for official affiliation to the CI before the Second World Congress in 1920. The question was how to get rid of the reformist minority in the leadership without losing the majority

22: There was already conflict about the KAP at the Second World Congress of the CI in 1920, but the Russian delegation shied away from an all-out confrontation. But it sharpened again after the unification of the KPD and left USPD in December 1920.
23: Koch-Baumgarten, 1986, p83; Reisberg, 1971, p91.
24: Broué, 2006, p479.

of party members who were reluctant to expel them. Levi and Zetkin distrusted the right wing but argued that the left in the Italian party should essentially work along the lines of "concentration" they themselves had practised in Germany, drawing a larger number of workers around them in mass campaigns and thereby exposing the right wing leaders in practice. This process of common political experience should improve the left's position before a split. The ECCI on the contrary decided to support the far-left wing of the PSI that favoured an immediate split even at the cost of losing the majority of party members. It championed this line at the Congress of the PSI in Livorno at which Levi was also present.

Levi protested in an article against the tactics of the ECCI. Radek replied and accused Levi of placing the authority of the ECCI in question. This hitherto unspoken public accusation finally turned the ongoing conflict into an all-out struggle. At the end of February the plenary session of the ECCI decided that there was a need for a reshuffle of the KPD Zentrale. The ECCI had finally decided to push Levi out.[25] Levi was informed about that discussion from the KPD representative in Moscow.[26] He lost the debate about Italy in the German leadership and decided to resign from the German Zentrale. He was followed by a number of his collaborators. This finally provided the opportunity for the theory of the offensive to be put into practice in Germany.

Levi's general perspective in 1920-1—even after leaving the party leadership—was not to break with the CI altogether. He still believed that his existing differences with the ECCI could be resolved, but he already saw that there was more at stake than mere personal disagreements. He understood the ECCI's misjudgement of the situation in Western Europe as a consequence of the Russian comrades' desire to relieve pressures at home. But as the conflict dragged on he posed the problem in more general terms: he saw the possibility that a gap could develop between the interests of the Russian state and the interests of the international workers' movement, which could become a serious obstacle for the further development of the CI in the long run.[27] Only one year after his expulsion he would argue that

---

25: Koch-Baumgarten, 1986, p84.

26: Angress, 1972, p133 (quoted in the German edition).

27: "The Russian comrades are a state power and a mass organisation. As a state power, they have to undertake in relation to the bourgeoisie measures which they would never undertake as a party for the sake of the proletarian masses... We can, of course, theoretically conceive that there is a risk here, the risk that if the link between the Communist International and the state power became very close, the Communist International would no longer act as a party or a super-party, as it were, inspired solely by the standpoint of Communism, but that it would

the internal tensions in Russian society had already begun to change the class nature of Soviet society.[28] But in spring 1921 Levi was not yet fully aware of the far-reaching implications of his questions.

The March Action and Levi's critique

Even before the March Action a decision had been made by the ECCI that the KPD leadership should get rid of Levi. The controversy following the March Action therefore seems to have delivered only a pretext for taking this campaign a step forward.

As the March Action itself has been covered in depth in various analyses, it will be sufficient only to outline the basic story here.[29] The newly formed KPD leadership wanted to utilise a minor local conflict between the Prussian police and miners in the Mansfeld region in central Germany to incite a general uprising on a national scale. It assumed that an escalation of this conflict would draw larger numbers of non-Communist workers alongside the KPD into direct confrontation with the state. This prediction proved to be completely wrong. A substantial part of the party membership took the call to arms seriously, but there was only a small positive reaction from the workers outside the party's ranks.[30] For about two weeks the party centre tried to fuel the fire, appealing to its members to go on strike, procure weapons and blow up railway bridges. Finally it even issued threats against workers who refused to join the struggle. Physical fights broke out between Communists who wanted to carry out the decision of their party leadership and other workers who saw no reason to go on strike.

In the end the unrest was suppressed relatively easily, although the police spilled a lot of blood in the process. Thousands of people were injured in the fighting, and 180 were killed. Some 6,000 Communists were imprisoned, four of them sentenced to death, and thousands more

---

become involved in the diplomatic game between the bourgeois forces of which the Bolsheviks must take account not as a party but as a state apparatus"—Broué, 2006, pp456-457.

28: For his full arguments see his Introduction to *The Russian Revolution* by Rosa Luxemburg, in Fernbach, 2011, pp220-265. In 1922 Levi saw the main danger to workers' power in Russia coming from the peasants in the first place and the merchants and foreign capitalists getting business concessions in Russia in the second place. He clearly did not foresee the later development in Russia. Still he was asking the decisive question already in 1922: which class will determine the politics of the Bolshevik Party in the long run?

29: For more detailed accounts read Broué, 2006, Harman 1997, Koch-Baumgarten, 1986, and Angress, 1972.

30: Lenin's claim that "hundreds of thousands of workers" in Germany were waging a heroic defensive struggle in March 1921 was based on a misjudgement. For an assessment of the numbers involved in different areas see Koch-Baumgarten, 1986 .

lost their jobs for trying to go on strike while their workmates were not ready to follow them. The party lost nearly two thirds of its membership. The SPD leadership gleefully accused the KPD of "putschism" and argued that the KPD would achieve its goals through the use of violence against other workers. The feeling of distrust against the party among trade unionists and social democrats grew. Well-known Communist militants were purged from union organisations. The March Action weakened the industrial base that the KPD had patiently built up over two years, and so it was no wonder that a large number of those who left the party in disappointment were trade union veterans. The KPD press was banned in a state of emergency. Virtually nobody outside the party was prepared to stand up for the KPD against this kind of repression.

In a literal sense it was incorrect when Levi later characterised the March Action as simply the "biggest Bakuninist putsch in history". The initial unrest in the Mansfeld region that had led to the police campaign in the first place was not caused by party appeals. But there can be no doubt that the appeals of the KPD had contributed strongly to the bloody outcome. There was no need for the party to force this limited conflict into open insurrection. A number of small-scale skirmishes between workers and the police had taken place all over Germany in the years 1919 to 1923. Although the party had sometimes argued fiercely over how to relate to them, it had never before taken decisions like that taken in March 1921. The party could have protested against the intervention of the police and resorted to more limited methods of mobilisation against them—as it had repeatedly done in the past. The KAP would have criticised the KPD (as it had also done before), but in the long run the KPD could have continued to build its influence much more successfully by the united front approach until the conditions for open confrontation were more favourable.

Levi argued that in a political sense the ECCI was responsible for the disaster. This was basically correct, even if the ECCI did not give direct orders for insurrection. Without the pressure of its emissaries in Germany the March Action would not have taken place in that way. They had systematically encouraged the KPD left to action and at the same time bullied the more cautious members after the retreat of Levi and Zetkin from the leadership. The party undoubtedly felt itself under immense moral pressure in March 1921 because of its boasting about the "revolutionary offensive" in the preceding weeks. It had become, as Levi put it, "the prisoner of its own slogans". It felt it could not take a more cautious stance in March 1921 without losing radical face, and for this the ECCI was to blame to a large degree.

Fernbach's collection includes Levi's pamphlet about the March

Action in its entirety.[31] It is one of the most systematic accounts of the political tactics that had inspired the KPD leadership between 1919 and Levi's resignation in February 1921. It includes an assessment of the political balance of forces in the German working class at the time and in addition Levi outlines his own approach to the strategic problem of insurrection here. In doing so he borrowed heavily from Lenin's famous pamphlet *"Left-Wing" Communism: An Infantile Disorder.* In that sense it was not original in its theoretical essence, but was nevertheless one of the most serious attempts to apply Lenin's general approach to the specific circumstances in Germany in 1921. Levi's pamphlet thus surpasses by far most writings of his party opponents at the time and his later slanderers.

The cover-up at the Third CI Congress

On 15 April 1921, three days after the publication of *Our Path*, Levi was officially expelled from the KPD for slander.[32] He protested against this decision and a whole number of Communist veterans, most prominently Clara Zetkin, spoke in his defence and testified to the depiction of events he had given in his pamphlet. Members of the KPD Zentrale wanted to expel them all but decided not to do so after the intervention of the ECCI.

The debate about the March Action was put on the agenda of the Third World Congress of the CI, which took place some two months later in Russia. The general line which was decided at the Congress confirmed the essentially defensive line which Levi, Zetkin and their followers had been consistently pursuing with the open letters. The "Theses on Tactics" adopted there declared: "It is absolutely incontestable that on a world scale the open revolutionary struggle of the proletariat for power is at present... slowing down in tempo. But in the very nature of things, it was impossible to expect that the revolutionary offensive after the war, insofar as it failed to result in an immediate victory, would go on developing uninterruptedly along an upward curve".[33] The tactic of the open letter was explicitly approved by another resolution,[34] while Lenin condemned the theory of the offensive before the German delegates in the strongest terms.[35] This sounded much like Levi's previous arguments.

31: *Our Path: Against Putschism*, in Fernbach, 2011, pp119-165. See also *What is the Crime? The March Action or Criticising it?*, pp166-205, published shortly afterwards—Fernbach, 2011, pp166-205.
32: Broué, 2006, p506.
33: Hessel, 1983, p203.
34: Hessel, 1983, p289.
35: He called it "an absurd theory which offers to the police and every reactionary the chance to depict you as the ones who took the initiative in aggression"—Broué, 2006, p539.

But when it came to the March Action itself, the decisions of the Congress were remarkably weak. It was portrayed as an essentially defensive struggle that the German party had wrongly turned into an offensive due to an incorrect assessment of the situation. The resolution declared that the struggle had been "forced upon" the party, implying that there had been no real alternative to bold engagement. At the same time, it was called a "step forward" for the party. There was not a word in the resolution about the role of the ECCI.[36] It was designed primarily to allow those responsible keep their face in front of the Congress, and not to decisively answer the questions at stake.

The theory of the offensive had already been defeated in Russia at the very same time that the preparations for the March Action were beginning in Germany. The "concessionist" camp in the Bolshevik Party had won the debate about the theory of the offensive in Russia itself at the Bolshevik Party Congress in mid-March, which had voted for the NEP and for peace with Poland just as Kun and Rakosi were pressing for action in Berlin. It had also introduced the infamous ban on factions in the party for the first time. This made it difficult for the Soviet delegation to be honest at the subsequent World Congress. After complicated negotiations in the Russian delegation Zinoviev and Bukharin remained silent there in order to preserve the impression of closed ranks in the Bolshevik leadership towards foreign delegates. They could not defend their cause in the Comintern even if they had wished to do so. Their inner-party opponents Trotsky and Lenin would attack the theory of the offensive in general terms, but at the same time were cautious in order to preserve the newly found unity in their own party. The resulting cover-up of the role of Bukharin and Zinoviev was only possible if Levi's criticism was silenced. The need to find a compromise formula about the March Action stemmed, therefore, at least partly from the need to preserve the unity of the Russian party.

Levi's expulsion was confirmed by the Congress, although it was now based on the accusation of having "broken party discipline". At the same time there were considerable efforts to prevent his supporters from leaving with him. The formalistic argument about breaking discipline was obviously designed to cool down the debate over the *political* arguments raised by Levi. The custom of criticising supposed errors of the party in public had been well established in both the KPD and the Bolshevik Party in the preceding years. Even Zinoviev himself had committed this "crime"

36: Hessel, 1983, pp290-291.

in a far more serious situation than March 1921, in the days before the October insurrection in 1917.

Lenin had argued a hundred times before that it would be far worse for the party to hide its errors from the public, for fear of playing into the hands of the class enemy, than to openly admit them and enable a necessary learning process. Similar reasoning also led Levi to reject the demand to stay silent about the March Action. He argued:

> It's a completely false attitude that Communists can sort out their mistakes in a quiet little room. The errors and mistakes of Communists are just as much a component of the political experience of the proletariat as their achievements. Neither the one nor the other should be withheld from the masses. If they made mistakes, they did not make these for the party, and even if the party collapses as a result—if *this* is the only way in which the proletariat can draw the lessons from experience—then it has to be so, as the party exists for the sake of the proletariat and not the other way round. [37]

Levi's attempts to join the party again were not handled honestly. He was not allowed back in at the World Congress but behind the scenes was given some vague promises about later—provided that he agreed not to make any further public criticisms of the March Action. Meanwhile the Communist press started—for the first time in the history of the German party—a vicious personal slander campaign against Levi, thereby making his return effectively impossible. Levi tried for a few months following his expulsion to be allowed back into the KPD but finally gave up his efforts after one year in early 1922. A short time later he decided to go back to the SPD broken-hearted.[38]

Long-term consequences of Levi's expulsion

The outcome of the Levi affair at the Third World Congress had some important long-term consequences for both the CI and the KPD.

The most obvious was that during the faction fight the KPD lost not only one of its most gifted leaders but a whole layer of experienced trade union veterans, which seriously weakened the party in the following campaigns for the united front. However one might judge Levi's own later

---

37: Fernbach, 2011, p205.

38: Lenin—in contrast to Radek and Zinoviev—seriously hoped to win Levi back and decided to hold back further public polemic for some time. He changed his mind definitely just after Levi published Rosa Luxemburg's critique of Bolshevik policies in 1922. An account of the discussions going on behind the scenes is given by Zetkin, 1934.

political trajectory (this would be another broad topic in itself, to which Fernbach's book provides some sources), it simply cannot be separated from his experience of the cover-up and the slander campaign by the Comintern.

There were also other consequences of the Levi affair that seriously affected the KPD in subsequent years. The decisions at the Third World Congress hampered what could have been a potentially healthy process of political clarification about the tactical questions at stake inside the KPD as it set strict limits on the debate from the beginning. Although the World Congress finally called for the united front approach, essentially generalising what Levi, Zetkin, Radek and others had begun in Germany in 1920, the legitimate questions about the inner workings of the ECCI and the role of the Bolshevik Party leaders in the conflict were never openly discussed in the KPD afterwards.[39]

The distorted depiction of the roots of the March Action itself—the story of the "enforced defensive struggle"—blurred some decisive points about tactics. When debating the lessons of the March Action the various factions in the German party would point to the resolution of the World Congress to argue their case. But the grave differences that had existed before the March Action continued to exist. The party was not permitted to learn from past errors through honest and open debate, which led to an unclear outcome in the KPD leadership itself. In the following two and a half years it consisted of a somehow artificial and uneasy alliance of ultra-leftists and supporters of the united front approach. This was basically bound together by the overarching authority of the ECCI.

This leads directly to the third long-term consequence of the Levi affair: it was the first major step in a process by which the Russian party would slowly but irreversibly become the all-decisive last instance in all internal conflicts of the Comintern. The relative weight of the Russian-dominated ECCI against the Western European party leaders increased significantly with the expulsion of Levi, previously acknowledged as one of the most capable "Western Bolsheviks", and the ECCI became the generally accepted referee in all future party disputes.

The habit of "turning to Moscow" to decide internal disputes had been largely unknown before 1921, but became regular practice in the following years. It undermined critically the ability of the national leaderships

---

39: An instructive case is Clara Zetkin. She shared many of Levi's criticisms, but finally decided not to attack the ECCI in public. She stayed in the KPD and would later become a sharp critic of the politics of the Stalinists in the CI—but always just in her private letters, never in public.

to judge and act by themselves, even where the rapidly changing dynamics of revolutionary crises demanded it. This was especially true in the summer of 1923, when the leadership of the KPD repeatedly travelled to Moscow to let the ECCI mediate between the ultra-lefts and the supporters of the united front approach while a political and social crisis of world historical dimensions was ripening in Germany itself. And this also meant that the German party leadership ultimately remained helpless when the rise of the Stalinist dictatorship in Russia itself began to gain momentum after 1924.

Finally, the political prestige of Zinoviev and Bukharin as leaders of the CI was preserved by the treatment of the Levi affair at the Third World Congress. Both would play a nasty role in the Stalinisation of the CI only a few years later by providing critical support for Stalin's rise (only to fall into disgrace themselves shortly afterwards).

It would, however, be wrong to attribute all these long-term consequences to a conscious plot by the Bolshevik leaders in 1921. The later degeneration of the KPD into an obedient tool of the Stalinist dictatorship in Russia cannot be traced back in a straight line to the Levi affair in 1921, as some have implied.[40] The road to Stalinism was certainly not yet paved in 1921 and it would be some years before the top leadership of the Bolshevik Party would become a self-conscious ruling class. In 1921 neither the destiny of Soviet Russia nor the future of bourgeois Germany had been decided irrevocably. But the outcome of the Levi affair certainly narrowed the options for the development of the KPD in Germany as well as the CI as a whole significantly.

David Fernbach's book makes plenty of source material available for socialists who want to obtain a deeper understanding about the relationship between the CI and the Communist movement in Weimar Germany. It should be read alongside the existing general studies on the history of the KPD and the CI.[41]

40: This is the core argument in Löwenthal, 1960, and Koch-Baumgarten, 1986.
41: Broué, 2006, is highly recommended for further reading on Paul Levi. It contains—next to a broad account of the general development—a sophisticated assessment of Levi's politics. Harman 1997 gives a more general overview.

References

Angress, Werner T, 1972, *Stillborn Revolution: Communist Bid for Power in Germany, 1921-23* (Princeton University Press).

Bois, Marcel, and Florian Wilde, 2007, "Modell für den künftigen Umgang mit innerparteilicher Diskussion? Der Heidelberger Parteitag der KPD 1919", in *Jahrbuch für Forschungen zur Geschichte der Arbeiterbewegung*, number 2.

Broué, Pierre, 1997, *L'Histoire de l'Internationale Communiste 1919-1943* (Fayard).

Broué, Pierre, 2006, *The German Revolution 1917-1923* (Haymarket).

Carr, Edward H, 1953, *The Bolshevik Revolution 1917-1923*, volume 3 (Penguin).

Cliff, Tony, 1985, *Lenin 1917-1923: Revolution Besieged* (Bookmarks).

Harman, Chris, 1997, *The Lost Revolution: Germany 1918-1923* (Bookmarks).

Hessel, Bertil (ed), 1983, *Theses, Resolutions and Manifestos of the First Four Congresses of the Third International* (Ink Links).

Koch-Baumgarten, Sigrid, 1986, *Aufstand der Avantgarde. Die Märzaktion der KPD 1921* (Frankfurt/Main. Campus).

Lenin, V I, 1965, "Letter to the German Communists", 14 August 1921, in *Collected Works*, volume 32 (Progress), www.marxists.org/archive/lenin/works/1921/aug/14.htm

Levi, Paul, 1969, *Zwischen Spartakus und Sozialdemokratie: Schriften, Aufsätze, Reden und Brief*, edited and introduced by Charlotte Beradt (Europäische Verlagsanstalt).

Löwenthal, Richard, 1960, "The Bolshevisation of the Spartacus League", in David Footman (ed), *International Communism*, www.questia.com/library/3658821/international-communism

Reisberg, Arnold, 1971, *An den Quellen der Einheitsfrontpolitik, Berlin GDR* (Dietz).

Riddell, John, 2011, "The Origins of the United Front Policy", *International Socialism 130* (spring), www.isj.org.uk/?id=724

Zetkin, Clara, 1934, *Reminiscences of Lenin* (International Publishers).

The Bradford riots: responses to a rebellion

Amy Leather

A review of Janet Bujra and Jenny Pearce, **Saturday Night and Sunday Morning: The 2001 Bradford Riots and Beyond** *(Vertical Editions, 2011),* £13.99

Visiting Bradford in 1986, the novelist Hanif Kureishi observed that "Bradford seems to be a microcosm of a larger British society". George Galloway's landslide victory in the Bradford West by-election thrust the city back into the national limelight. The significance of a defeat on this scale in a seat held by Labour since 1974 has not been lost on politicians and commentators alike as they struggled to explain such a political earthquake.

Although it has a large geographical spread, at the heart of the Bradford West constituency are the wards of Manningham and Toller. It was here where, over a decade ago, a major riot took place. Although subsequent events, including Galloway's appalling comments on rape, have changed the situation again, his election campaign was characterised by its youth and vibrancy, galvanising and exciting many young people in their twenties and thirties. Many of those in the driving seat of the campaign would have been part of a generation of young people in Bradford influenced in some way by the events of Saturday 7 July 2001.

This book aims to tell the story of the 2001 Bradford riot and its aftermath, ending with what happened when the English Defence League (EDL) came to the city in August 2010. In doing so Janet Bujra and Jenny Pearce also paint a picture of Bradford, its social, political and economic history as well as the politics and activism that have shaped the city. They set the events of 2001 and beyond in the context of the decline of a once great textile town with a history of immigration, especially from Pakistan, as workers were recruited to work in the city's mills.[1]

In the summer of 2001 Nazi thugs from the BNP, the National Front (NF) and other Nazi groups such as Combat 18 had targeted a number of former mill towns in the north, including Oldham and Burnley, where the BNP were also making electoral gains. They had rampaged through Asian areas smashing up businesses in an attempt to intimidate those living there as well as provoke retaliation. Bradford was the next town on their list, with the date set for their march as 7 July.

On the day despite a ban by the home secretary on the planned Nazi march, many known Nazis were in the town congregating and drinking. Although the council had cancelled the final day of a longstanding multicultural festival, the Anti Nazi League together with the trades council held an anti-fascist rally in Centenary Square outside the Town Hall. Thousands of young, predominantly Asian men came out to defend their city and community and joined the rally in the city centre. As reports of racist attacks spread, the police attempted to "kettle" those in the town centre. Then in full riot gear, police attempted to herd those protesting against the Nazis out of the city centre towards Manningham. People fought back as they responded to both the Nazis and the police's attempts to protect them.

Afterwards the full weight of the state was used against those who had defended their community and city from racists. As *Socialist Worker* subsequently reported, "In the end 200 jail sentences totalling 604 years were handed down".[2] These included someone given four years for throwing three stones, while another person was sentenced for 11 months for picking up, but not throwing, two stones. As the authors note, such harsh sentences were "designed to deter them and others from repeat performances". They make an interesting comparison with the sentences given for a similar, although less reported disturbance, which occurred two nights later on a predominantly white estate in the city. Those involved in the "Ravenscliffe riot" were charged with "violent disorder" rather than "riot", an offence which carries a much shorter jail term, resulting in much more lenient sentences. The conclusion that many drew was that the different reaction of the courts to these two events was driven by racism.

Bujra and Pearce started the project that led to the publication of

---

1:    Perhaps aptly, I first came across this book in Salts Mill, a former textile mill on the outskirts of Bradford that once employed over 3,000 people including my ancestors, now converted into a gallery for Hockney paintings and a space for expensive shops.

2:    *Socialist Worker*, 14 August 2010, www.socialistworker.co.uk/art.php?id=22063

this book in 2003. By that point 144 people had already been charged with riot and 107 adults had been given custodial sentences that averaged over four years. An interesting note is that, despite the hysteria whipped up at the time about the rioters and the fact that one of the judges made it clear he was "not concerned" with the origins of the riot, the authors' project was initially funded by a grant from West Yorkshire Police through its Neighbourhood Renewal Safer Communities Fund in order to try to understand "why the rioters rioted". The authors themselves were motivated by a strong feeling that the "rioters' voices needed to be heard". Initially they set out to talk to the rioters about their motivations but the project "soon expanded to other parties—the police in all ranks, the organisers of the initial ANL rally, people who had intervened to try and halt the violence and others who had observed". For the authors "this is a book of their stories": "our point is that all of them represent some 'truth' as seen from contrasting perspectives and social positions". A laudable aim perhaps, but the implicit postmodernist twang does not prevent the authors drawing their own, often unargued conclusions as we shall see later.

The authors did nearly 50 interviews about the 2001 riots, including with 21 men charged with riot and imprisoned at the time, and over 50 around the time of the 2010 EDL demo. This research was also "accompanied by hundreds of conversations and more importantly by living in and/or participating in the life of the city and engaging in its many struggles".

It is very clear from the interviews of those charged with riot that they were defending themselves and their communities from the Nazis of the NF. They believed that the NF would attack people and property in Asian areas, as had happened in Oldham and Burnley. Known Nazis were in the town centre and had attacked and provoked violence and the police were complicit in this. As one man explains, "They were protecting them and they should have been protecting us." Therefore, as another says, "it turned into a riot against the police". More than one rioter spoke of the police using racist language. As the authors highlight, there was a younger generation who were not prepared to accept the racism that their parents had experienced.

The rioters were very critical of the police's tactics—not only the way they acted to protect the Nazis, but how they provoked anti-racists and the perception that the police were just trying to protect the town centre and push them back into "Asian areas".

What make for an interesting and surprising read are the accounts from the police officers on duty that night, nearly all of whom "commented negatively on the tactics they were told to employ". It becomes clear that communication had broken down and tactical decisions were being made on the basis of rumour and speculation. The police found themselves at a strategic disadvantage after pushing the rioters out of the town centre: they were at the bottom of a hill, without food, water or breaks. As the authors conclude, "many officers lost confidence in their commanders whilst they continued to hold the line". Given the recent prevalence of kettling in recent years, the comments of one officer are particularly relevant. He makes it clear that they should not have cordoned off the crowd in the square to begin with. "Encircling a crowd does nothing apart from create confrontation," he insists. "There's no safety valve for people to go and when there's no safety valve you get a build of pressure, don't you?"

However, while the officers on duty may have been critical of their superiors they had no sympathy whatsoever for the rioters. As perhaps we would expect, the police reject the rioters' rationale that they were defending Bradford and their communities from the NF since "they (the far right) didn't come". Most of the police reject the idea that known Nazis were in the town centre, claiming those drinking in the streets "were just football supporters, not racists". Indeed one of the turning points on the day was when a young Asian man, Kasel Altaf, was attacked in the town centre. Astonishingly, the police interviewed imply that he was implicated in his own beating up and was "not an innocent bystander".[3] One police commander takes the view that Altaf was "not lily white...to my mind he started all that".

Instead to the police, since there was no legitimate cause for the riot, those involved were simply "attracted by violence". Police also blamed the ANL for fomenting trouble and "whipping up hysteria". One police officer defends the ANL, blaming instead violent extremists—when asked for examples he cites not only the Socialist Workers Party but also the Campaign for Nuclear Disarmament!

There is much valuable detail in Bujra and Pearce's book, from the events of the riot to how it was reported as well as the accounts of those involved. Indeed in piecing together the events of the day from different media reports together with interviews of those involved on all sides, this book provides a unique account of how the day unfolded, unavailable elsewhere. As such it is to be welcomed. Their evidence demonstrates that, even without police racism and the Nazis, there was plenty to riot about if you were young in Bradford in 2001. Some of those interviewed mentioned the lack of facilities and education. Over 35 percent of Bradford's adult population lacked any qualifications in 2001, while youth unemployment had reached 21.6 percent according to a city council report in October 1993.

3:    Bujra and Pearce, 2011, p62.

A survey in 1996 revealed that half of Pakistani and Bangladeshi households contained no one in full-time employment. Unemployment among young Asian men reached 45 percent in the early 1990s.[4]

But although the interviews offer interesting insights, and the statistical information about Bradford is useful, there are some problems with the book. The authors' use of language is particularly irritating. For example, the term "lads" is constantly used to describe those involved in the riot. Perhaps the authors think this is the correct Yorkshire term for young men. However, given the average age of those involved was 24 and thus many were older, in some cases married and with children, this is not an accurate term to describe grown men. Instead it becomes patronising.

Even more grating is, for want of a better word, the authors' "accenting" of those they interview: that is, they quote them not only as they speak, which by definition can be grammatically incorrect, but they also change the spelling of words to show the speaker's accent, for example "yer" for "you", "outa" for "out of". It might be argued that there are good reasons to do this, for example, to allow those interviewed "to speak in their own voice". I initially speculated that the authors had done this to show just how integrated British-born young Asian men are in that they had Bradford accents, but what would happen if they had to quote someone with poor, perhaps broken, English?

When they do, this method becomes even more patronising and takes away from what is being said. The question of who is "accented" also arises. Everyone has some sort of accent. Although there is a slight "accenting" of the police quotes it is much starker for the rioters. It is also true that spoken language is very different from written language, in terms of sentence structure etc. To quote some people in accents, and also to quote directly so that the written sentence structure is poor, not only distracts the reader but can serve to make the person quoted look less articulate than those who are not accented and contrasts harshly with the written text in which the quote is contained.

There is also a problem with the book's lack of academic rigour. Early on the authors state that "as the audience for the book is non-academic we have avoided jargon and extensive referencing". Yet when a book is based on research of some kind, being able to check the references is crucial. Although many of the interviews were anonymous and there would be some problems identifying who is being quoted, it is very frustrating not knowing where certain "facts" and indeed opinions come from.

4:    Bujra and Pearce, 2011, p105.

And this definitely does not excuse unsubstantiated assertions that appear throughout the book. For example, in a discussion about why Nick Griffin, the leader of the BNP, lost the 2005 parliamentary election in Keighley, the authors simply assert that "mothers from the local Sure Start, who had all voted BNP at the last election, turned the tide. Griffin lost".[5] No figures are given and there are no references to check this. Unfortunately such assertions make the reader less inclined to trust other "facts".

Indeed these other unsubstantiated "facts" often seem to reflect the authors' own political stance, despite their claim to simply be telling everyone's stories. Of course, nothing takes place in a vacuum without a standpoint but it would be far better to be honest about this from the start and not pretend otherwise.

So, for example, Manningham is described as a "bohemian quarter" in the 1970s and there is a discussion about the left and the divisions within it. The authors assert, with no preamble, "The International Socialists, later the Socialist Workers Party, expelled various members for wanting to open up gay and other sections." There are no references for this and no source is given. So where has such a damaging accusation come from? What it has to do with race relations in Bradford? If the authors wanted to have a discussion about socialists and the issue of gay liberation during the 1970s then that might be interesting and would no doubt involve some conflicting views and accounts from the time. However, this sort of writing is simply lazy and falls back on personalised, stereotypical accounts of the left.

Similarly, on the history of anti-fascist organisations we again encounter lazy research. It becomes clear that the authors' sympathies lie with strategies advanced by Hope Not Hate (who in a departure from the norm actually have their website referenced in the book) but for obvious reasons, they can't avoid mentioning the Anti Nazi League and Unite Against Fascism. The authors claim that the Anti Nazi League (which organised the 2001 rally) "was not active in the 1990s".

Clearly the authors were not involved in the 1993 Unity demo of over 60,000 which marched to shut down the BNP's "bookshop HQ" in south east London shortly after the murder of Stephen Lawrence, and which the ANL was at the heart of organising. Nor were they present at the 100,000-plus strong ANL festival in 1994 in Brockwell Park, south London. They can't have participated in the myriad "Don't vote Nazi" campaigns initiated by the ANL which leafleted and knocked on doors across the country after the Nazi Derek Beackon was elected in the Isle of

---

5:   Bujra and Pearce, 2011, p187.

Dogs and which succeeded in stopping the election of other BNP candidates at the time and eventually got rid of Beackon himself.

No, instead they claim that the SWP was "on another journey", and having shut down the ANL, the SWP argued that "anti-fascism must be led by those directly threatened by fascism". The authors don't expand on what they mean by this but say of Unite Against Fascism that "some suspected it was a recruitment front for the SWP", although unfortunately, there is again no reference for this quote. One can only conclude that the authors just took the opportunity to air their own views. They thus fail to seriously highlight and assess the real debates that have taken place in the anti-fascist movement about what strategy is needed to stop the Nazis.

This brings us to the biggest weakness of the book—the coverage of what happened when the EDL targeted Bradford in August 2010. The starting point for the authors, mirroring that of many of those in positions of power and authority in Bradford at the time, seems to be: "How can we prevent young Muslim men from being provoked into causing a riot like that of 2001?" rather than: "How can we prevent the growth of a far-right street fighting organisation that has known Nazis at its heart?" Although there is a brief acknowledgement of previous EDL demonstrations, the EDL mobilisation in Bradford is taken out of any national context and becomes purely a problem that Bradford had to face alone.

The implicit consequence of this is that the authors essentially accept the mainstream view that Asian people are themselves to blame if they respond to the Nazis trying to whip up race hatred. So when they depict the efforts made to keep people out of Bradford town centre on the day of the EDL protest in August 2010 they describe how "lads had been taken out of the city or enticed into snooker halls to remove them from potential *trouble making*" (my emphasis). We have to be clear it is the racists who are the real "trouble makers", that they are the ones who provoke violence and those who seek to defend themselves and areas are not to blame.

However, the legacy of 2001 had been that young men, defending themselves against Nazis and police racism, were criminalised. As a result, a cloud of fear hung over Bradford in the run-up to the EDL protest in 2010, as the council, the mosques, even the youth service urged people to stay at home and not be "provoked". The problem is that is exactly what the Nazis and thugs of the EDL want—people cowering at home while they rule the streets. It is a testimony to many in the anti-racist movement in Bradford that so many people did come out to join the counter-protest on the day.

At the time there was much debate in Bradford over how to respond to the EDL, from whether it was enough to ban the EDL from marching, though this still enabled them hold a static protest in the city, to whether it was enough to hold a counter-event, outside the city centre or even on another day. It would have been more interesting if the authors had examined these differing strategies.

Instead the conclusion seems to be that everyone, from the police to local councillors to the youth service to potential rioters, had learned from 2001 and came together to prevent a riot. The overriding message is that if a Nazi organisation comes to your town, don't be provoked and all will be fine as long as you don't have a riot. Thankfully, not every city has responded in that way.

Towards the end of the book the authors describe how it "has taken us on a journey". But neither the journey for Bradford nor the fight against the EDL ended in 2010. On the one hand, the riot of 2001 can be seen perhaps as a forerunner of those in 2011 when cities across Britain erupted in response to police racism and massive inequality and lack of hope for the young. One newspaper quoted George Galloway's success as "Bradford's version of the riots", and indeed much of what fuelled frustrations in 2001 still exists.

The gap between the most and the least deprived areas in Bradford was the largest in the country in 2010. Out of the 30 wards in Bradford, two are ranked in the 15 percent least deprived in the country, while Manningham and Bradford Moor fall within the 5 percent most deprived. In Manningham 35 percent of households had incomes less than £15,000, while in 2010 one in three people of working age were out of work in Bradford.[6]

It is also worth noting that the deputy leader of Bradford council in the summer of 2010, Imran Hussain, was the Labour candidate beaten so massively by Galloway. Hussain was part of the strategy led by the council that urged self-restraint against EDL provocation, in particular calling on young people to "trust the police". Perhaps his message was not so popular after all.

6:    Bujra and Pearce, 2011, p204.

The impact of the crisis on the working class in Britain

Laura Cooke

Throughout the crisis sensationalist claims have emerged on both the right and the left that the crisis would lead to a catastrophic and immediate rise in joblessness or, conversely, that it is really not that bad. This article examines exactly what has, and what hasn't, happened to the labour market during the latest recession and how this compares to the labour market impact of previous crises.

Large quarterly falls in employment in the first half of 2009 led commentators to predict a jobless total exceeding 3 million by the end of that year.[1] In reality, this did not materialise, and the three-month employment level actually rose, compared to the preceding three months, for 22 out of the 33 three-month periods between July to September 2009 and the latest set of data.[2] The unemployment level has so far peaked at 2.69 million in the three months to November 2011, falling back since then, to 2.58 million in the latest set of figures.

Although this figure is almost a million higher than it was before the crisis took hold, the fact that unemployment has not risen as quickly or as far as expected has itself prompted claims that the impacts of the recession are not as bad as they could or should have been, given the depth of the crisis.[3]

1:     Faulkner, 2009.
2:     For the three months to May 2012.
3:     For example, Gregg and Wadsworth, 2011.

While it is true that crisis has not thus far translated into long-term job losses on the scale witnessed in previous recessions, the economic recovery is the weakest on record, and the world economy remains precarious. Other countries are witnessing unemployment on the scale we might expect, while economists in the UK are puzzling about why this is not the case here. It may well be the case that there is worse in store for British workers as the economy continues to stall.

What has happened?
In December 2007, at the beginning of the crisis, there were 29.4 million people in employment in the UK.[4] Of these, 23.4 million worked in the private sector and 6 million in the public sector. In March 2012, as the economy went into double-dip recession, there were 29.2 million people in employment, of which 23.4 million were employed in the private sector, and the remaining 5.9 million in the public sector. Between these two dates the figures have fluctuated, with total employment reaching a low of 28.8 million in the three months to February 2010. Private sector employment fell by almost a million between December 2007 and December 2009, before rising to just 20,000 short of 2007 levels by the first quarter of this year. In the public sector the pattern was reversed, as employment grew by 300,000 in the first two years of the crisis and then fell by 600,000 during 2010 and 2011. The latest figures show that the overall level of employment in the three months to May 2012 is just 50,000 lower than it was in the three months to December 2007.

Overall employment declined rapidly from the start of 2008, with this decline intensifying in 2009. Job losses at this point were confined to the private sector, with manufacturing suffering most heavily, but other industries, particularly retail, distribution and construction, also seeing sizeable reductions. Parts of the financial sector, saved from collapse by government intervention and merger, also made large numbers of workers redundant. Between the final quarter of 2007 and the third quarter of 2010, there was a decline of 137,000 in the number of people employed in financial and insurance activities. Although the decline reversed slightly through 2011, recent announcements of further job losses in the sector (HSBC 3,100 jobs, National Australia Group 730 jobs, Royal Bank of Scotland 600 jobs) suggest a potential return to declining employment in the sector in the coming months.

4:   All statistics, unless stated, are taken from Office for National Statistics, 2012b. Any disparity between whole-economy totals and the sum of their constituent parts is due to rounding.

In wholesale and retail,[5] which is now the largest industrial sector in the UK in employment terms, employment grew throughout 2008, before falling by around 300,000 in 2009. Employment in the sector is currently 200,000 lower than it was at the end of 2007, standing at 4 million, with many of the large supermarkets promising job creation in the 2012/13 financial year.

The pattern of employment in the manufacturing sector over this period is particularly interesting. Since 1997, when comparable data on employment by industry began, manufacturing employment has been in steady decline. There were 4.4 million workers employed in manufacturing in the three months to March 1997, falling to 3.2 million by the three months to December 2007. Although the speed of this decline increased throughout 2008, from the beginning of 2009 onwards manufacturing employment appears to have stabilised, remaining at around 2.8 million.

There is an apparent disparity between the sustained rise in unemployment and the change in the employment level since the start of the recession, with close to a million extra unemployed people but the employment level only 50,000 lower than it was at the end of 2007. This is explained by a growth in the number of people looking for work. Unemployment figures are best understood not simply as the number of people out of work, but as the number of people who are out of work who are actively looking for work. This is a significant distinction, because it explains how there can be a rise in unemployment with no corresponding fall in employment. If, for example, the introduction of university fees meant that a million extra students needed to work while at university, there would be a rise of 1 million in the number of people looking for work (the economically active population). If no existing workers lost their jobs, but no new jobs were created, this would lead to a rise in the unemployment level of 1 million. There has been an overall rise of 920,000 in the economically active population between 2007 and 2012, of which 435,000 are men and 486,000 are women.

Have women workers borne the brunt of the crisis?

It has been claimed that women have been more heavily impacted by the crisis in employment terms than men. The figures for the unemployment levels of men and women respectively do not appear to support this. Women's unemployment has increased by 412,000 since the end of 2007 to 1.1 million, while male unemployment is 563,000 higher in the three

---

5:    This industrial sector also includes the repair of motor vehicles.

months to the end of May 2012 than it was at the end of 2007. The figures for total employment for men and women show that women's employment has actually risen by 74,000 since the end of 2007, while male employment has fallen by 129,000 over the same period.

But headline employment levels may not be the best way to measure the recession's impact on women. As I will explain in detail below, the impacts of the current recession are being felt more as a general squeeze on pay and terms and conditions of employment, rather than on employment per se. As some of the lowest-paid workers in the economy, women will be disproportionately affected by attacks on wages. Women also continue to shoulder the bulk of caring responsibilities, so are more likely to rely on precisely the types of employment benefits, such as holidays and flexible working, that are being attacked.

Underemployment

Although the total number of people in employment does not appear to have seen a lasting decrease so far, this does not mean that the types of jobs that people are doing have not changed. There has been a shift, since the start of the recession, in the number of people working full and part time. Between the end of 2007 and the latest set of data there has been an increase of 500,000 in the number of people working part time, and a corresponding fall of just under 600,000 in the number of people working full time. There has also been a significant rise in the proportion of part-time workers who are working part time because they are unable to find a full-time job, from just under 10 percent at the end of 2007 to just under 18 percent (4.8 percent of all people in employment) in the three months to May 2012.

The number of self-employed people has increased by about 350,000 since the start of 2007, with 200,000 of these newly self-employed people working part time. There is something of a debate around what this signifies. John Philpott, of the Chartered Institute of Personnel and Development, argues that this is a sign of the worsening effect of the crisis on employment, pointing out that, according to the Office for National Statistics (ONS), a quarter of the rise is accounted for by people working on a self-employed basis in the lowest occupational category, "elementary occupations". This signals an increase, he argues, in "odd-jobbers", people working part time in low-skilled occupations providing childcare, home tutoring or handyman-type services. But the ONS figures also show that over 50 percent of the rise has taken place among the top two occupational categories, "managers and senior officials" and "associate professional and technical". This accounts for the other side of the argument, that many of the people who are losing their jobs in the recession are setting up their own business or providing consultancy services.

Looking at the figures by industry, the most significant increases in self-employment have taken place in education (75,000), information and communication (45,000) and administrative and support services (39,000). By contrast, the three industries with the typically largest shares of self-employment—construction, professional, scientific and technical activities and wholesale, retail and repair of motor vehicles—have seen relatively little change. Although this appears to indicate that much of the new self-employment may be accounted for by consultancy-type roles, there are some indications that part of this growth is accounted for by employers taking advantage of the current economic situation to force new employees to accept bogus "freelance" contracts. This is a sort of phoney self-employment, which often means being paid less than other workers in the company as well as having no entitlement to paid holidays, pensions or other benefits and having to pay tax and National Insurance contributions independently.

Long-term unemployment

The Claimant Count is an alternative measure of unemployment, showing the number of people claiming Jobseeker's Allowance (JSA). The figures for Claimant Count flows show the number of new claimants, and the number of people who stop claiming, each month. These figures show that while around 300,000 are beginning claiming JSA each month, the same number are stopping claiming, for one reason or another. The main reason for people stopping claiming is usually that they have found a job.

Despite this churn in the labour market, figures for long-term unemployment show a worrying trend. Long-term unemployment is often experienced by the most vulnerable workers, those whose skills have become outdated or unneeded, older workers, and women. At present, the majority of unemployed people have been out of work for less than six months. But since the start of the recession the numbers of workers unemployed both for more than a year and for more than two years have more than doubled, with 878,000 unemployed for more than a year and a further 438,000 unemployed for more than two.

A young people's recession

Although media reports of almost two in five young people unemployed are somewhat sensationalised, it is certainly true that young people are bearing the brunt of the crisis in employment terms. In the three months to May 2012 the unemployment rate among 16 to 24 year olds was 36.7 percent, up from 25 percent at the end of 2007. This does not mean, as some reports have claimed, that 36.5 percent of all those aged 16 to 24 are unemployed, but that 36.5 percent of those looking for work in that age group are unemployed. This equates to 14 percent of all 16 to 24 year olds. Either way, the figure is exceptionally high. In real terms, the number of young unemployed people has risen by 340,000 since the end of 2007, surpassing the 1 million mark for the first time since comparable records began in 1992. Unlike the figures for the whole population, where rising unemployment has been accounted for largely by an increase in economic activity, rising youth unemployment is coupled with a fall in employment levels for this age group, signalling that young people are having difficulty entering the labour market. As the crisis began in 2007 there were 4.23 million people aged 16 to 24 in employment. This figure has been falling more or less steadily since then, and has stood at around 3.6 million since the end of 2011.

These figures are likely to be exacerbated by the recent announcement of a 9 percent fall in university applications among English students, as the hike in tuition fees to £9,000 a year comes into effect in September. The removal of the Education Maintenance Allowance paid to post-compulsory students from impoverished backgrounds is already believed to have impacted negatively on the participation rate in further education among 16 to 19 year olds.[6] Figures from the ONS on the number of 16 and 17 year olds in education show that the steady increase in this number that had been happening since around 1994 has stalled from 2010 onwards.

Labour market impacts of previous recessions
The recession of the 1970s had very little impact on employment compared with the recessions that have followed it. The employment level remained more or less stable throughout the recession period (1973-5) and thereafter, though unemployment rose by 400,000 following the end of the recession to 1.4 million, a level at which it would remain until the crisis of the 1980s.

The recession of 1980-2 had the most profound impact on employment of the crises covered by current labour market data. Unemployment had doubled by the end of 1982 and continued to rise after the recession had officially ended. By the end of 1983 unemployment had surpassed 3 million (3.2 million in October-December 1983). A corresponding fall of 1.5 million in the number of people in employment signalled that the rise in unemployment was being sparked by job cuts, not just an increase in people looking for work. Unemployment continued to rise, reaching

6:    House of Commons Education Committee, 2011.

a peak of 3.3 million in March to May 1984, before falling slightly, but would remain above the 3 million mark until the middle of 1987. It then began to fall, reaching 2 million by the autumn of 1989. Unemployment stayed at this level until the autumn of 1990, when it began rising again.

The crisis of the early 1990s saw unemployment once more surpass the 3 million mark, again coupled with a fall in employment. Unemployment had increased by 900,000 by the end of the 1990s recession, and peaked at just over 3 million in the first quarter of 1993, staying above 3 million for just two consecutive months. It fell only slightly during 1993, and remained at 2.9 million in the final quarter. The unemployment level then began on a slow downward trajectory, bottoming out at around 1.4 million in the mid-2000s. Only as the latest recession began to take hold did unemployment once again start to rise.

How women and young people fared in the past

At 13.6 million, there are currently more women in employment than ever before. The proportion of women who are economically active has risen from 44 percent in 1971 when comparable records began, to 56 percent today. There are an extra 4.5 million women in work than there were in 1971. An increase in the number of single parent families over the last 30 to 40 years means that more families rely on the wages of women to survive, and in two-adult households women's earnings now account for a greater proportion of overall income. These factors alone mean that women are feeling the impact of the current recession more directly than they did in the past.

Looking at unemployment levels, the current recession has now surpassed the 1990s recession in the number of women unemployed, but at 1.1 million, the unemployment level for women is still some way off its 1984 peak of 1.4 million. This may change. A third of all women in work are employed in the public sector, compared to 15 percent of men. The fact that current attacks on jobs appear for the time being at least to be confined to the public sector means that job cuts are likely to begin impacting on women in a much more pronounced way than to date. Recent reports showing that only between 10 and 20 percent of the planned public sector cuts have yet taken place means we might expect to see women's unemployment increase markedly over coming months.

Although the figures for unemployment by age group only go back as far as 1992, a report[7] by the ONS in February this year showed that youth unemployment, both as a proportion of all young people and as an

---

7:    Office for National Statistics, 2012a.

absolute number, has not reached the peak of the 1980s recession. Youth unemployment currently stands at 1.02 million, higher than the 1990s peak of 924,000, but still below the level it reached in the 1980s recession of 1.2 million in 1984. But the ONS points out that the shift into full-time education that has been taking place over the last 20 years is largely from employment, meaning that a lower participation rate in education among 16 to 24 year olds is likely to mean an increase in jobseekers in this age group.

How particular industries were affected

It is sometimes claimed that the current recession is more widespread than the recession of the 1980s, with the fact that job cuts in the 1980s were concentrated in manufacturing held up as evidence. The current figures for employment by industry do not go back as far as the 1980s, but a separate series, called "Workforce jobs by industry", does shed some light on this argument. This series shows that, in fact, jobs were lost in 11 out of the 19 industrial sectors between December 1979 and December 1983, compared with nine out of 19 between December 2007 and December 2011. Large numbers of job losses were indeed concentrated in the manufacturing industry in the 1980s recession, but this is to be expected, given that manufacturing accounted for 25 percent of UK jobs at the time, compared to less than 10 percent today.

What lies behind the current state of the labour market?

Different crises have had differing impacts on employment in Britain. This has tended to be a result of the industrial makeup of the country at the time of each crisis, and whether it has been possible for the capitalist class as a whole to allow certain industries to die off while expanding other ones. The crisis of the 1980s in particular came at a time when what had become low-profit manufacturing industries accounted for a large proportion of both GDP and employment, and these low-profit industries could be cleared out and replaced with newer service industries.

At present it is unclear where British capitalism can go next. In the private services sector investment in new technology has not yet allowed capital to do away with workers on a mass scale, though some steps in that direction do appear to be being taken (automated tills in shops, for example). It is also difficult for employers in the retail, distribution, food service and hospitality industries, which together account for around a quarter of UK employment, to simply close down their UK operations and move them to a developing economy, in the way that manufacturers have tended to do.

As a result, rather than leading to lasting changes to the industrial makeup of the private sector of the economy, and the permanent or semi-permanent job losses that such changes incur, the current crisis has led to a full-scale attack on pay and hours and on terms and conditions of employment in both the public and private sectors. Plant shutdowns and short-time working were widespread in the car industry in 2009, for example. At its Ellesmere Port plant in Cheshire, Vauxhall introduced a short working week between February and July 2009. Shifts or hours were also cut at BMW, Toyota, Ford, Jaguar Land Rover and Honda, as well as at various car components plants. Although working time was later restored at all of these companies, there are signs that short-time working may be starting to re-emerge as the recession continues.

Attacks on pensions have been widespread in both the public and private sectors, especially where final salary pension schemes are still in place. Workers at Unilever, BT and Ford, as well as workers across the public sector, have seen their pensions come under fire since the start of the crisis. More generalised attacks on other terms and conditions of employment, such as holidays, overtime rates and shift premiums, have also been common, at Superdrug, Boots and local authorities, for example.

Although actual wage cuts have been rare (with the exception of those related to short-time working), and have so far been mainly confined to the public sector, real wages, that is, wage rises adjusted for inflation, have been falling since 2010. Pay freezes were instituted at a third of organisations across the economy in 2009, mainly in the private sector. This was followed by pay freezes across the public sector from 2010 onwards. In the private sector wage freezes have become much less frequent from 2010 onwards, but in both 2010 and 2011 wage rises were far below the level of inflation, meaning real-terms pay cuts for most workers. And in some cases employers have been introducing new, lower rates of pay at the bottom end of pay structures, though this has often been an attempt to avoid the Agency Workers Regulations, rather than being a direct response to the crisis.

The driving down of real wages, coupled with benefit changes that are forcing people onto JSA from other types of social security benefit, such as Disability Living Allowance, goes some way to explaining the increase in the numbers of people looking for jobs. And as we saw earlier, increased economic activity has led to an inflated unemployment rate.

The fact that capital is attempting to recover from crisis through a generalised attack on pay and conditions, rather than through job cuts, may also explain why young people are facing such a high unemployment rate, despite large increases in unemployment not being seen elsewhere. Young people appear to be fulfilling the role of the "reserve army of labour" deliberately harnessed by the capitalist class in order to drive down the pay and conditions of workers across the economy. Employers are playing up the threat of unemployment in order to drive through cuts in pay and conditions that otherwise workers may not allow to be pushed through. It is much easier for your boss to tell you he's cutting your pay by 5 percent if he can also point to a million young workers poised to replace you if you protest.

The fact that capital has as yet not been able to reverse the crisis, and the knowledge that the majority of public sector cuts are yet to come, means that attacks on workers look set to continue for the immediate future at least. It is important for socialists to understand where we are at now, in terms of the impacts of the crisis, if we are to come up with an effective strategy for fighting further attacks on workers as the crisis continues.

References

Faulkner, Neil, 2009, "From Bubble to Black Hole: The Neoliberal Implosion", *International Socialism 122* (spring), www.isj.org.uk/?id=536

Gregg, Paul, and Jonathan Wadsworth (eds), 2011, *The Labour Market in Winter* (Oxford University Press).

House of Commons Education Committee, 2011, "Participation by 16-19 year-olds in education or training" (July), www.educationengland.org.uk/documents/pdfs/2011-CESC-16to19-year-olds.pdf

Office for National Statistics, 2012a, "Characteristics of Young Unemployed People" (February).

Office for National Statistics, 2012b, "Labour market statistics—July 2012", www.ons.gov.uk/ons/rel/lms/labour-market-statistics/july-2012/statistical-bulletin.html

Round-up on political economy

Joseph Choonara

The global capitalist crisis has now reached its half-decade point, and the months leading up to this unhappy anniversary saw the publication of a number of interesting papers on Marxist political economy. Here I will briefly survey some of them, focusing on those dealing with themes that have featured prominently in *International Socialism*.

A paper by Andrew Kliman and Shannon D Williams, "Why 'Financialisation' Hasn't Depressed US Productive Investment", builds on one of the controversial arguments in Kliman's latest book.[1] It challenges the idea that from the early 1980s financialisation caused the fall in the rate of accumulation (the rate at which profits are ploughed back into investment).

Over the past three decades the scale of financial payments (interest, dividends, etc) and financial assets swelled enormously, including in the non-financial sector. Kliman and Williams argue that this growth was not caused by firms diverting profits away from productive investment as people generally assume. Instead, "the substantial increase in corporations' financial acquisitions has been funded by means of borrowing". If this is the case, an alternative explanation for the slowdown in accumulation

---

1: Kliman, 2012. The paper is available from Kliman's website: http://akliman. squarespace.com/writings. Elsewhere on the same site (http://akliman.squarespace.com/ crisis-intervention) is his talk and PowerPoint presentation from the recent Marxism 2012 conference in London, which covers some of the themes in his book.

in the US is required. The authors argue that the major cause was the long-term decline in the rate of profit during the post-war period.

While it is also true that the *share* of profits going towards accumulation has declined somewhat since the early 1980s, they argue this is not due to financialisation; it is instead because in the 1970s the share had risen to unsustainable levels. The decline simply meant it had fallen back to levels similar to those between 1949 and 1971.

Another paper examining the relationship between finance and the wider economy is by Alan Freeman.[2] Its central claim is that the profit rate should be "corrected" to take into account the growth of financial assets.

Government statisticians do not publish a "Marxist profit rate". It is usually approximated by dividing some measure of the profits corporations make by their investment in fixed assets. Freeman's argument is that their total investment in financial assets should be added to their fixed assets. He shows that if it is calculated this way the rate of profit for the UK economy falls steadily in the post-war period, and the US rate of profit falls faster and further than in most other estimates. Without this "correction", Freeman argues, the UK profit rate would appear to have rebounded substantially from the early 1980s.

It is true that the competing financial claims over the profits generated by capitalist firms can become a problem for the system. "Deleveraging", destroying some of the debts created prior to a crisis, is one of the ways that crisis itself can help to pave the way for a new boom, alongside the bankruptcy of unprofitable firms and attacks on workers.

However, there are problems with throwing financial assets together with fixed assets.[3] As Freeman acknowledges, we are dealing here with what Karl Marx calls *fictitious capital*. This consists of paper claims over profits expected in the future—shares and bonds, for example. Marx argues that these claims circulate according to their own laws of motion through financial markets. But if their market prices happen to rise, I do not see why the rate of profit should be reduced. Even more problematic, in the case of shares, Marx argues that "the capital does not exist twice over, once as the capital value of the ownership titles, and then again as the capital actually invested in or to be invested in the enterprises in question".[4] This apparent multiplication

2:   "The Profit Rate in the Presence of Financial Markets: A Correction". I have only seen an early draft. A later version will hopefully be published this autumn in the *Journal of Australian Political Economy*.

3:   Freeman actually uses "financial derivatives, investment position, all sectors" to measure financial assets.

4:   Quoted in Freeman's paper.

of capital means that in the world of finance we have to be careful to avoid "double counting". Freeman is right to raise the issue of what to do with financial assets, but I suspect a great deal more work remains to be done.

A third paper considering some of these themes is a fascinating piece in *Historical Materialism* by Tony Norfield, formerly executive director and global head of currency strategy at ABN AMRO bank and now a PhD student researching Marxist crisis theory![5] He presents an admirably clear explanation of how derivatives work. These are financial contracts whose market price changes based on something else—the movement of interest rates or the price of oil, say. They are traded without the underlying "something" they are based on changing hands.

He takes issue, rightly in my opinion, with the influential account by Dick Bryan and Michael Rafferty in their book *Capitalism with Derivatives*.[6] Norfield argues that, contrary to the claims made by Bryan and Rafferty, derivatives cannot be seen as a new form of money. In addition, the price of derivatives can be highly unstable. Often the underlying "something" is itself a form of fictitious capital and, writes Norfield, a "derivative on fictitious capital...has a value that is regulated in yet another independent manner, even further removed from the underlying capital or commodity on which it is ultimately based". The market in derivatives brings together capitalists who want to "hedge" against a particular risk (for instance, by purchasing a derivative contract that pays up if the price of a commodity they are planning to buy in the future changes, covering any losses they incur) and those engaged in speculation (buying derivatives in the hope that their price will rise), and in practice it is difficult to draw a precise line of demarcation between hedging and speculation. But both flow out of the logic of capitalism, rather than being an anomaly that can be regulated away.

Norfield argues that the recent growth in derivatives flowed out of the period of subdued profitability—"banks and other corporations", faced with low profitability elsewhere and, after 2001, taking advantage of a wave of cheap credit, looked "for other sources of profit". He traces the explosion of these markets in the run-up to 2008 and criticises the proposed regulation of derivatives since as "attempts to install fire-doors in an earthquake-damaged skyscraper". Such reforms are, he argues, likely to

---

5:   "Derivatives and Capitalist Markets: The Speculative Heart of Capital", *Historical Materialism*, volume 20, issue 1. Those wishing to read the article will need to buy a copy of the journal or obtain it via a library as it does not appear to be freely available online.
6:   Bryan and Rafferty, 2005.

fail and in any case will not resolve the underlying laws of motion driving capitalism towards crisis, and the speculative bubbles it periodically creates.

Guglielmo Carchedi, who has an article in the current issue of this journal, has produced an interesting paper on the relationship between the general tendencies driving world capitalism towards crisis and the specific problems faced by the eurozone.[7] The first part of his paper covers the decline in the rate of profit, making this central to his explanation of the crisis.[8] Carchedi goes on to look at the structural problems built into the euro, which he argues was conceived as a potential competitor to the dollar as a world currency, and the dilemmas facing ruling classes across Europe.

Interestingly, he also challenges the view commonly held on the left that the imbalances that have grown up between Germany and weaker European economies reflect the more successful repression of wages imposed on German workers since the euro was launched.[9] He instead sees it primarily as the result of greater *rises* in efficiency in German industry (everyone accepts that the German economy *started from* a higher level of productivity than, say, Greece). He concludes by arguing that, while leaving the euro and devaluing the currency might help weaker countries to export more, this would come at the price of reducing the amount of value they can appropriate at an international level (because their new currency would fall rapidly in value) and potentially even reducing their profitability.

Michael Roberts, who runs the magnificent blog "The Next Recession", has written a paper entitled "A World Rate of Profit".[10] His average global rate is painstakingly estimated by combining data from the big G7 economies, plus Brazil, Russia, Indian and China (the so-called "BRICs"), which, taken together, make up a large chunk of the world system (see figure 1). Roberts concludes that "there was a fall in the world rate of profit from the starting point of the data in 1963 and the world

---

7:   "From the Crisis of Surplus Value to the Crisis of the Euro", available from http://tinyurl.com/GC-euro

8:   Carchedi, 2011, sets out his position on the crisis in some detail.

9:   This is the argument, for example, of Lapavitsas and others, 2012, and the papers by the same authors available from www.researchonmoneyandfinance.org. Lapavitsas compares nominal unit labour costs across the eurozone, showing that the total compensation going to workers has stayed in line with productivity in Germany, but risen for the weaker economies; furthermore, he presents evidence that productivity growth for Germany was modest compared to many other economies. See Lapavitsas and others, 2012, pp23-28. Carchedi, by contrast, looks at GDP divided by labour hours, and the total labour hours, for just Germany and Italy.

10: http://thenextrecession.files.wordpress.com/2012/07/roberts_michael-a_world_rate_of_profit.pdf

rate has never recovered to the 1963 level in the last 50 years. The rate of profit reached a low in 1975 and then rose to a peak in the mid-1990s. Since then the world rate of profit has been static or slightly falling and has not returned to its peak of the 1990s." This is useful confirmation, for those of us who concentrate on the US data, that patterns globally were not entirely dissimilar.

However, I think the paper tends to overstate the degree to which the global economy is integrated by the flows of capital between national economies. Of course, capitalism is a global system—no major economy has been able to exempt itself from the consequences of the crisis, for example. But, despite low wages in less developed countries, it remains the case that capitalists in the most developed economies direct the bulk of their investment towards themselves or other highly developed economies, or to quite specific regions elsewhere (notably in recent decades the coastal regions of China) in particular sectors.[11]

Figure 1: A world rate of profit (index: 100 = 1963)

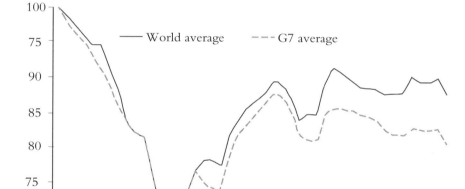

11: Roberts also appears to accept the idea of "super-exploitation", by which he means that workers in less developed countries receive less than the value of their labour power and that there is appropriation of surplus value from poorer nations by richer ones. The first concept implies a single universal standard for the value of labour power; the second seems to suggest exploitative relations between nations, as opposed to classes. I remain sceptical about such approaches.

In other words, either capitalists do not generally anticipate obtaining higher profits from less developed economies or there are significant barriers to the flow of capital to these economies. There may be a tendency towards the formation of a global rate of profit, but this remains a tendency, and an uneven one, so what we are looking at is an average of different, but interacting, national profit rates. Roberts' paper is useful in looking in broad terms at the global economy and its general health; it would be complemented by more detailed analyses of where capital does actually flow and the sectors of the world economy in which there is convergence of profit rates. Unfortunately, few Marxists seem to have delved deeply into this area.[12]

Roberts has also made available a collection of ten attempts to explain the crisis in 1,000 words or fewer—"Radical Economic Theories of the Current Crisis"—prepared for a joint summer conference involving the Occupy movement and the Union for Radical Political Economics in the US.[13] This contains a range of Marxist, left wing Keynesian and other heterodox approaches, with contributions from Steve Keen, Andrew Kliman, David Kotz, Arthur MacEwan and John Miller, Fred Moseley, Thomas Palley, Jack Rasmus, Anwar Shaikh, Richard Wolf and Roberts himself. Though the quality of these essays is uneven, their brevity and their intended audience mean that they form an easy introduction to the various contending accounts of the crisis on the left.

Those wanting a more sophisticated survey, covering just Marxist explanations, should look at the recent paper by Deepankar Basu and Ramaa Vasudevan.[14] The authors write, "A survey of literature is confronted by a daunting excess of conflicting characterisations".[15] They focus on the US profit rate and present a huge range of potential measures.

One issue in measuring profit rates is whether to value the assets of corporations at their historical costs (the value that they were purchased at) or their replacement costs (the value that would have to be spent to replace them with similar assets today). The authors are quite dismissive of historical cost calculations. However, such a measure allows us to compare

---

12: Though one recent noteworthy attempt to grapple with some of the issues is George Liodakis's "Transformation and Crisis of World Capitalism: Long-run Trends and Prospects", available from Roberts' website: http://thenextrecession.files.wordpress.com/2012/07/liodakis_george-transformation_and_crisis_of_world_capitalism.pdf

13: http://thenextrecession.wordpress.com/2012/08/16/ten-views-on-the-causes-of-the-crisis/

14: "Technology, Distribution and the Rate of Profit in the US Economy: Understanding the Current Crisis", available from: http://people.umass.edu/dbasu/BasuVasudevanCrisis0811.pdf

15: See Choonara, 2009, for my own, much earlier, survey of Marxist accounts.

the amount capitalists actually invested at a certain point with the profit they subsequently realise. Kliman has put the strongest arguments for historical cost calculations. Kliman also argues that various different measures are possible on this basis—for instance, using broader or narrower conceptions of profit, depending on the question you are trying to answer. In this spirit, Basu and Vasudevan's paper is interesting as it presents figures that show what happens to the profit rate if you deduct corporate taxation, interest payments, depreciation costs, etc from the broadest possible measure (figure 2 shows their results using historical costs)

Figure 2: Various measures of % rate of profit using historic costs

The historical cost profit rates appear to fall or stay more or less trendless from the early 1980s. On that basis I cannot agree with the authors when they argue that the current Great Recession is not the result of a crisis of profitability. Their argument makes a lot of the differences between the years preceding 2007 and the run-up to the Great Depression in 1929. But why assume that all crises of profitability will manifest themselves in the same manner? Most writers associated with this journal have seen the Great

Recession as the product of a long period of subdued profitability in which crisis was deferred by the expansion of credit, finally erupting when this process reached its limit.[16]

Figure 3: The share of unproductive labour and wages

Finally, in autumn 2011 *Review of Radical Political Economics* published an interesting paper by Dimitris Paitaridis and Lefteris Tsoulfidis, entitled "The Growth of Unproductive Activities, the Rate of Profit, and the Phase-Change of the US Economy".[17] This considers the impact of the growth of areas of the economy in which labour does not generate surplus value (the source of profit), a theme that authors such as Fred Moseley have explored in the past.

The authors note, "The growth of unproductive activities is induced by the intensification of competition which forces capital to spending increasingly more resources in sales promotion, administration

---

16: The authors also offer an attempt to decompose the changes in the profit rate into their constituent factors, though their narrative depends on their preferred reading of the movement of profit rates. Despite this it does suggest that to a large degree the decline in profitability is a result of an increase in the value of fixed assets required to generate a given level of output.

17: *Review of Radical Political Economics*, volume 44, number 2. Unfortunately, this paper does not seem to be freely available online.

and supervision... Furthermore, social cohesion requires increasingly more resources to be devoted to the provision by the government of social security benefits... Finally, international competition...exerts a permanent pressure on governments to increase their military expenditures." They claim that this kind of employment has risen to very high levels in the US in the post-war period (see figure 3), though they also indicate some of the difficulties in calculating the numbers. They argue that the "net" rate of profit, taking these expenditures into account, has never returned to the kinds of levels it experienced in the 1960s.

Together this new body of writing on the causes and nature of the crisis show that the revival in Marxist political economy we have seen in recent years continues, even if it seems to generate as many new questions and controversies as answers.

References

Bryan, Dick, and Michael Rafferty, 2005, *Capitalism with Derivatives: A Political Economy of Financial Derivatives, Capital and Class* (Palgrave Macmillan).

Carchedi, Guglielmo, 2011, "Behind and Beyond the Crisis", *International Socialism 132* (autumn), www.isj.org.uk/?id=761

Choonara, Joseph, 2009, "Marxist Accounts of the Current Crisis", *International Socialism 123* (summer), www.isj.org.uk/?id=557

Kliman, Andrew, 2012, *The Failure of Capitalist Production* (Pluto).

Lapavitsas, Costas, and others, 2012, *Crisis in the Eurozone* (Verso).

Roberts, Michael, 2009, *The Great Recession* (Lulu).

THE POINT IS TO CHANGE IT!

an introduction to
Marxist philosophy

by John Molyneux

Out now £7

John Molyneux provides a great
introduction to key concepts and
themes in Marx's philosophy, including historical materialism and
the dialectic, morality and justice,
human nature, truth and ideology.
Using contemporary examples he
shows how Marx's ideas can be useful in understanding our
21st century world. This book is a must for anyone who's ever
been afraid to approach "philosophy".

John Molyneux is a socialist writer and activist, formerly a
lecturer at Portsmouth University and now living in Dublin. His
books include *Marxism and the Party* (Bookmarks 1978), *What
is the Real Marxist Tradition?* (Bookmarks 1985), *Will the Revolution be Televised?* (Bookmarks 2011) and
Anarchism: A Marxist Criticism (Bookmarks 2011).

BOOKMARKS PUBLICATIONS

Bookmarks the socialist bookshop
1 Bloomsbury Street, London WC1B 3QE
020 7637 1848 www.bookmarksbookshop.co.uk

A comment on Greece and Syriza

Richard Seymour

The "strategic perplexity" of the left confronted with the gravest crisis of capitalism in generations has been hard to miss.[1] Social democracy continues down the road of social liberalism. The far left has struggled to take advantage of ruling class disarray. Radical left formations have tended to stagnate at best. Two exceptions to this pattern are the Front de Gauche in France and Syriza in Greece. While the Front de Gauche did not do as well as many hoped, it did channel a large vote for the radical left in the presidential elections won by Hollande. Meanwhile, Syriza is potentially a governing party in waiting.

In Alex Callinicos's piece for the last *International Socialism*, he offered a complex analysis of these developments.[2] At the most general level, he argued that the capitulation of social democracy to neoliberalism in combination with the capitalist crisis is opening up a space to its left. He suggested that the reason why Syriza and the Front de Gauche had succeeded was that they were dominated by "left reformists". They speak the language of an older reformist tradition with deep roots in the working class and are thus far better placed to capitalise on workers' discontent than revolutionaries.

This analysis is a rebuke to the notion that there is nothing between the far left and social democracy. That diagnosis may have been appropriate in

---

1: Kouvelakis, 2011.
2: Callinicos, 2012.

the period of revolutionary growth beginning in 1968.[3] This period, marked by the long-term decomposition of once dominant social democratic parties, is quite different. A typical feature of emerging radical left parties and coalitions is the involvement of a left breakaway from the old reformist parties, as well as a realignment of some of the Communist parties associated with them. There is a structural gap between what such forces represent on the ground and what they can project in elections, which makes any success extremely fragile. Nonetheless, today there *are* quite serious forces between us and social democracy. And in the circumstances, this is no bad thing.

Syriza and "left reformism"

On the face of it, the characterisation of "left reformism" is a reasonable depiction of the rough balance of forces—provided national specificities are not lost in such generalities. Unfortunately, I think some of the discussion of Greece and Syriza in particular glosses over some important details.

First of all, Syriza's specificity as a "left reformist" organisation isn't persuasively dealt with by Alex. Acknowledging the existence of a revolutionary pole inside Syriza, he suggests that its only function is to "allow [Syriza] to project a very radical image when it suits", although "these organisations have little influence on the determination of policy". This hardly does the subject justice. It implies that the coalition is simply an integument for Synaspismos, the dominant ex-Eurocommunists.

The decision by Synaspismos to launch Syriza was part of a general turn to the left under the influence of the anti-capitalist and anti-war movements. For example, while in 1992 Synaspismos supported the Maastricht Treaty, by the time Syriza was formed it had repudiated this stance. It later campaigned against the European Constitutional Treaty, and joined the Greek Social Forum in 2006. It was the only parliamentary party to support the student rebellions in 2009, and played an important role alongside Antarsya in the "movement of the squares". Synaspismos's traditional openness to the social movements played an important role.

The revolutionary left, a minority in Syriza, is by no means negligible. The Maoist group, the Communist Organisation of Greece (KOE), is the second largest organisation in the coalition. Alongside it are smaller Trotskyist and communist groups such as the International Workers' Left (DEA). In addition, Synaspismos possesses its own internal differentiations, a corollary of its effort to act as a broad canopy of left forces, and the result

---

3: Such a political vacuum was part of Chris Harman's explanation for the growth of the revolutionary left after 1968. See Harman, 1979.

is that the revolutionary left inside it is not completely lacking in influence. It has representation in the national bodies and leadership and is able to work with the left inside Synaspismos to achieve its goals.[4]

Ecumenicism

Whatever Syriza's limits, it has been open to forces to its left and has been willing to work with them in a democratic way. In this light, a surprising omission in Alex Callinicos's detailed analysis of Syriza's rise is the role of the slogan calling for a united left government to block austerity measures. Alex points out that for a time before Syriza's ascendance the more moderate Democratic Left was ahead in the polls. But he concludes from this only that Syriza's "political ambiguity" allows people to believe "what they want to believe". This misses the far more salient point that the balance shifted to Syriza as the crisis radicalised, and Syriza's advantage crystallised after Alexis Tsipras's call for a left government to resist austerity measures.

The slogan of a united left government was consistent with Syriza's general ecumenicism towards the left, combined with its opposition to an alliance with pro-austerity forces.[5] This contrasted it with its two main electoral rivals, the Democratic Left and the Greek Communist Party. The result was that both rivals lost ground significantly to Syriza in both May and June elections.

As a part of this approach, Syriza met with Antarsya following the 6 May elections, to discuss the prospects for an electoral united front. Syriza guaranteed Antarsya visibility in the campaign and its political independence. Antarsya declined, as was its right. It decided instead to stand separately, arguing that it could raise a more coherent programme for resistance to austerity. However, Antarsya was in no position to capitalise on its basis in industrial struggles through electoral intervention and was always destined to get a tiny proportion of the vote. At best, it would use the election to raise propaganda but make zero impact on polling day, and would be in no position to relate positively to the popular call for a government of the left.[6]

The fact that the call for left unity pivoted on the question of governmental power may be difficult for revolutionaries. But in the absence of

---

4:   For background on Syriza, see Marlière, 2012; Davanellos, 2008; 2012; and MacFhearraigh 2012.
5:   See Alexis Tsipras's comments in Gilson, 2011.
6:   Worse than this, the logic of *some* of Antarsya's supporters was ridiculously sectarian. Thus Syriza represents "a rather right reformism" and is "the last chance of the national as well as the international system...to save the situation with something akin to 'normal' methods". See Kloke, 2012.

soviet power or any equivalent, this demand resonated with Greek workers. The same call is likely to reverberate in other situations, where austerity combines with the breakdown of social democracy. Finding a way to respond to it constructively is extremely important. This is the problem with the analysis hinging on the typology of "left reformism". It isn't fundamentally incorrect; it's just that insofar as it allows one to explain the success of certain types of formation without referring concretely to what they are saying and doing, it leads one to overlook vital details.

"Fundamental contradiction"

Central to the critique of Syriza's programme is its incoherent position with regard to the EU. Syriza promises to combat austerity measures within the framework of the eurozone, which is hardwired for neoliberalism. I agree that this "fundamental contradiction", as Alex Callinicos describes it, is a real limitation in Syriza's approach. However, matters are not so simple.

First of all, there is a real dilemma for leftist forces operating in the "peripheral" countries of the eurozone. As the Irish Socialist Workers Party argued:

> Support for the EU is often fairly high in peripheral countries like Greece and Ireland. This is because the euro and the membership the EU symbolises arise out of an underdeveloped status. Many workers fear that an exit will represent a return to poverty and lower living standards.

This does not mean the revolutionary left should capitulate to such fears. Rather it should "defend working class interests—no matter what the EU thinks".[7] Tactically, then, it makes sense for the left to axe its slogans not on the question of eurozone membership, but rather on the immediate issue of resistance to austerity measures which press against the limits of what the eurozone rulers can tolerate. In which case, the logic of running a no-hope electoral campaign that differentiates primarily on the question of a voluntary exit from the eurozone is all the more mysterious.

The only detailed programme for a "Grexit" that we as a party or tendency have identified with is that outlined by Costas Lapavitsas and others.[8] Formally, this is a left-populist agenda for rescuing Greek capitalism by resituating it on a national path of redevelopment outside the eurozone. However, Alex Callinicos has identified it as potentially a

---

7:   SWP Ireland, 2012.
8:   See Lapavitsas and others, 2012.

"transitional programme", as its demands imply a confrontation with capitalism. But as Grace Lally has suggested, it depends on the context and by whom such demands are raised.[9] Greece is not in a revolutionary situation, and revolutionaries are not in a position to take the leadership of the working class. Nor is the "Grexit" agenda a likely basis for united front action or a government programme. The question, then, is what is concretely gained by making such an agenda a point of division on the left?

This is not to say that Syriza's position should not be criticised. Within Syriza itself there is growing support for more critical policies towards the EU—both among revolutionaries and on the Synaspismos left. The most pro-EU forces actually split with Fotis Kouvelis to form the Democratic Left. Prior to the elections Syriza had settled on the formulation "Not one sacrifice for the euro". In practice, leading Syriza politicians tended to adopt a more conciliatory stance during the elections. But even then they held to commitments such as repealing the memorandum which implied a confrontation with the EU's leaders. I think the revolutionary left ought to have taken Syriza up on its promises and struggled to make that confrontation a reality— first, by supporting Syriza's call for the election of a left government.

Conclusion

The key problem posed by this conjuncture is how we can, as Stathis Kouvelakis put it, articulate a series of "workable intermediate objectives" between reformist minimum programmes and revolutionary maximalism. This journal's debate on "transitional programmes" represents one possible attempt to square the circle. However, no one on the left has as yet alighted on a coherent solution. In practice, we are all pursuing "left reformist" agendas, in the hope that the ensuing class struggles and crises will provide the means (popular self-organisation, workers' rebellion) to turn them into tools for transition. Until such a time as institutions of popular power develop which are capable of posing a threat to capitalism, the question will recur, and it will focus mainly on the question of governmental power.

In this context, I think that Syriza's attempt to answer the question by proposing a united government of the left is a valuable step in a pedagogical process. It is a step that I think revolutionaries ought to have supported wholeheartedly.

9: Callinicos, 2010; Lally, 2011.

References

Callinicos, Alex, 2010, "Austerity Politics", *International Socialism 128* (autumn), www.isj.org.uk/
?id=678

Callinicos, Alex, 2012, "The Second Coming of the Radical Left", *International Socialism 135*
(summer), www.isj.org.uk/?id=819

Davanellos, Antonis, 2008, "Greek workers move left", *International Socialist Review*, 59 (May-
June), www.isreview.org/issues/59/rep-greece.shtml

Davanellos, Antonis, 2012, "Where did Syriza come from?", *Socialist Worker* (US) (17 May),
http://socialistworker.org/2012/05/17/where-did-syriza-come-from

Gilson, George, 2011, "Warding Off a 'Social Catastrophe'", *Athens News* (2 October),
http://www.athensnews.gr/issue/13463/48402

Harman, Chris, 1979, "Crisis of the Revolutionary Left", *International Socialism 4* (spring),
www.marxists.org/archive/harman/1979/xx/eurevleft.html

Kloke, Andreas, 2012, "Answer to the statement of the FI on Greece" (1 June),
http://4thinternational.blogspot.co.uk/2012/06/andreas-kloke-answer-to-statement-
of-fi.html

Kouvelakis, Stathis, 2011, "Facing the Crisis: the Strategic Perplexity of the Left", *International
Socialism 130* (spring), www.isj.org.uk/?id=727

Lally, Grace, 2011, "Discussing the Alternatives", *International Socialism 129* (winter),
www.isj.org.uk/?id=708

Lapavitsas, Costas, and others, 2012, *Crisis in the Eurozone* (Verso).

MacFhearraigh, Donal, 2012, "SYRIZA and the Rise of Radical Left-Reformism in Europe",
Irish Marxist Review, volume 1, number 2, http://irishmarxistreview.net/index.php/imr/
article/view/21

Marlière, Philippe, 2012, "Syriza est l'expression d'une nouvelle radicalité à
gauche", interview with Stathis Kouvélakis, Le blog de Philippe Marlière (6 June),
www.blogs.mediapart.fr/blog/philippe-marliere

SWP Ireland, 2012, "Greece and the advance of the left" (21 May), www.swp.ie/content/
greece-and-advance-left

Greece after the elections

Panos Garganas

Less than three months into its term, the new Greek government is faced with a "hot autumn" of resistance. Helena Smith predicted this in the *Guardian* in early August and by the end of the month it was more of a reality than a prophecy.[1]

Bank workers at the Agricultural Bank (ATE) and the Hellenic Postbank (TT) came out on strike against privatisation. Then 24 August saw the largest anti-racist/anti-Nazi demo in Athens yet, as thousands of immigrants and locals (5,000 according to the police, probably four times as many in reality) took to the streets to protest against mass arrests, beatings and one murder. A national demonstration against the cuts on 8 September in Thessaloniki set the tone, and on 12 September, the day primary schools started, a teachers' strike turned into a broader movement involving hospital and local government workers. The unions have called for another general strike on 26 September to coincide with the vote in parliament on the new austerity package.

Back in June there had been a collective sigh of relief in the ruling circles across Europe when the Greek Tories of New Democracy (ND) narrowly beat the Coalition of the Radical Left (Syriza) into first place at the polls. The coalition government of ND with Pasok (the Greek equivalent of New Labour) and Dimar (the Democratic Left party that had split from Syriza) was formed on the basis of renegotiating the terms of the

---

1:    Smith, 2012.

Memorandum of Understanding with the Troika (the European Central Bank, European Commission and International Monetary Fund) with a view to lightening the unbearable burden of austerity.

In practice, the new prime minister, Antonis Samaras, promised to try to convince the Troika to agree to an "elongation", ie spreading the next round of cuts over four rather than two years. But, he argued, before the Greek government can convince its creditors, it has to prove its credibility by showing determination in the implementation of the existing memorandum.

This means a package worth about €11.9 billion in cuts in 2013-14. The cuts may have to be revised for the worse, as the recession is hitting the fiscal deficit and the memorandum insists on its reduction. There is a clause in the memorandum that opens a window for an "elongation" and Samaras was pinning his hopes on the German chancellor, Angela Merkel, agreeing to activate this. An official visit to Berlin and Paris on 24-25 August drew a predictable reply: first must come the pain and then we shall see.

So Samaras is stuck with the same old task that proved the undoing of his predecessors, George Papandreou and Lucas Papademos: lifting the economy out of recession while imposing massive new cuts in the face of bitter resistance from the working class. In private he must be praying that the *Financial Times* got it right when it wrote at the end of August:

> If markets doubt that the euro will survive intact, it is because they are pessimistic about Germany's willingness to let the ECB deploy its full power to keep the governments of peripheral Europe liquid. More than many appreciate, that disagreement has been settled—and won by Mario Draghi [president of the ECB]... Madrid's and Rome's short-term borrowing costs have dropped precipitously.[2]

Apart from keeping his fingers crossed, Samaras has set about attacking workers' resistance viciously. He sent the police to attack the steel workers' strike and to tear gas local government workers when they tried to lead a demo with garbage collection vehicles. But the worst campaign was against immigrants. Nikos Dendias, the minister for public order, has tried to disorient anger with such an attack. "The country is perishing," he claimed on television. "This is the biggest invasion since the Dorians entered Greece 4,000 years ago."

During the first three weeks of August police rounded up 7,500 black and Asian people and detained 2,000 for deportation. This gave the signal for

---

2:   *Financial Times*, 2012.

a series of attacks by Nazis, some in police stations. A young Pakistani worker in the oil refineries of Aspropyrgos had his nails squeezed with a pincer by police. Nazi thugs carried out other attacks on the streets. A young Iraqi was killed on 12 August in a knife attack near Omonoia Square in Athens.

It was this brutality that provoked the anti-Nazi explosion on 24 August and put the government on the back foot. It is now up to the left to seize the initiative as the strike movement revives.

How is the left responding? The Communist Party (KKE) is in retreat after its poor showing in the parliamentary elections. It doesn't see the class advancing after the massive swing to the left. Accordingly, it instructed the steel workers' leadership to call an end to the strike. It also supported the ATE union officials stopping the bank workers' strike in the middle of August. There was a tiny report of the 24 August demo in the party daily, *Rizospastis*.

What about the victorious wing of the left, Syriza? Here it is the right wing of the leadership that has made the running. The party spokesperson Panos Skourletis instructed Syriza cadre that they must be careful when they make statements to the press: "We cannot speak in the same way as we did when we had 4 percent of the vote now that we have 27 percent." This piece of advice was targeted at left wingers who spoke of a "people's default" as a last weapon for the poor.

There was no similar rebuke for George Stathakis, a new deputy and one of Syriza's key economic strategists, who argued in an interview that the best course is to support EU plans for a banking union. Syriza had campaigned on the promise that there must be a strong nationalised sector in the Greek banking system, but Stathakis watered this down, explaining, "This wouldn't be a nationalisation properly speaking, just one person to supervise the system".[3]

Syriza leader Alexis Tsipras had been interviewed by Reuters immediately after the 17 June election:

Asked about strategy after Sunday's election, Tsipras signalled that Syriza would not call its supporters onto the streets to protest against the austerity measures. The bloc of 12 leftist groupings would instead focus its energy on creating "a shield of protection for those on the margins".

"Solidarity and resistance are both important, but right now solidarity is the most important," he said. "Our role is to be inside and outside parliament,

---

3:    Perrigueur, 2012.

applauding anything positive and condemning all that is negative and proposing alternatives".[4]

A little later Tsipras went on to have a meeting with Shimon Peres, the president of Israel, without any official statement on what was discussed. This provoked an angry letter from Tasos Kourakis, a Syriza MP who was on the flotilla that tried to break the blockade of Gaza in May 2010. Nine activists were killed when Israel attacked the flotilla.

All in all, the Syriza leadership has been trying to formulate the familiar tactic of posing as a "government in waiting", an opposition that has responsible policies and calls on people to use their vote rather than mobilise to change things through direct action. This, of course, is a line that is difficult to impose on an angry, militant and radicalised working class. Syriza trade union officials too called for an end to the ATE strike. This did not stop Postbank workers from starting their own strike. Tsipras joined the demonstrators in Thessaloniki. It will be a tug of war between a rebellious rank and file and a leadership set on winning over the "moderate voters".

Where should revolutionaries stand on this? Richard Seymour suggests that the characterisation of Syriza as "left reformist" is a reasonable depiction of the rough balance of forces but thinks that it may be glossing over important details. I agree that we need to move from the general to the concrete but when he attempts to do that his sources let him down. He seems to have an idealised version of Syriza in mind.

Synaspismos is by far the dominant component of Syriza and was created on an explicitly reformist strategy that remains to this day. The founding father was Leonidas Kyrkos, the architect of a coalition government with the Greek Tories back in 1989. The Maoist group, the Communist Organisation of Greece (KOE), is *not* the second largest organisation in the coalition. The people who had the courage to break from Pasok and join Syriza play a far more important role, but it is not fair to say they represent a non-reformist element.

Finally, we have to keep in mind that the proposal for a government of the left was addressed mainly and concretely to Dimar, as the only other pro-European section of the left. Syriza's position on the EU and the euro means it can work with Dimar but not with the KKE. The thought that Dimar ministers who now serve under Samaras would be part of a government of the left is not very encouraging.

4:   Stott and Kyriakidou, 2012.

I agree with Richard that the question of governmental power may be difficult for revolutionaries. All the more reason why we should be careful to avoid the mistakes of the past. Chris Harman reminds us what happened in Italy and France back in the 1970s when revolutionaries tried to base their perspective on an electoral left victory leading to socialist or revolutionary change. We need to take that experience on board.[5] Richard's argument that it is a mistake for revolutionaries to highlight the necessity of breaking with the eurozone because this currently lacks popular support is a dangerous one because it assumes that consciousness will remain static in a situation that continues to polarise between the radical left and the extreme right.

The Front of the Anticapitalist Left (Antarsya) with its small forces and the Socialist Workers Party (SEK) among them have been at the forefront of the efforts to bring the movement in Greece back onto the streets, and to build the strikes and occupations. Our role in developing the anti-Nazi movement and defending immigrant communities from racist attacks is widely acknowledged. The urgency of this task became even clearer as the first opinion polls after the summer show Golden Dawn rising to near 10 percent of the vote. This is the result of a desperate government pushing a viciously racist agenda through both propaganda and police attacks. But the same polls show the swing to the left continuing with Syriza overtaking New Democracy and KKE above Dimar. The potential both to resist the austerity onslaught and to counter the fascist threat is there. We are actively seeking to involve every force on the left for joint action in this direction, so that we can make the Samaras government even more short-lived than its immediate predecessors.[6]

5:    Harman, 1979, and 1988, chapter 16.

6:    Just to set the record straight, a delegation of Antarsya met with Tsipras three days after the 6 May elections, while Alexis had a mandate to form a government, after Samaras had failed to do so (the Greek constitution empowers the President of the Republic to invite in turn the leaders of the first, second and third parties in that order to form a government). Tsipras was attacked by New Democracy for this meeting, as Antarsya was not a parliamentary party and therefore "he was wasting everybody's time". Contrary to what Richard suggests, no electoral pact was on the agenda. The main point of agreement between the two sides was a decision to mobilise people if the pro-memorandum parties attempted to form a government. Eventually such attempts failed and fresh elections were called for 17 June. The report on this meeting in *Avgi* (the daily of the left that supports Syriza) is here: www.avgi.gr/ArticleActionshow.action?articleID=687642 and the communiqué of Antarsya is here: www.antarsya.gr/node/354.

References

Financial Times, 2012, "A Berlin-Frankfurt Alliance for the Euro" (30 August), www.ft.com/cms/s/0/5337f500-f295-11e1-86e0-00144feabdc0.html

Harman, Chris, 1979, "The Crisis of the European Revolutionary Left", *International Socialism 4* (spring), www.marxists.org/archive/harman/1979/xx/eurevleft.htm

Harman, Chris, 1988, *The Fire Last Time: 1968 and After* (Bookmarks).

Perrigueur, Elizabeth, 2012, "Syriza est favorable à une union bancaire en Europe", *La Tribune* (29 June), www.latribune.fr/actualites/economie/union-europeenne/20120629 trib000706497/-syriza-est-favorable-a-une-union-bancaire-en-europe-.html

Smith, Helena, 2012, "Greece braced for 'hottest autumn yet' over round of new spending cuts", *Guardian* (9 August), www.guardian.co.uk/world/2012/aug/09/greece-braced-protests-spending-cuts

Stott, Michael, and Dina Kyriakidou, 2012, "Greek Rage to Force Bailout Changes", *Reuters* (19 June), www.reuters.com/article/2012/06/19/us-greece-election-tsipras-idUSBRE85I13820120619

Emancipation by dispossession?
A rejoinder to Federico Fuentes

Jeffery R Webber

In his response to my recent article on the TIPNIS conflict in Bolivia, Federico Fuentes characteristically positions himself well to the right of Uruguayan social democrat and prominent political ecologist Eduardo Gudynas.[1] For if Gudynas never offers a satisfying critique of capitalism in his analytical interventions on the "new extractivism" of centre-left governments in South America, he does, at a minimum, understand the role played by the Morales regime within the logic of endless accumulation and expansion inherent in the world system as it is currently organised.[2] In 2010 and 2011 South America achieved an average growth rate of 6.4 percent, with Paraguay hitting 15 percent, Argentina 9.2 percent and Uruguay 8 percent. After a dip in 2009 Bolivia's economy picked up again to 4.1 percent in 2010, and grew at 5 percent in the first semester of 2011.

A set of unique regional dynamics in South America over the last decade, related to patterns of accumulation elsewhere in the world market (notably high rates of growth in China), has set off a concerted shift towards the acceleration of mining, oil and gas extraction, and agro-industrial mono-crop cultivation throughout the continent. In other words, the uneven mutations of the ongoing economic crisis on a world scale have not resulted in low growth rates on an aggregate level across South America—at least not yet. Similar to the

1:   Fuentes, 2012, responding to Webber, 2012.
2:   Gudynas, 2012.

period normally described as "neoliberal", massive multinational corporations are deeply imbricated in the extension of extraction at the heart of this primary commodity led growth everywhere in the region. Those cases in which centre-left regimes have entered into joint contracts between state-owned enterprises and multinationals, and negotiated relatively higher royalties and taxes on these extractive activities, are no exception.

Compensatory states

Skimming from the rent generated, many South American governments have established what Gudynas terms "compensatory states", whose legitimacy rests on the modest redistribution achieved through the priming of often already existing cash-transfer programmes to the extremely poor, without touching the underlying class structure of society. Indeed, the very reproduction of these political economies depends upon states prioritising the maintenance and security of private property rights and juridical environments in which multinationals can profit. Is this what Fuentes means by "regaining sovereign control over vital natural resources and initial steps towards endogenous industrialisation" and "rolling back the neoliberal project in Bolivia"?

Because the legitimacy function of relatively petty handouts runs on the blood of extraction, the compensatory state increasingly becomes a repressive state, on behalf of capital, as the expansion of extraction necessarily accelerates what David Harvey calls accumulation by dispossession, and the variegated forms of resistance it regularly spawns.[3] In the representative case of the TIPNIS in Bolivia, the steamrolling of the rights to self-governance of indigenous communities resisting highway construction through their territory illustrates the coercive wing of the compensatory state in action—somehow, though, I've missed, according to Fuentes, the ways in which Morales has established and protected novel "forms of

---

3:   Geographer David Harvey's concept of accumulation by dispossession is an elaboration of Marx's "primitive accumulation". Marx writes of those epoch-making "moments when great masses of men are suddenly and forcibly torn from their means of subsistence, and hurled onto the labour market as free, unprotected and rightless proletarians. The expropriation of the agricultural producer, of the peasant from the soil, is the basis of the whole process. The history of this expropriation assumes different aspects in different countries, and runs through its various phases in different orders of succession, and at different historical epochs." See Marx, 1977. For Harvey, Marx rightly highlighted these processes of capital accumulation "based upon predation, fraud, and violence", but incorrectly imagined them to be exclusively features of a "primitive" or "original" stage of capitalism. With the concept of accumulation by dispossession, Harvey wants to point rather to the continuity of predatory practices that have risen dramatically to the surface once again in the era of neoliberalism. See Harvey, 2003, p144.

self-government by indigenous communities". Indigenous self-government in Bolivia is to be defended by Morales, it would seem, only when the claims are to territories marginal to the state's development project.

The compensatory state co-opts and coerces in response to such signs of opposition, and builds an accompanying ideological apparatus to defend multinationals—an ideology in which communities of resistance are vilified as internal enemies acting in concert with the interests, or even in the pay, of various instruments of imperialism. The discursive gestures of state officials, of course, safely set to one side the obvious imperial character of the dispossessing activities of multinational corporations—now called "partners" rather than "bosses" in development—within the matrix of the new extractivism. Fuentes is, within the relatively small English language world of the international far left, an important functionary on behalf of this ideological production. As such, he is one of very few leftist intellectuals knowledgeable about Bolivian dynamics who persist enthusiastically in citing the recent musings of the country's vice-president Álvaro García Linera as if they were credible analytical outputs.[4]

The people, social class and imperialism

One pillar of this theoretical point of departure is the subsuming of social class within the category of "the people", the latter, in turn, finding its unproblematic expression in the Morales government. "Whether we, like García Linera, regard the TIPNIS controversy [in Bolivia] as a conflict within the people," Fuentes concludes, "or like Webber take sides against the Bolivian government in this matter, we must not fail to oppose the intrusion of imperialist governments and agencies into the internal affairs of the Bolivian people".[5]

4:   See, in particular, García Linera, 2011. The recent work of García Linera needs to be distinguished from his often luminescent writings of the late 1990s and early 2000s. Again, consistent with the rest of Fuentes' work on Bolivia, in his critique of my TIPNIS article one will struggle in vain to find a source cited by Fuentes on the ostensible "advances" of the "process of change" that isn't directly linked to the government itself or to journalists (in this case Stefanoni) with a long and well-known connection to official sources. Stefanoni is a close friend of Álvaro García Linera and his frequent collaborator on books and articles on Bolivian politics.

5:   One nefarious implication here, obviously, is that unlike Fuentes I am not really against imperialism because I also speak of class contradictions within Bolivia. It is worthwhile to reiterate here the opposition to this perspective I offered in the original article: "The implied lesson here—it is not sufficient for activists and intellectuals in the Global North to condemn and fight the imperialism of our governments; we must also close our eyes to contradiction, shut our mouths, and play the role of Evo's loyal soldiers abroad. International working class

Because Fuentes proceeds without any conceptualisation of the specificity of capitalist social relations, or any rootedness in the history of Marxist engagement with the question of the peasantry, he doesn't see anything novel about intensifying class stratification and the effect it has had on the unfolding dynamics of the TIPNIS conflict. For Fuentes, its rhythms, logic and dynamics are mysteriously incomprehensible and utterly contingent. Out of this confusion emerge astonishingly ahistorical claims about the basically unchanging character of rural life across millennia and different modes of production, and an absurd charge that my entire analysis rests on crudely moralistic foundations: "One of the most questionable aspects of Webber's piece is his effort to divide indigenous movements between 'good' ones [his words, not mine], which he says are 'non-capitalist' communities[6] waging class war...and 'bad' ones [again, his words] allied with the MAS." For Fuentes, "peasant populations have always, everywhere, been stratified along class and income lines", so it is safe to ignore entirely my summary of changes in the country's agrarian relations over the last several decades, which indicates, among other things, an acceleration of what Marx called primitive accumulation during the neoliberal epoch that has not stalled under Morales. It's best not to try to understand the complexity of social relations driving the TIPNIS conflict at different scales—local, regional, nation-state and international—but rather to defer to the government and its defence of "the people".

Another strange absence recurs throughout Fuentes' text—the hierarchical world market and multinational capitals in his thinking on imperialism. To select one especially telling example, readers of his critique will have been

solidarity, on this view, means parroting the communiqués of the presidential palace in La Paz and aligning ourselves with Bolivian embassies in our countries. The palace and the embassy almost *become* the Bolivian masses. We must observe a stern silence as regards explosions of independent working class, peasant and indigenous resistance against the impositions of a reconstituted neoliberalism in Bolivia. Better still, when faced with a struggle like that in TIPNIS, we ought to tip our hats to their legitimate demands, while portraying the movement as largely a by-product of 'green imperialism'. The endogenous linear developmentalism of García Linera's Andean-Amazonian strategy—a veritable green light for the steamrolling of TIPNIS—is magically eclipsed in this view."

6:    It would be interesting to know if Fuentes would challenge the empirical basis of what I argue, precisely: "On the other side, that is in TIPNIS to the North, we encounter the largely non-capitalist social relations of the Mojeños-Trinitarios, Chimanes, and Yuracarés—that is, communities based on collective self-reproduction through small-scale agricultural activities, the extraction of forest resources, and artisanal production." Fuentes may be conflicted here, as my argument draws on the empirical evidence of a book on the TIPNIS written by Pablo Stefanoni and Álvaro García Linera, before the latter became vice-president.

interested to learn that the imperatives of the world market have no bearing on prices of natural gas produced in the country, and multinationals operating in the country simply take orders from the Bolivian government: "While transnationals technically extract the majority of Bolivia's gas, they do so as contractors hired by the state, which determines the quantity and the price of every single drop of Bolivian gas that is produced".[7] The only agents worth considering in Fuentes' understanding of imperialism are the multifaceted tentacles of the US state. I'm charged, here as elsewhere, with "overlook[ing] the real role of the Santa Cruz oligarchy and US imperialism".[8]

From the other sides of the analysis, the only anti-imperialist agent of note, it appears, is the Bolivian state, which, again, embodies the people insofar as significant parts of it are under the control of Morales's party, the *Movimiento al Socialismo* (Movement Towards Socialism, MAS). From these first principles, then, Fuentes rules out the possibility that the indigenous communities of resistance in the TIPNIS are themselves on the front line of anti-imperial struggle in direct confrontation with extractive capital, the property and investment rights of which are being protected by the Bolivian state, not out of an "error" committed by the MAS government, but rather because its political economy depends on this capital for its very reproduction. He also rules out the possibility of the complexity of a situation in which the Bolivian state sometimes finds itself simultaneously acting as partial antagonist vis-á-vis the US state, and facilitator vis-á-vis different multinational capitals and other imperial and sub-imperial states. These are elementary points made by many critical observers of Bolivia's intensifying extractive sectors. But they won't be unearthed in the pamphlets of García Linera.

The new extractivism in Bolivia

The logic of the new extractivism has its particular expressions in the Bolivian case, most of which are made entirely invisible through the analytical prism adopted by Fuentes. In terms of natural gas extraction, it pays to remember that in the first administration of Gonzalo Sánchez de Lozada (1993-7) the Bolivian state attempted to extend the area designated for gas exploration and exploitation to approximately 13 million hectares. When this initiative was defeated through indigenous resistance in different areas of the Amazon, the multinational petroleum corporations were forced to

---

7:    For a realistic account of the gas sector and the role of multinationals therein, see Fernández Terán, 2012.
8:    For a more extensive refutation of Fuentes' consistent manipulation and simplification of my arguments, as well as his radically reductionist treatment of imperialism in the current period, see our exchange in *International Socialist Review*, Fuentes, 2011, and Webber, 2011.

concentrate on their mega-gasfields in the south of the country, above all in the department of Tarija. At the end of 2011, however, Morales had taken up the defeated mantle of Sánchez de Lozada, and proposed the extension of gas exploration and exploitation to roughly 12 million hectares—an area four times as great as that in 2009. Of this area, close to 50 percent was conceded entirely to multinationals. New government measures introduced in 2012 will likely amplify this area significantly, bringing the level of extraction of gas in the country to unprecedented levels.[9]

Likewise, in mining, spokespeople for the Morales government have announced initiatives for the large-scale expansion of mining activities beyond those in the traditional zones of the *altiplano*, or western high plateau, where mining has been under way since the colonial era. Much of this new mining will involve opening new frontiers into the Amazon.[10]

Similar to other cases of dispossession from Mexico to Chile, the geographies being encroached upon in Bolivia for extending gas and mineral extraction, together with the growth of agro-industrial production (the majority of which is soya production under the control of Brazilian capital), include protected areas of biodiversity and indigenous territories which are currently among the last regions of the country relatively free of industrial and commercial activity, and which are, at the moment, governed by ecologically sustainable economies. It is the logic of accumulation by dispossession at the heart of this tripartite process—mining, gas and agro-industry—that has generated the TIPNIS conflict, and which is likely to generate many more social conflicts into the future. It used to be the case that the theoreticians of the Latin American left opposed enclave economies ruled by the interests of multinational capital, and argued instead for building paths towards socialist revolution; but today the likes of Fuentes are dangerously reversing this axiomatic point of departure, accepting as the parameters of transformation the crumbs dispensed by a compensatory state, which in Fuentes' vision of the world appears capable of regulating capitalism, a mode of production that can be benevolent if only the government is on the side of "the people".

Agrarian reform?

In challenging my characterisation of the extreme limits of agrarian reform under Morales, Fuentes poses a rhetorical question: "Is it 'inconsequential' that in its first five years the Morales government presided over the redistribution or titling of 91 million hectares of land to over 900,000 members of

9:   Gandarillas Gonzales, 2012, pp29-31.
10:   Gandarillas Gonzales, 2012, p30.

indigenous peasant communities?" And, elsewhere in his critique Fuentes claims that "over 35 million hectares of land has been handed [sic] as communitarian property or placed under the direct control of the original indigenous inhabitants".

Now, it is undoubtedly true that with the election of the MAS in December 2005 land reform was placed squarely back on the political agenda by the social movements. The debate around agrarian reform and what form it would take was among the most heated components of political life in the first few months of Morales's first administration. Rumours and threats proliferated, with various right wing, large landowners' organisations rooted in the lowland departments of Santa Cruz, Pando and Beni even threatening to take up arms against the state in response to any state initiative that might impinge upon their property rights.

According to the MAS government, there were three legitimate agrarian sectors that deserved state support: (i) large-scale agro-industrial exporters; (ii) small-scale family peasant production, partially for the market and partially for subsistence; and (iii) communal indigenous landholdings. The government's contention was that a certain harmonious balance, or virtuous circle of mutual benefit, could be maintained across these different sectors, rather than there being an inherently conflict-ridden class antagonism structured into their competing interests.[11] This position has been essentially maintained throughout both administrations of the Morales regime to date, as expressed in the Plan Nacional de Desarrollo.

For the MAS government, the construction of a new model of agrarian development signifies a commitment to a "plural and diverse" agricultural economy, with state, communitarian, cooperative and capitalist forms of social property relations coexisting alongside one another. However, the plural economy, from the government's perspective, can only act as the basis for a sustainable and integrated model of rural development if it prioritises the strengthening of the economic, technical and institutional capacities of those social groups historically subject to social and economic exclusion: indigenous communities, peasants and the landless.[12] By 2010 the Ministry of Rural Development and Land claimed that the distribution of rural properties undertaken to that point had already achieved a "communitarian renewal of agrarian reform" and in a short while would achieve "an equitable and inclusive structure for all economic actors", which would result in "practically two thirds of the national territory being in the hands of the country's

---

11: See *La Prensa*, 17 May 2006.
12: MDRAyMA, 2007, p19.

majority, with the state having control of a half of the remaining third part of the national territory, and the sector of individual property owners linked to agro-industrial activity having access to the other half of the last third".[13] The notion of a conflict-free, plural agrarian economy appears in the new constitution as well as in the two major pieces of legislation introduced by the government to address agrarian reform—the *Ley de Reconducción Comunitaria de la Reforma Agraria* (Law for the Communitarian Renewal of Agrarian Reform, LRCRA) passed in late 2006, and the *Ley de la Revolución Productiva Comunitaria Agropecuaria* (Law of Productive Communitarian Agricultural Revolution, LRPCA), passed in 2011.

If this is the transformative discursive apparatus of the government's agrarian policy framework, in practice the continuities with neoliberalism in the implementation of such legislation have been rather sharper than any ruptures. Indeed, a pattern of reconstituted neoliberalism has been quite decisively demonstrated in the most detailed report on the political economy of the Bolivian countryside under Morales available to date, Control Ciudadano's *Reconducción comunitaria de la reforma agraria y producción agrícola*, published in March 2012. Putting it mildly, it offers an interesting contrast to García Linera's inflated account of agrarian reform on which Fuentes, as in other areas of his analysis, relies heavily.

Of the many insights in this report, I'll indicate but two. First, empirical trends in crop production demonstrate that the neoliberal export-oriented model of agrarian capitalism—initiated in earnest in the late 1980s, rooted in large-scale agro-industrial enterprises and geographically situated in Santa Cruz—has been consolidated rather than overturned under the MAS administration. Small-scale peasant production has continued to lose relevance. The LRCRA amounted to little more than the introduction of a select number of modest reforms to the neoliberal INRA law of 1996, and it was designed to better operationalise its predecessor rather than to undo its underlying logic. Crop patterns are one indication of continuity. Since the mid-1990s the aggregate trend in agricultural production in Bolivia has been slow and moderate expansion. The slow but relatively steady uptick in agricultural production can be explained essentially through the growth of four specific industrial crops: sugar cane, soya, corn and sorghum. If these four crops are removed from the equation, agricultural production has been in a transparent process of stagnation.[14] During the government of the MAS crops that are usually catalogued as industrial—because

---

13: Quoted in Control Ciudadano, 2012, p12.
14: Control Ciudadano, 2012, pp2-3.

they undergo some level of manufacturing or industrial processing in preparation for human or animal consumption and are produced, by and large, under capitalist relations of production—account for the bulk of agricultural production in the country (79.1 percent in the 2005-6 agricultural season, and 80.4 percent in 2010-11). Moreover, two export-driven crops alone—soya (40 percent) and sugar cane (36 percent)—account for 76 percent of the total growth in volume of production between 2005 and 2011.[15] On the other hand, the portion of overall agricultural production of those crops in which peasant production continues to be important (fruit, vegetables, tubers and fodder) has trended toward irrelevance.[16]

Second, to return for a moment to the passage from the Ministry of Rural Development and Land quoted above, it may be close to true that soon roughly two thirds of the national territory will be formally in the hands of the indigenous peasantry of the country. This tells us nothing of the quality of the land they will control, however. Nor does it tell us anything relevant about the third of the territory that will remain in the hands of the medium and large agro-industrial firms. This third, in reality, constitutes the best lands for agricultural production and ranching in the country. Because, as the report demonstrates in exhaustive detail, the MAS government has not touched their monopolisation of this territory and has no plans to do so, the alleged "equality" of distribution in the plural economy will not translate into "equality" of quality lands.[17]

Conclusion

Even those Marxists like Emiliano López and Francisco Vértiz, who insist on emphasising the differences between at least three emergent national development models in Latin America since the regional crisis of neoliberalism began in the late 1990s,[18] recognise that in the current world conjuncture,

---

15: Control Ciudadano, 2012, p5.

16: Control Ciudadano, 2012, p3.

17: Control Ciudadano, 2012, p13.

18: The first of these, according to this account, is that which maintains a clear continuity with the policies associated with the neoliberal ideal. In this group we encounter Mexico, Chile, Perú, Colombia and large chunks of Central America. A second group of countries—which principally includes Argentina, Brazil and Uruguay—is that which has adopted a national-popular rhetoric directed against international financial capital and certain domestic oligarchic sectors. In embracing such rhetorical positions, these countries have distanced themselves from the neoliberalism of the 1990s. Lastly, there are those countries—Bolivia, Ecuador and Venezuela—with transitional projects. In this category the rhetoric of anti-neoliberalism and anti-imperialism is more pronounced, and the positive position advanced by these governments is potentially anti-systemic.

above and beyond their differences, each of these three models fall into line with a "new international consensus" which assigns Latin America to the role of exporting natural resources. Such an insertion in the world market restores, if in novel ways, the role the region played historically in the geopolitical order at an international level.[19]

More interestingly still, we need to seriously entertain the hypothesis, recently advanced by José Seoane and Clara Algramati, that the particular logic of expression of the global crisis in the periphery of the world system is a radical deepening of processes of accumulation by dispossession.[20] That is to say, more specifically, between 2008 and 2011 we have witnessed a new cycle of commodification, appropriation, and assertion of control on the part of large capitals of a series of collective goods across the global periphery, but especially the commodification and appropriation of the common goods of nature. According to Seoane and Algramati there is still a direly insufficient consciousness of the scale and magnitude of this offensive, as well as the forces behind it. Reflecting on the trends of foreign direct investment (FDI) into Latin America since the world crisis began to unfold in 2008, we can at least begin to understand the necessity of further exploration of the issue. With the exception of 2009, when aggregate GDP across Latin America and the Caribbean momentarily dipped, the period between 2008 and 2011 witnessed record volumes of FDI coming into the region—depending on the year, an increase of between 70 and 130 percent compared to the average levels obtained between 2000 and 2005.

In the mining sector FDI in 2011 reached a record high of approximately US$140 billion, a 40 percent increase on the figure for 2010 (already a massive year) and a 250 percent increase on the volume registered in 2003.[21] Seoane and Algramati stress the fact that, regardless of variations in political ideologies, most governments in the region appear intent on deepening this model, and justifying it through the suggestion that it is a logical response to the instability of the global economy, the deceleration of growth on a global scale, and the possible impacts upon public budgets and trade balances, pillars of the preceding economic cycle. This relative commonality, furthermore, finds expression in projects such as the Initiative for the Integration of the Regional Infrastructure of South America (IIRSA), the supreme importance of which Fuentes cannot seem to understand.[22] IIRSA

19: López and Vértiz, 2012.

20: Seoane and Algramati, 2012.

21: Seoane and Algramati, 2012.

22: IIRSA was launched in 2000 with the participation of 12 of South America's governments at the time. Brazil took the lead from the beginning in the initiative's planning

needs to be understood, according to Seoane and Algramati, in the context of this intensification of accumulation by dispossession in the areas of mining, gas and agro-industry throughout the region. The priority of this public infrastructural project of regional integration is to facilitate the commercial export of raw commodities. IIRSA is, therefore, yet another expression of the increasing hegemony of the extractivist-export model of development, even if it is today cloaked in an ideological guise of neo-developmentalism and growing trade with China rather than the US.

In the face of this extractivist offensive, there has been a veritable wave of protest and social resistance emerging and developing at a regional level. A vast number of movements and struggles are calling into question the extractivist-export model and its attendant violence, looting, environmental devastation and recolonisation in the form of multinational capital's power.[23] At the close of 2010, for example, one conservative estimate suggested at least 155 active mining conflicts across the region.[24]

This is the wider imperial logic that needs to be understood in order to grasp its specific manifestations on a local scale in the context of TIPNIS. Discerning the players on all sides, and their descending relations of importance, is obviously a difficult and complex matter of investigation. But Fuentes' response has taught us, at least, the path our analysis should avoid if we want a minimum of clarity regarding contemporary Bolivian dynamics.

and financing. With a current budget of just under US$1 trillion, the vision is to increase access to remote regions of South America and to spike energy-generation capacity through the construction of highways, railways, bridges, seaports and waterways—see Friedman Rudovsky, 2012. I briefly discuss the role of Brazilian sub-imperialism acting in and through IIRSA in the original article to which Fuentes is responding.

23: Seoane and Algramati, 2012.
24: Delgado Ramos, 2012, p4.

References

Control Ciudadano, 2012, *Reconducción comunitaria de la reforma agraria y producción agícola: evaluación y perspectivas* (CEDLA).

Delgado Ramos, Gian Carlo, 2012, "Extractivismo, fronteras ecológicas y geopolítica de los recursos", *América Latina en Movimiento* (March).

Fernández Terán, Roberto, 2012, "El reacomodo del poder petrolero transnacional en Bolivia", in Alejandro Almaraz and others (eds), *La mascarada del Poder* (Textos Rebeldes).

Friedman-Rudovsky, Jean, 2012, "The Bully from Brazil", *Foreign Policy* (20 July), www.foreignpolicy.com/articles/2012/07/20/the_bully_from_brazil?page=full

Fuentes, Federico, 2011, "Government, Social Movements, and Revolution in Bolivia Today", *International Socialist Review*, 76 (March-April), www.isreview.org/issues/76/debate-bolivia.shtml

Insert: Fuentes, Frederico, 2012, "The Morales Government: Neoliberalism in Disguise?', *International Socialism 134* (spring), www.isj.org.uk/?id=803

Gandarillas Gonzales, Marco A, 2012, "La ampliación de las fronteras extractivistas en Bolivia", *América Latina en Movimiento* (March).

García Linera, Álvaro, 2011, *El "onegismo", enfermedad infantil del derechismo; O cómo la reconducción del Proceso del Cambio es la restauración neoliberal* (Vicepresidencia del Estado), www.rebelion.org/docs/133285.pdf

Gudynas, Eduardo, 2012, "Estado compensador y nuevos extractivismos: Las ambivalencias del progresismo sudamericano", *Nueva Sociedad* 237 (January-February), www.nuso.org/upload/articulos/3824_1.pdf

Harvey, David, 2003, *The New Imperialism* (Oxford University Press).

La Prensa, 2006, "El Estado promoverá desarrollo de tres 'plataformas' agrarias" (17 May).

López, Emiliano, and Francisco Vértiz, 2012, "Capital transnacional y proyectos nacionales de desarrollo en América Latina: Las nuevas lógicas del extractivismo neodesarrollista", *Herramienta* 50 (July), www.herramienta.com.ar/revista-herramienta-n-50/capital-transnacional-y-proyectos-nacionales-de-desarrollo-en-america-latin

Marx, Karl, 1977, *Capital*, volume I (Vintage), www.marxists.org/archive/marx/works/1867-c1/

MDRAyMA, 2007, *Revolución rural, agraria y forestal* (Ministerio de Desarrollo Rural, Agropecuario y Medio Ambiente).

Seoane, José, and Clara Algramati, 2012, "La ofensiva extractivista en América Latina: Crisis global y alternativas", *Herramienta* 50 (July), www.herramienta.com.ar/revista-herramienta-n-50/la-ofensiva-extractivista-en-america-latina-crisis-global-y-alternativas

Webber, Jeffery R, 2011, "Fantasies Aside, It's Reconstituted Neoliberalism in Bolivia under Morales: A Rejoinder to Frederico Fuentes", *International Socialist Review*, 76 (March-April), www.isreview.org/issues/76/debate-bolivia.shtml

Webber, Jeffery R, 2012, "'Revolution Against Progress': The TIPNIS Struggle and Class Contradictions in Bolivia", *International Socialism 133* (spring), www.isj.org.uk/?id=780

Book reviews

After Carthage was destroyed
Nick Evans

Chris Wickham, **The Inheritance of Rome: A History of Europe from 400 to 1000** *(Penguin, 2009), £14.99; Peter Sarris,* **Empires of Faith: The Fall of Rome to the Rise of Islam, 500–700** *(Oxford University Press, 2011), £35*

When Chris Wickham's monumental study, *Framing the Early Middle Ages* (2005), was reviewed by Chris Harman in this journal, readers put off by its size were advised to wait for his new contribution to the *Penguin History of Europe*. Now, with the appearance of Peter Sarris's volume for the new Oxford History of Medieval Europe, they will be spoilt for choice. Sarris claims in the introduction to *Empires of Faith* that he deliberately avoided looking at Wickham's *Inheritance of Rome* for fear of "simply paraphrasing it". He need not have worried. Both books provide more in the way of continuous political narrative than some of the authors' other publications. Both chart a period which saw the collapse of the Roman Empire in the west in the 5th century and the rise of Islam in the 7th over a geographical area stretching from Ireland to Iran, and do so in ways that reveal how ordinary people participated in and experienced these extraordinary developments. However, their approaches are different, and not just because of the narrower time frame in Sarris's book.

Wickham is more explicit about his theoretical framework and methodology than Sarris. Readers of *Framing the Early Middle Ages* will recognise his characterisation of underlying social and economic changes, his simultaneous control over archaeological, documentary and literary evidence, and his clear but detailed comparisons between different European societies in the early Middle Ages. Here, though, we get an account of what change *looked* like: there are some pictures in this book. In the middle of *The Inheritance of Rome* is a chapter on architecture. Descriptions of buildings such as the 8th century Great Mosque in Damascus and a 7th century palace complex in Northumbria provide the basis for comparison between the different ways elites dealt with the Roman legacy.

We also find comparison of village sites, ranging from the stone houses of the olive oil producing peasants of Serjilla in Syria, to the simpler wooden structures in Vorbasse in Denamrk. Wickham shows that peasants in Serjilla, no less than elites in Constantinople, used buildings to score points against neighbours. Wickham as cultural historian even tells us what change *tasted* like (at least for some: western aristocrats started eating more meat), but he never lets his readers lose sight of underlying structures. At the heart of his comparison between the different villages is the question of if, when and where aristocrats were in control. The fact that they don't seem to have been in control in Serjilla may explain not only why the peasants were so rich, but also why they were so competitive: "There was more to play for" (p246).

In some ways, Sarris's book feels more old-fashioned. There is little in the way of theoretical exposition in the introduction or conclusion. The book as a whole is more dominated by accounts of coups and battles, engages slightly less with archaeological evidence, and its claim to be "unashamedly an 'Oxford' book" may not endear it to all readers. However, it makes a series of significant contributions to a historical materialist understanding of the period. For example, Sarris argues there was a far greater level of hostility to the Christian church among peasants in societies from Northumbria to Byzantium in the early Middle Ages than historians have tended to suggest. According to Sarris, this reflected anger at attempts to impose cultural change from above, but was also the product of class tensions over the process of production itself, as the church was becoming an increasingly important landowner in its own right. Sarris provides vivid examples. We are told of a 7th century Byzantine saint's life, which reports how the peasants of one village armed themselves to prevent the bishop's agent from entering, and an 8th century account of a Frankish "holy man" stabbed in his sleep by his dependent peasants for overworking them. This is a challenge to the influential argument that ascetic "holy men" helped to heal social tensions in the post-Roman world.

Class struggle is at the heart of both of these books, but Sarris and Wickham differ on where the balance of forces lay in this period. Both are agreed that the Roman senatorial aristocracy with estates scattered across the empire—"possibly the richest private landowners of all time", according to Wickham (p29)—lost most from the fragmentation of the empire in the West,

but the question is what happened below that level. In *Framing the Early Middle Ages* Wickham talked about a "peasant mode of production" operating in certain parts of Europe and the Mediterranean in this period, where peasant producers were not subjected to exploitation by aristocratic neighbours. This terminology is not used in *The Inheritance of Rome*, but the argument remains: Wickham explicitly claims that, "in the last two millennia, the period 500 to 800 was probably when aristocratic power in the west was least totalising" (p216). Perhaps the most powerful section of Wickham's book is where he shows how peasant autonomy became increasingly restricted in the following period, from 800 to 1000, although in different ways in the various regions he surveys. He argues the process happened especially dramatically in England, which he sees as having moved from being the post-Roman province with least peasant subjection in 700, to that with the most in 900.

Sarris is not so sure. First of all, he argues that provincial aristocrats below the super-rich were able to cling on to much of their landed possessions and their political power in the new "Romano-Germanic" kingdoms that emerged as the Roman Empire crumbled in the west. The institution of the church provided positions for family members who would previously have been absorbed into the imperial bureaucracy. Sarris is more inclined than Wickham to see the provincial aristocrats as active participants in the collapse of the Roman state, opting to ally themselves with "barbarian" leaders once their tax obligations to Rome seemed to outstrip its usefulness to them in providing stability. He is not only interested in elite protagonism: we read of overtaxed 4th century gold miners in the Balkans who happily point out hidden grain stores to the invading Gothic armies.

On the whole, though, the picture is one of continued aristocratic dominance. The second element of Sarris's argument, which is clearly influenced by the work of Jairus Banaji, concerns relations at the point of production itself. Sarris, unlike Wickham, argues that direct management of agricultural production by landlords in the early Middle Ages was a legacy of the late Roman period. Sarris and Banaji have developed their arguments about the exploitation of landless agricultural workers (ie wage labourers) on the basis of estate records from Egypt, but they show evidence of it happening in northern Europe too. By weaving it into a complex argument that links monetary developments, changes in the structure of the aristocracy and basic relations of exploitation, Sarris suggests a way towards a multilayered understanding of the underlying dynamic of social change in this period.

It is perhaps surprising that two books with such apparently similar aims should end up presenting such different pictures of this period. Wickham is more upfront: with his arguments and methodology, with his use of his sources and their limitations, and with his comparisons of different types of societies. Sarris moves rapidly between written sources from such different contexts and between different types of explanation, so you feel that Wickham's criticism of Marxists who "have found their focus slipping as the blurred edges of the vast cultural and political superstructure of the Roman swim into their vision" might apply to Sarris at times.* Even more bizarre is Sarris's claim, at the end of an account of the 7th century Islamic conquests which had placed them in the context of social and economic changes in the region, that the "ultimate factor behind Arab success" was

"zeal" (p274). But at his best, Sarris hints towards something that seems sometimes to be lacking in Wickham's account: a sense of change as the product of a society's internal contradictions. Wickham is so good at presenting accounts of the internal structure of societies quite different from our own that at times we seem to be left with a series of rigorously differentiated static models. The task for Marxist historians should be to find the motors for change.

The trouble with tribunals
Sarah Robertson

David Renton, **Struck Out: Why Employment Tribunals Fail Workers and What Can be Done** (Pluto, 2012), £19.99

In this new book developed from his earlier article in *International Socialism*,[†] socialist barrister David Renton examines the disparity between the ambitions of workers who bring tribunal claims and the outcomes they are likely to receive. "Where the law creates problems", he argues, "the answers are outside the law."

One of the biggest failures of the tribunal system is the failure to reinstate unfairly dismissed workers. Of over 40,000 unfair dismissal claims in 2010-1, only eight resulted in orders for reinstatement.

Where compensation is awarded, arbitrary statutory caps mean claimants are often

---

* Chris Wickham, 1984, "The Other Transition: from the Ancient World to Feudalism", *Past and Present*, 113.

† David Renton, 2009, "Tribunals and Tribulations", *International Socialism* 124 (autumn), www.isj.org.uk/?id=589

awarded significantly lower payments than their actual calculated loss. One claimant says: "I became financially in debt because I wasn't able to meet my regular domestic bills... I'm still trying to catch up on bills and things that got left. I'm trying to clear up this mess. The £3,000 was like a month's wages; it went back against the bills. It wasn't luxury money. Financially, I'm still struggling."

On top of statutory caps, employment judges tend to over-use their powers to reduce compensatory awards as a result of "deep lying anxieties that a tribunal system which was more generous to claimants would upset the proper relationship between workers and employers in the workplace".

Employment judges are overwhelmingly male, middle-aged, white, educated at public school and Oxbridge. Renton argues that this "encourages a general approach of deference towards existing property rights and towards the rights of both professionals and managers".

These judges often have to decide whether an employer acted *reasonably*. As Renton points out, "tests of reasonableness leave judges a wide discretion to decide the law according to notions of what seems right to them in a given case". Toby Topham of the Institute for Workers' Control anticipated in 1971: "An employer can, by reason of his status...always find reasons for a dismissal which a bourgeois court will accept as reasonable...in crucial cases, where legal protection may be needed by victimised workers, the tribunals would prove quite inadequate."

Policy makers, by establishing Employment Tribunals and making dismissals "a legal question rather than a trial of industrial strength" sought to reduce strikes and weaken unions. However, Renton argues

against the conclusion that the increasing number of tribunal claims since 1971 explains the falling number of strikes. He shows the major causes of strikes in the 1960s—wages and hours—continue to be resolved by industrial action rather than litigation.

More important in explaining the fall in strikes "are the legacy of the unions' setbacks in the battles of the 1980s, the anti-union laws adopted in the same period, and the failure of such union victories as there have been in recent years to give such confidence to the workers as to transform the mood in the workplace".

Rather, he argues, tribunals have filled a space left by the partial decline in industrial bargaining, "so that someone who has a genuine grievance about their work increasingly has no option but to sue".

Although Renton suggests some legislative and procedural reforms that would improve the tribunal system for workers, he concludes: "Real reform must mean taking decisions out of the hands of judges and putting them back into the context of workplace bargaining."

A question of ethics
Sean Sayers

Paul Blackledge, **Marxism and Ethics: Freedom, Desire and Revolution** *(SUNY, 2012), $80*

Ethics has been a problematic area for Marxism ever since its beginnings. Marx himself wrote very little on the topic, and what he did write seems paradoxical. On the one hand, he appears to deny that his outlook involves ethical values at all. Socialism, he insists, is not a mere ethical ideal; it is rather the real and concrete form of society that will result from the revolutionary forces currently at work in capitalist society. "The working classes have no fixed and perfect utopias to introduce…they have no ideals to realise; they have only to set at liberty the elements of the new society which have already been developed in the womb of the collapsing bourgeois society".* On the other hand, there is quite clearly a moral dimension to his criticisms of capitalist society and his vision of a socialist alternative.

These apparently conflicting strands of Marx's thought have given rise to an enormous amount of controversy among subsequent Marxist philosophers. Blackledge gives an impressively comprehensive and detailed account of these debates in this major new study. After describing the views of Marx and Engels on ethics, he then traces these controversies from the ideas of Second International figures such as Bernstein and Kautsky, and the responses of Lenin and Lukács, through the work of the Frankfurt School (Adorno, Marcuse), Sartre and the British New Left (EP Thompson, Perry Anderson, Alasdair MacIntyre), to the debates in contemporary academic philosophy. He deals not only with the ideas of recent analytic philosophers like GA Cohen and Steven Lukes, but also gives an excellent account of recent discussion by continental philosophers, including Simon Crichley, Alain Badiou and Slavoj Žižek. Interestingly, he shows how similar the ideas of these camps have been, though superficially they appear to be so different and disconnected.

* Karl Marx, 1871, *The Civil War in France*, www.marxists.org/archive/marx/works/1871/civil-war-france/index.htm

Blackledge's own position emerges from this historical account. He rejects the view that capitalism is pregnant with the socialist future as a form of historical determinism that denies human freedom and political choice, and leads to ethical "nihilism". He associates this "obstetric" view (as GA Cohen called it) particularly with the dogmatic certainties of "Stalinism", though in fact it is more widespread than anything that can be encompassed even by such a catch-all term, and comes from Marx himself as the quotation above illustrates.

However, as the revolutionary potential of the working class has increasingly come into question, many have argued that the Marxist critique of capitalism and its vision of socialism are embodied in universal ethical principles rather than on problematic historical grounds. Blackledge rejects this sort of ethical approach as well. Marxism does involve an ethic, he maintains, an ethic of freedom—but this is not an abstract moral doctrine derived from disinterested or universal principles. The values of Marxism arise out of the concrete situation and actual struggle of the working class to overthrow capitalism and to create socialism. When Marx says that the working class has "no ideals" to realise "he should not be understood…as suggesting that Marxists have no vision of a better future", but rather that their values are "immanent" and "rooted in the real movement of things" (p133).

This may seem to lead inevitably to relativism. However, the revolutionary working class is not simply one particular and sectional interest group in capitalist society. As the agents that are struggling to create socialism and transcend class divisions, workers are "the potential agents, not only of their own liberation, but also of the universal liberation of humanity" (p53). Thus, like Lukács, Blackledge argues that the working class is potentially the "universal class". Moreover, the values that it represents have not been imposed upon it externally from on high, but are immanent in society itself. "Freedom is best understood as an immanent potential which evolves over time through a process of collective struggles" (p57).

The idea that the working class is a revolutionary force in modern capitalist conditions is widely questioned. It is mainly because of doubts on this score that many Marxists have abandoned the revolutionary basis of Marxism and settled instead for an abstract, ethical utopianism of a sort that Marx himself explicitly repudiated. It is one of the main strengths of Blackledge's book that he confronts this issue so directly. In response to the non-revolutionary conditions that now exist, Marxists should adopt what Lucien Goldmann called a "tragic vision": without a basis for hope, they should nevertheless continue to hope (p141). They should look beyond the limits of the present through a "wager" on future possibilities of change. "Marxism involves not a deterministic prediction of the socialist future of humanity but rather a wager on the revolutionary potential of the proletariat" (p142). This wager is based ultimately on the solidarity that develops in working class struggles. These require and exhibit the socialist "virtues" of community and cooperation. They prefigure a future socialist society and demonstrate its feasibility.

In making these arguments, Blackledge draws heavily on some early writings by Alasdair MacIntyre. At first, this may seem a surprising source. MacIntyre is now a Catholic social philosopher steeped in Aristotelianism who rejects Marxism. However, in an earlier period he was an active Marxist—initially as a member of the Communist Party, then in the British New Left, and then as a Troskyist

in the Socialist Labour League and the International Socialists (pp185-186).*

The Aristotelian language of "virtue" seems an anachronistic way to describe the ethics of Marxism. More importantly, it is doubtful whether the social psychology of small scale struggles can provide a sufficient basis for a socialist ethics. Feelings of solidarity are a feature of many kinds of protest movement. A socialist ethic needs a more specific grounding.

Fundamental to Marxism is the insight that there are far larger, objective—economic, social and historical—forces at work within capitalism, creating the contradictions that will lead towards a specifically socialist society in the future. The operation of these is largely passed over in Blackledge's account, which portrays Marxism in political terms as primarily a philosophy of revolutionary struggle.

Marx is referring to these objective forces with the "obstetric" picture that Blackledge is so critical of. No doubt Blackledge is right to question the simple determinism that can easily be read into this picture. But we must be careful not to throw out the baby with the bathwater. Marxism is not simply a philosophy of political commitment and struggle. It essentially involves a historical theory according to which capitalism is only a particular and limited stage that, because of the objective conflicts at work within it, is destined to come into crisis and to generate the forces that will lead to its overthrow and to a new and better form of society ("better" in the sense of freer, as Blackledge argues).

Though he objects to Marx's "obstetric" language, Blackledge cannot so easily

---

* See Paul Blackledge and Neil Davidson (eds), 2009, *Alasdair MacIntyre's Engagement with Marxism: Selected Writings, 1953-1974* (Haymarket).

reject the aspect of Marx's thought that it describes. Indeed, he relies on it when he argues that the working class is a revolutionary force "immanent" within capitalism. True, this is not a purely mechanical process guaranteed automatically to deliver a better society. Nevertheless, according to Marx this will happen as a matter of fact. And, if it does, it will do so partly because the capitalist system will generate increasingly severe and incapacitating crises,* and partly because political forces will arise to abolish capitalism and build a new society.

For Marx, the main component of this force will be the working class. That is where the problem lies. Though capitalism has led to recurrent and severe crises, there is no sign of the emergence of a revolutionary working class. It cannot be conjured up by political commitment alone. If it does emerge that will be because larger—social, economic and historical—forces are at work, driven ultimately by the increasing socialisation of the means of production and exchange.

That is to say, the "wager" on the emergence of revolutionary forces that Marxism makes is not based only on the experience of solidarity in struggle, but on the existence of objective forces at work in capitalist society. To say this is not to deny freedom or to exclude a role for ethics, as Blackledge fears. Correctly understood, freedom does not exist only in the absence of determining conditions; it is not a merely negative phenomenon. It depends not only on the removal of the restraints of capitalist society; it requires also the creation of positive conditions which enhance people's abilities and

give them the power actually to exercise freedom and choice. This has been, and will be, the effect of the social and historical developments that Marx describes.

These are large and fundamental issues. The most important thing about Blackledge's book is that it raises them. It moves beyond what has become the well-worn ground of the dispute within Marxism between ethical nihilism and universalism and takes the debate onto more substantial and promising new ground.

Cuba Libre?

Dave Sewell

Sam Farber, **Cuba Since the Revolution of 1959: A Critical Assessment** *(Haymarket, 2011), $24*

Discussions around Cuba have an unfortunate tendency to generate more heat than light, particularly on the left. Sam Farber's new book, in the same spirit as Jeffery Webber's recent works on Bolivia, provides much-needed clarity.

Farber starts from the simple premise that it is both possible and necessary to oppose US imperialism and the imposition of neoliberalism in the island without buying into the Castro brothers' mythology. And he backs this up with a wealth of detailed information about the state of the island over the past five decades.

Many persistent myths are put to rest in these pages. Cuba's "anti-imperialist" foreign policy is dissected and found wanting, not least for its alliance with General Franco's Spain. Workers and peasants

---

* There is a quasi-mechanical aspect to the occurrence of economic crises, in that the market is an alienated system out of people's power to control.

remain disenfranchised—and inequality and underdevelopment remain rife.

Even Cuba's celebrated health and education systems aren't all they are cracked up to be. The university system has been thrown into chaos by Castro's policies. And while Cuban doctors provide the backbone of the island's diplomacy, they haven't been able to stop patients freezing to death in substandard hospital buildings.

Perhaps the gravest failings of the Cuban revolution are its inability to challenge oppression. The pre-revolutionary consensus of denying the very existence of racism on the island has been upheld, and anti-racist organisation suppressed as much as possible.

The role of women has been transformed, with far more women being integrated into the workforce than was previously the case. This has, of course, been the case in many other countries with no pretensions of Communism—and it has coexisted perfectly well with old-style sexism, placing a double burden on Cuban women. Farber can even point to government officials who refuse to recognise the concept of marital rape, and state schools where girls are expected to wash the boys' clothes or risk being denounced as lesbians. And the Castro regime's persecution of gay men has been particularly extreme, from raids and show trials in the 1960s to what were effectively mass expulsions in 1980.

Farber puts this in the context of a society that was never transformed from the bottom up—that was only ever converted to "Communism" by decree from on high, with all its reactionary prejudices left intact. It has been left to Castro to pander to these prejudices at best, and at worst to mobilise them in search of a scapegoat.

Such a society is, of course, not without its discontents, especially as the seemingly terminal decline of Castro's economic model sets in. One chapter takes us on a tour of the various dissident movements. Farber doesn't sow any illusions—from tame internal critics of the Communist Party to fellow travellers of the Catholic church or the vicious Miami right wing, the opposition is considered warts and all—but he shows that there is, at the least, a debate under way about what a post-Castro Cuba could look like.

Raul Castro clearly has a vision of his own. The policies declared at the sixth congress of the Cuban Communist Party last year point ineluctably towards the Chinese model of state capitalism. The imminence of such far-reaching reforms, and the eagerness of US imperialism to shape such a transition lend urgency to the discussion of the reality of Cuba's situation.

In his predictions for this "transition to capitalism", it's frustrating that Farber refuses to recognise Cuba as *already* being state capitalist, as having never really left capitalism behind. He may show no mercy to the Cuban regime—or to those leftists abroad who would rather give it a free ride than shatter their own illusions—but nor does he ever stop referring to the country as Communist. But this doesn't stop him from recognising the potential for class conflict which the Cuban situation presents. Farber concludes that "resistance is not futile, since there is an alternative to both capitalism and the failed 'Communism' of Cuban history" and that this "will not be handed down as a gift by the people in power but will have to be obtained by struggles from below".

With this vivid portrait of the real Cuba, Farber has done a valuable service to all those who would seek to understand and to support these struggles.

Pick of the quarter

There are rich pickings in the two issues of *Historical Materialism* published since we last appeared. In the first (no. 20.1) we have the Marxist classical scholar Richard Seaford exploring the parallels between the structure of ancient Greek philosophy and the money economy developing in the city states of Greece and Asia Minor during the 6th century BC. This is a thesis that he first developed in *Money and the Early Greek Mind* (2004), but here Seaford relates it to the earlier work of the Marxist philosopher Alfred Sohn-Rethel. Elsewhere Tony Norfield offers an analysis of financial derivatives that differs sharply from the pioneering Marxist study by Dick Bryan and Michael Rafferty. His central claim is that "derivatives did not cause the crisis; they gave it a peculiar intensity and financial form. Low growth and low profitability were the reasons for the boom in derivatives-trading and 'financial innovation'."

The following issue (20.2) starts with David Harvey's 2011 Deutscher Memorial Lecture, "History versus Theory: A Commentary on Marx's Method in *Capital*". As one would expect, Harvey offers many rich insights, but his overall interpretation rests on a strained reading of a passage in the *Grundrisse* and ignores Marx's effort carefully to construct and order the categories he uses to analyse capitalism. Other treats include Mariano Féliz arguing that the economic strategy pursued by Argentina under Néstor Kirchner and Cristina Fernández represents a modification of neoliberalism,

and Alex Levant on the brilliant Soviet Marxist philosopher Ewald Ilienkov (one of whose texts is also translated in this issue).

The latest *New Left Review* (II/76) has useful pieces on those uneasy neighbours Turkey and Greece. Cihan Tuğal dismantles the so-called "Turkish model" of neoliberal Islamism that Recep Tayyip Erdoğan's government offers to Egypt and Tunisia but is perhaps too sympathetic to the fears of the Islamophobic wing of the Turkish left.[*] Yannis Mavris focuses on Greece's two watershed elections in May and June. He stresses "the massive campaign to intimidate the population" that contained the advance of Syriza on 17 June, but stresses that Syriza nevertheless "has emerged as the dominant political formation among the middle- and working-class strata who have been impoverished by the crisis". Greece, he concludes, is seeing "the formation of a new large-scale party of the left" unparalleled since the late 1950s. Elsewhere Robin Blackburn remembers the radical journalist Alexander Cockburn, who died in July.

The 2012 issue of *Revolutionary History* is a celebration of the 50th anniversary of the Algerian Revolution. The journal's guest editor (and frequent *International Socialism* contributor) Ian Birchall has amassed a wide range of materials on the theme of "European Revolutionaries

[*] http://newleftreview.org/II/76/cihan-tugal-democratic-janissaries

and Algerian Independence, 1954–1962". The journal offers the fullest account in English of the role of the revolutionary left in giving political and practical solidarity to the Algerian liberation struggle. Included are substantial extracts from *Les Camarades des Frères*, Sylvain Pattieu's book about the role of Trotskyists and anarchists during the war, and other accounts which draw on documents by and interviews with participants.*

The Canadian socialist scholar John Riddell picks up from Ian Birchall's review of of his book on the Fourth Congress of the Communist International (Comintern) in our last issue to discuss "The Comintern as a School of Socialist Strategy" on his excellent website.[†] John takes up Ian's advice that "if we study [the Comintern records] carefully, without trying to read off simple slogans or directives, they can be of great value" in order to look at how the lessons of the Comintern might inform socialist strategy today.

There are a number of interesting pieces in the September/October issue of the US socialist journal *Against the Current*. In the aftermath of the massacre of striking miners at Marikana, the journal collects a number of articles examining the left and social movements in South Africa. Elsewhere in the issue Kim Moody looks at the history of mass strikes in the US to examine why the Occupy movement's call for general strikes met with only limited success.[‡]

Finally, the summer issue of *Socialism and Democracy* has a symposium on the "Promise and Challenge of the Occupy Movement". The 14 articles it collects cover topics ranging from the links between Occupy and the post-Seattle anti-capitalist movement to the role of social media in Occupy.

AC & JJ

---

* The journal can be ordered from the website www.revolutionaryhistory.co.uk/
† http://johnriddell.wordpress.com/2012/09/03/the-comintern-as-a-school-of-socialist-strategy/
‡ All articles are available at their website www.solidarity-us.org/atc/160